IF IT'S RAINING IN BRAZIL, BUY STARBUCKS

The Investor's Guide to
Profiting from News and
Other Market-Moving Events

Peter Navarro

McGraw-Hill

New York   Chicago   San Francisco   Lisbon   London
Madrid   Mexico City   Milan   New Delhi
San Juan   Seoul   Singapore
Sydney   Toronto

Library of Congress Cataloging-in-Publication Data

Navarro, Peter
    If it's raining in Brazil, buy Starbucks : the investor's guide to profiting from news and other market-moving events / by Peter Navarro.
      p.   cm.
    ISBN 0-07-137369-1
    1. Investment analysis. 2. Portfolio management. 3. Investments. I. Title.

HG4529 .N38   2001
332.6—dc21

                            2001031702

McGraw-Hill

A Division of The **McGraw·Hill** Companies

1 2 3 4 5 6 7 8 9 0   DOC/DOC   0 9 8 7 6 5 4 3 2 1

ISBN 0-07-137369-1

This book was set in Times New Roman by Joanne Morbit of McGraw-Hill's Professional Book Group composition unit, Hightstown, N.J.

Printed and bound by R. R. Donnelley & Sons Company.

This publication is designed to provide accurate and authoritative information in regard to the subject matter covered. It is sold with the understanding that neither the author nor the publisher is engaged in rendering legal, accounting, or other professional service. If legal advice or other expert assistance is required, the services of a competent professional person should be sought.

—From a Declaration of Principles jointly adopted by a Committee of the American Bar Association and a Committee of Publishers.

McGraw-Hill books are available at special quantity discounts to use as premiums and sales promotions, or for use in corporate training programs. For more information, please write to the Director of Special Sales, McGraw-Hill, Two Penn Plaza, New York, NY 10121-2298. Or contact your local bookstore.

To the wonderful women in my life,
Evelyn and Leslie. And to that mischievous
little prince named Alex.

Acknowledgments

The manuscript greatly benefited from the comments of Rafat Abbasi, Nick Bok, Art Jeppe, Merlin Rothfeld, Pedro Sottile, John Stocco, and Ed Urbano.

Keith Loh did a superb job assisting with the analytical framework and research assistance. Gregor Jovanovich went the absolute extra mile in reviewing the manuscript. eGoose's Pej Hamidi provided many brilliant, wonderful, and valuable insights.

Finally, many thanks to McGraw-Hill's Gary Burke and the dynamic editing duo of Stephen Isaacs and Jeffrey Krames—Jeff and Gary for making it possible and Stephen for his wonderful stewardship.

Any errors and omissions remain, of course, my own.

Money supply, government deficits, trade deficits, inflation figures, the financial markets, and government policy. I look at all those things for the U.S. and key foreign countries as well. It is one big, three-dimensional puzzle. However, if you had a three-dimensional puzzle, you could eventually put it together. But this puzzle is not one in which you can spread out the pieces on a great big table and put them all together. The picture is always changing. Every day some pieces get taken away and others get thrown in.

Jim Rogers*

*Jim Rogers is a legendary international investor in stocks, bonds, commodities, and currencies—both on the long and short sides—and one of the leading pioneers in the art of macrowave investing.

Contents

Prologue

On March 10, in the year 2000, the Nasdaq stock market index burst exuberantly through the 5000 barrier and reached an all-time high of 5132. But even as the Nasdaq was reaching this historic peak, powerful macroeconomic forces were gathering to bring this raging bull to its knees.

The first macrowave blow struck was a regulatory one. It came during the weekend of April 2 when lawyers from Microsoft and the U.S. Department of Justice tried to hammer out an eleventh-hour compromise in the government's antitrust suit against the software giant. The talks collapsed amid arrogance and acrimony, and when the Nasdaq market reopened on Monday, it wasn't just the stock of Microsoft that went into the tank. The Nasdaq index plummeted a record 349 points.

The second macrowave blow came quickly on the heels of this Bill Gates debacle, and it was an inflationary one. On April 14, the Bureau of Labor Statistics released data indicating that the Consumer Price Index had taken an unexpected, sharp upward jump. This bleak macroeconomic news sparked a widespread market panic and caused the Nasdaq to plunge 355 points.

With the Nasdaq reeling, Federal Reserve Chairman Alan Greenspan came in with what, in hindsight, would be the knockout macrowave punch. On May 16, Greenspan's Fed raised the discount rate by 50 basis points. This was not only the sixth Fed interest rate hike in 11 months, it was also the largest. For those traders and investors who had already suffered large paper losses but who still hoped against hope that the Nasdaq would shrug off its fears and quickly regain its lofty heights, this was a stake through the heart.

Indeed, the Nasdaq index would wind up falling over 2000 points in less than three short months. This massive, 40-percent decline not only erased billions of dollars in paper profits for millions of investors, it also completely wiped out thousands of investors who had ridden the Nasdaq wave up on a sea of margin buying and who had been caught without enough cash to cover their margin calls. In the process of this Nasdaq wipe-out, hearts were broken, homes were lost, dreams were shattered, and the biggest of chills descended over an entire generation of investors weaned on upward momentum and extravagant dot-com wealth.

Sad to say, the macrowave worst was still not over. Not by a long shot. For six months more, the market tried desperately to rally—even as thousands of equally desperate traders and investors hung on for dear life. But every time the Nasdaq tried to pull its bloodied and beaten index off the canvas, another roundhouse macrowave punch would come along to slam it back down.

First, there was an avaricious OPEC cartel and a sharp spike in oil prices. This particularly battered transport and technology stocks. Next, there was a severely weakening euro and a dollar far too strong for its own good. This lethal combination not only hit America's export industries and trade deficit hard, it also threatened to provoke an international currency crisis. Finally, even as Greenspan's ever-higher interest rates began to take a heavy toll on the earnings of virtually every big-name stock, the nation was hit with the ugliest of presidential election controversies. The ensuing storm cloud of legal and political uncertainties over whether George W. Bush or Al Gore would ultimately be president turned out to be absolutely toxic for both the economy and the stock market.

The result was nothing like the elegant soft landing that Alan Greenspan had futilely tried to engineer. Rather, it was a harsh recession, a Nasdaq sliced in half, a whole army of New Economy stocks left garroted along the information superhighway, and a whole new generation of online traders and investors left gutted by the roadside.

Out of this cataclysmic experience, one lesson has emerged with crystal clarity: Any trader or investor who ignores the power of macroeconomics over the world's financial markets will, sooner or later, lose more than they should—and perhaps more than they have.

The purpose of this book is to help you become a *macrowave investor.* This is an individual who not only can learn to jump out of the way when the macroeconomic freight train is coming, but who can also jump on that train and ride it for a profit—whichever direction it is going.

Introduction

The Federal Reserve hikes interest rates, consumer confidence falls, war breaks out in the Balkans, drought shrinks the coffee crop in Brazil, oil prices spike sharply in Rotterdam, Congress passes new Medicare legislation imposing price controls on prescription drugs, and the U.S. trade deficit reaches a new record high. Each of these macroeconomic waves—some of them thousands of miles away—will move the U.S. stock market in very different but nonetheless systematic and predictable ways. If you come to fully understand these macrowaves, you will become a better investor or trader—no matter what your style of investing or trading is. That's the power of macrowave investing, and that's what this book is about. Let me show you what I mean with just a few examples of some fictional microinvestors in very real situations.

- Jim Fleet is a day trader and a very good one. Typically, he follows a momentum strategy to "scalp teenies." That is, he buys or shorts large volumes of a stock based on a stock's up or down momentum. He never holds the stock for more than a few minutes, and he makes his money when the stock goes up or down by a "teenie"—1/16 of a point—or more. With working capital of $50,000, Jim usually rakes in about $2,500 a week. Yesterday, however, he lost $20,000 on a Wal-Mart stock play after a computer glitch cut off his access to the market for a few minutes. During that time, the Conference Board released data showing a very sharp and unexpected drop in consumer confidence. Minutes after CNBC reported this news, stocks in the entire retail sector swooned. By the time Jim got back online, Wal-Mart was way down and Jim was out a month's profits.

- Jane Ellington is a swing trader who typically buys or shorts a stock over a one-to-five-day period. Her strategy is to use technical analysis to identify higher-volume and moderately volatile stocks that are trading comfortably in a range. Then, she "buys on the dip" and "sells on the peak." Over the last year, Jane has used this strategy to make about $500 a week, which is a very nice supplement to her regular salary as a marketing executive. However, last week, she lost $8,000 on one trade after the government released the monthly Consumer Price Index data. These data showed the core rate of inflation spiking sharply upward. The entire market promptly tanked, and Jane—oblivious to the news—got caught in the downdraft.

- Ed Burke is an ex–Navy petty officer and a retired petroleum engineer. He's a pretty conservative buy-and-hold investor who likes to hold a large portion of his portfolio in blue-chip oil stocks like Chevron and Exxon. Last May, in the space of just three weeks, he made $40,000 in paper profits when the price of a barrel of oil rose steadily from $26 to $39, and Jim's oil stocks moved up sharply. However, after the OPEC cartel met in June and relaxed its production quotas, oil prices began to fall back down. By July, when oil prices had sagged to $20 per barrel and dragged oil stocks down with them, Ed's $40,000 paper profit had turned into a $10,000 paper loss—a swing in the value of his portfolio of some $50,000.

Now obviously, these three investors are as different as night and day in both their trading strategies and investing styles. However, they all share one thing in common. They all lost money because they chose to ignore the powerful impact that macrowave forces can have on the stock market.

Sure, it was bad luck that Jim had computer problems. However, Jim also knew, just like any good day trader knows, that computers can crash at any time. Knowing this, Jim could have easily avoided trading a retail sector stock on a day when data on a major economic indicator like consumer confidence were to be released—if only he had been thinking like a macrowave investor.

As for Jane, the worst thing a technical trader can do is to ignore broader macroeconomic signals like a possible inflationary spike or sharp rise in the unemployment rate. This is because it is precisely such macroeconomic shocks that can throw all stocks abruptly out of their trading ranges and, at least temporarily, render technical analysis meaningless.

Of course, Ed may have been doing the right thing—at least for Ed. That's because, by temperament, he is a long-term investor who likes to buy and hold blue-chip stocks with strong fundamentals and not worry about fluctuations in paper profits. On the other hand, if an investor like Ed is going to have a portfolio that is so heavily weighted in a particular sector like oil, rather than be diversified, it borders on foolishness to ignore macrowaves that can strongly influence that sector. Indeed, in this case, if Ed had simply been paying attention to price movements in the world oil market, he'd be $40,000 richer rather than $10,000 poorer.

The broader point of these examples—and the ultimate point of this book—is that regardless of what kind of trader or investor you are, a deeper appreciation of the systematic effects of macroeconomic events on the stock market can help you in your trading and investing decisions. Moreover, such a macrowave perspective can help you in two very specific and very profitable ways.

First, by adopting a macrowave perspective, you will be much better able to predict and anticipate broad trends in the market. Will the stock market be up or down today? Or next week? Or even next year? This is powerful information to arm yourself with because you never, *ever* want to trade or invest against the trend. That was Jane Ellington's mistake, and it cost her dearly.

The second way that a macrowave perspective can help you is equally powerful. As we shall soon see, even in an up-trending bull market, some sectors like computers or electronics may rise much faster than others like chemicals or autos. Moreover, in a bear market, some sectors like housing and technology may fall much farther and faster than other so-called "defensive sectors" like food and pharmaceuticals that can provide you with much safer investing havens.

The good news here is that a macrowave perspective will help you identify the key sectors to trade in—or stay away from!—given particular kinds of macroeconomic news. In this sense, a macrowave perspective serves as a powerful trading compass, and it is just such a compass that both Jim Fleet and Ed Burke in our examples above could have used to a very profitable advantage. Here's the roadmap we will be following:

Part One lays down the analytical foundations of macrowave investing. This begins in Chap. 1, where we will systematically work our way through the various kinds of macrowave forces that can bear down, buffet, or buoy the various U.S. and global financial markets. These macrowaves range from inflation, unemployment, and slower economic growth to earthquakes, wars, and international currency crises.

In Chap. 2, we turn to what should be both an entertaining and very useful history of the warring schools of macroeconomics. These schools range from Keynesianism, monetarism, and supply-side economics to the latest school of new classical thinking, which is based on the controversial idea of rational expectations. This chapter is important because so many of the decisions on macroeconomic policy that are made in Congress and the White House and at the Federal Reserve are driven by which particular school of economics happens to be in vogue at any particular time.

Chapters 3 and 4 then tackle the crucial task of examining the major tools of macroeconomic policy, principally fiscal and monetary policy. In these chapters, which complete Part One, we will come to understand not only how these policies work but also what their often far-ranging effects can be on global financial markets. For example, when Chairman Alan Greenspan sneezes at the Federal Reserve, Europe very often catches a cold—along with the stocks of U.S. companies that export heavily to Europe. We need to understand why. Similarly, when the OPEC oil cartel raises prices or the Japanese economy goes into a tailspin, the U.S. economy is likely to falter and pull the stock market down with it. Again, we need to understand why.

In Part Two, we get down to the nuts and bolts of macrowave investing. This begins with Chap. 5, which examines the major principles of macrowave investing. Here, we illustrate how a firm grasp of these principles generates profit opportunities. Then, in Chaps. 6 and 7, we examine the stock market from the macrowave investor's perspective. In these key chapters, we will see that when the macrowave investor looks at the stock market, he or she not only sees *companies* like Chevron, Compaq, or Wal-Mart. He or she also sees *market sectors* like energy, computers, and retailing. This is because many of the biggest moves in the stock market are sector-driven rather than company-driven. Quite literally capitalizing on the systematic differences between the various market sectors is at the core of the macrowave investing approach.

In Chaps. 8 and 9, we move on to the crucial topics of protecting your trading capital and managing your investment risks. Then, in Chap. 10, we reaffirm one of the major themes of this book, namely, that *any* kind of trader or investor can benefit from the power of macrowave investing. This chapter does so by illustrating how macrowave investing can be applied to different styles and strategies of trading and investing.

To complete Part Two, Chap. 11 presents the macrowave investor's checklist. Here, we see that just as a good pilot methodically goes through an extensive checklist before every flight, so too does the macrowave investor go through a checklist before every trade.

In the third and final part of this book, we turn to the all-important task of illustrating macrowave investing in action. Each of the chapters in Part Three focuses on a specific macroeconomic force such as inflation or recession or productivity. Importantly, the architecture of each of these chapters is the same.

We first learn about *which* economic indicators like the Consumer Price Index and the Jobs Report are the most important to follow and *when* the data for these indicators are regularly released. Then, we move to the crucial task of examining how each particular macroeconomic force might affect different sectors of the stock market. This analysis is the heart and soul of this book; it is from this analysis that you, the savvy macrowave investor, are most likely to profit.

For example, when we look at inflation in Chap. 15, we will see that interest-rate sensitive sectors like banking, brokerage, and retail typically react the strongest to inflation news, while defensive sectors like utilities, energy, and consumer staples react the weakest. Using this kind of information, you can buy into the strongest-reacting sectors on good inflation news or short-sell on bad news—or simply flee to the defensive sectors for shelter.

It is important to note that each of the chapters in Part Three is modular. That is, each stands alone and, in fact, the chapters can be read in any order. Because of this, you should find this book to be a very useful reference volume for your financial market shelf once you've read it. This is because you'll be able to consult the book every time you want to refresh your memory as to how the markets are likely to react to the latest piece of impending macroeconomic news.

With this, then, as our roadmap, let me provide you with one cautionary note. Because Part One of this book lays down our macroeconomic foundation, it may, at times, be a very challenging section to read. But take heart. Once you get to Parts Two and Three, it will be all smooth sailing. And all that hard work you did getting through the important conceptual material in Part One will pay off for you many, many times over. That's my promise to you, and it's a promise based on my years of experience developing the ideas in this book. So with that said, let's get started with the power of macrowave investing!

P A R T

1

Laying the Foundation

1

RIPPLES AND
MACROWAVES

Despite excellent management and a solid fundamental outlook, Starbucks's stock has dropped more than 8 points in the last several months. At this point, the savvy macrowave investor notices a small article on the back pages of the Wall Street Journal indicating that the rains have come to break a deadly drought in Brazil—the world's largest coffee producing nation.

On this news, the savvy macrowave investor buys several thousand shares of Starbucks. She's betting that the rains will save the Brazilian coffee crop, that this will cause coffee prices to fall dramatically, and that this, in turn, will drive up Starbucks's profit margins as well as its stock price.

Over the next week, Starbucks's stock falls 2 more points, but the macrowave investor sits tight. Finally, the stock begins to rise— and quickly—10 points in three days. She sells her shares and is out with an $8000 profit.

E very time a new macroeconomic wave hits the economy, its impact
ripples through the U.S. and global financial markets in both systematic and predictable ways. For large and unexpected macroeconomic events, these ripples can turn into a tidal wave.

One example of a small ripple is offered up by our Starbucks example:
Rain in Brazil leads to lower coffee prices in the wholesale market, and coffee
retailers like Starbucks enjoy higher profit margins and a rising stock price.
On the other hand, one example of a macroeconomic *tidal wave* might be
something like the Asian financial crisis of the late 1990s, which was sparked
by the collapse of Thailand's currency. This crisis not only sent both the Dow
and the Nasdaq markets reeling, it also brought down stock exchanges around
the world—from the Nikkei in Japan and Hang Seng in Hong Kong to the
London "Footsie," Frankfurt Xetra DAX, and Bombay Sensex.

In this chapter, I want to introduce you to the major macroeconomic
waves that bear down on any economy. These macrowaves range from
inflation, recession, and falling productivity to war, drought, and burden-
some government regulations. In this chapter, I also want to show you how
you can use a powerful tool known as macrowave logic to help you calmly
navigate your portfolio through any rough macroeconomic seas.

THE POWER OF MACROWAVE LOGIC

Macrowave logic is about being connected to the markets. To understand
this kind of connection, consider these questions: If inflation increases,
what will happen to interest rates? If interest rates rise, will the value of the
dollar go up or down? If the dollar goes up, what happens to the level of
exports, imports, and the trade deficit? If the trade deficit increases, which
industry sectors and company stocks will be winners to buy and which will
be losers to avoid or sell short? These are precisely the kinds of questions
that the savvy macrowave investor seeks to answer daily as new macroeconomic events unfold. The primary tool in this thought process is
macrowave logic.

For example, the macrowave investor knows that if inflation increases,
the Federal Reserve is likely to raise interest rates. If interest rates rise, the
value of the dollar will, in turn, go up because higher interest rates will
attract additional foreign investment. The important link in this particular
chain of macrowave logic is that in order for foreigners to invest in the U.S.,

they must first exchange their foreign currencies for dollars. This increased demand for dollars will bid the price of the dollar up.

Now, what will a stronger dollar do to the trade deficit? The macrowave investor knows that the deficit must increase. This is because a stronger dollar will increase the price of U.S. exports and make foreign imports cheaper. So U.S. companies will export less, U.S. consumers will buy more imports, and voilà, the trade deficit swells.

So who wins and who loses in the stock market? Certainly, export-dependent sectors like agriculture, pharmaceuticals, and steel are likely to see lower profits as their exports fall, so loser stocks like Nucor and Merck may well be ones for the macrowave investor to avoid or sell short. On the other hand, foreign-based companies like BASF and BMW and Ericcson that import heavily into the U.S. market may see their profits rise. These winners from the stronger dollar may be good stocks to buy.

The broader point, of course, is this: Macrowave logic draws upon well-established relationships between key macroeconomic variables such as inflation, unemployment, and interest rates. It uses these relationships to visualize the often-lengthy chain of events that begins with a new macroeconomic event such as inflationary news and ends with a major move in an individual stock's price. Using this visualization process, the macrowave investor forms expectations about the direction of the market trend, movements among the market sectors, and the direction of stock prices themselves. These expectations form the heart and soul of his or her trading decisions or *macroplays*.

Our introductory Starbucks's macroplay was a relatively simple application of macrowave logic. Here are several more macroplays:

- *The U.S. Justice Department announces plans to break up the Microsoft monopoly. While the microtrading herd rushes for the exits and Microsoft stock plunges, the savvy macrowave investor quickly realizes that the share prices of both Sun Microsystems and Oracle should benefit from the news. This is because these companies are two of Microsoft's main rivals. So the macrowave investor quietly buys several thousand shares of each. Several weeks later, he exits the position with a $12,000 profit.*

- *United Airlines announces the acquisition of U.S. Air to make it the largest carrier in the world. While speculators are trampling over each other trying to get on the U.S. Air bandwagon, the savvy macrowave investor quietly buys Northwest Airlines. She knows that within days Northwest must become an acquisition target of either Delta Airlines or American Airlines—the main rivals to United. A lucky 13 days after the merger announcement, the macrowave investor exits her Northwest position with a 10-point gain.*

- *Tomorrow, the savvy macrowave investor knows that the government will release the latest Consumer Price Index data. Tame CPI numbers will likely have little impact on the market. However, if the CPI shows an inflationary spike, the market will drop sharply on fears that the Federal Reserve will hike interest rates. This looks like an excellent macroplay to the macrowave investor—one with a small downside risk and a very big upside. So just before the market's close, he shorts 2000 shares of QQQ—a stock that tracks the Nasdaq index. At 8:30 the next morning, the CPI numbers are a horror show, and the Nasdaq plummets. The macrowave investor cashes in half his position for a 10-point gain by noon. Three weeks later after the Federal Reserve hikes interest rates another 50 basis points and QQQ has dropped another 15 points, the macrowave investor cashes in the rest of his position for a total profit of $35,000. Time for a week in Maui. Thank you, Alan Greenspan.*

———————

I hope these macroplays have made the point that macroeconomic events move the markets. What we want to do next is briefly review each of the major macrowaves that you will want to follow closely as you plan your trading and investing decisions and strategies. These macrowaves are listed in Table 1-1 along with some of the major economic indicators or information sources used to track these waves.

THE INFLATIONARY TIGER

U.S. stock markets ended a volatile week with record single-day plunges in the Dow Jones Industrial Average and the Nasdaq Composite Index.... The free fall was ignited by the early-morning release of a monthly Labor Department report on inflation.... The inflation report raised fears that the Federal Reserve...would raise interest rates higher than an expected quarter-point increase at its upcoming session in May.

WORLD NEWS DIGEST

The inflationary tiger is the scariest cat on Wall Street. When this big, bad cat is on the prowl, the bears come out and the bulls run for cover. So what is this beast and how do we know when it has crept into our economic village looking for prey?

Technically, inflation is defined as an upward movement of prices from one year to the next. It is typically measured by the percentage change in price indexes such as the Consumer Price Index, the Producer Price Index, or the Employment Cost Index. In stalking the inflationary tiger, you must first be aware that there are at least three species of this very dangerous beast. There is the *demand-pull* variety that comes with economic booms and too much money chasing too few goods. This tiger is perhaps the most easily tamed—although with inflation, nothing is ever truly easy. Then, there is the *cost-push* variety that follows supply shocks such as oil price hikes or drought-induced food price spikes. This inflation moves with deadly swiftness, inflicts great pain, and often gives the Federal Reserve fits. Finally, there is *wage inflation.* It can be the most dangerous of all, slow and plodding though it may be, and it is often triggered by both demand-pull and cost-push pressures.

If you are unable to quickly and clearly distinguish between these three species of inflationary tigers, you will be prone to misinterpreting the *real* messages of economic indicators like the Consumer Price Index and Producer Price Index. The likely result will be that one of these inflationary tigers will eat your trading capital for lunch, belch loudly, and then move on with nary a thank-you. This will be true for one very simple reason: In the face of inflationary news, both the Federal Reserve and Wall Street are likely to react quite differently depending on *which* species of the inflationary tiger they actually fear.

For example, while the Fed is likely to raise interest rates very swiftly when demand-pull inflation is pushing up the core rate of inflation, it is likely to be much more cautious when supply side shocks like energy or food prices are creating cost-push inflationary pressures. If you get caught on the wrong side of such reactions, you will be doomed!

THE RECESSIONARY BEAR

The nation's unemployment rate, the most politically sensitive economic indicator in an election year, rose sharply in June. Minutes after the [jobs] report was released, the Federal Reserve responded by cutting its key

TABLE 1-1.   Major Macrowaves and Their Indicators

Macrowave	Indicators
The inflationary tiger	• Consumer Price Index
	• Producer Price Index
	• Employment Cost Index
The recessionary bear	• The jobs report
	• Consumer confidence
	• Personal income and credit
	• Retail sales
The god of economic growth and the business cycle	• Gross domestic product
	• Car and truck sales
	• Capacity utilization
	• Housing starts and construction spending
	• Standard & Poor's DRI forecasting
The archangel of productivity	• Productivity and costs
The budget deficit dragon	• U.S. Treasury budget report
The trade deficit trap	• Merchandise trade balance
	• Import and export prices

interest rate in an attempt to stimulate the sagging economy.... Concerned about the weak economy, stocks slid today on the New York Stock Exchange....

THE NEW YORK TIMES

The recessionary bear ranks second behind only inflation as a menacing macrowave force. Moreover, as any recession deepens, inflation becomes much less of a concern to worried politicians scrambling to put idle and angry voters back to work.

As for monitoring the economy's various recessionary signals, the savvy macrowave investor can do no better than to follow the jobs report cited in the news story above. This report, which is released monthly by the U.S. Department of Labor, not only tracks the nation's unemployment rate by different sectors, regions, and demographic groups, it also provides valuable information on factors like the average workweek and hourly earnings.

TABLE 1-1.   *(Continued)*

Macrowave	Indicators
Big Brother—Regulation, taxation, and antitrust	• *Barron's*
	• *Business Week*
	• CNBC
	• CNN
	• *Forbes*
	• *Fortune*
	• *Investor's Business Daily*
	• *Los Angeles Times/New York Times*
	• *Money*
	• *Wall Street Journal*
	• *Washington Post*
	• *Worth*
The Four Horsemen of the Apocalypse	• Bloomberg
	• *Economist*
	• *Financial Times*
The whip of technological change	• *Active Trader*
	• Changewave.com
	• *Individual Investor*
	• *Red Herring*

In addition to the jobs report, there are several other useful recessionary indicators as well. For example, macrowave investors will want to watch the monthly reports on both auto sales and housing starts very carefully. These reports track the first two economic indicators to turn down when the economy begins to slide into a recession. These "leading indicators" of recession fall first because when consumers begin to worry about the economic outlook, one of the first things they do is postpone or cancel decisions to buy big-ticket items like autos or homes.

In this regard, and as we shall learn throughout this book, not all sectors of the market are created equal. For example, so-called "cyclical sectors" like autos and housing and the airlines are much more likely to be hurt by recessionary news than other noncyclical or defensive sectors like food, drugs, and health care. The reason is simple: Even in a recession people still have to eat and buy medicine and go to the doctor, but they can postpone buying a new car or a house or taking a vacation.

THE GOD OF ECONOMIC GROWTH

> The Commerce Department said the nation's gross domestic product grew by an anemic 0.5 percent in the three-month period that ended June 30.... Most broad-market indexes took a beating....
>
> *THE TIMES-PICAYUNE*

Both Wall Street and Main Street worship the god of economic growth for one simple reason. Over the long run, the rate of economic growth is the single most important ingredient of a broad-based prosperity. One way to think about it is this: Slow economic growth plus rapid population growth provides a quick ticket to the poorhouse. If you don't believe me, try an extended vacation in Bangladesh—but bring your own food, water, and medicine.

It's not just the U.S. growth rate that is important, however. As a macrowave investor, you will also want to compare growth rates across countries, particularly major trading partners such as Germany, Japan, and Canada. Here's just one reason, which is firmly rooted in macrowave logic: If the U.S. grows at a faster pace than, say, Germany, this differential growth rate is likely to contribute both to increasing U.S. trade deficits and collateral inflationary pressures. This is because a country's import demand is directly related to income so that when income grows in, say, America, so too will America's demand for German imports. Accordingly, one macroplay on strong economic growth news might be to invest in European export industries.

STOCKS TO PEDAL DURING THE BUSINESS CYCLE

> Cyclical stocks are favorites of market timers. Catch them as the economy is coming out of a downturn, then cash out when economic growth peaks.... "Figuring out when to buy cyclicals is always tricky, and it's even more difficult right now," says Fred Taylor, chief investment officer at U.S. Trust. "You need to worry about where they are in their own

cycle, where you are in the business cycle, and where you are in the stock market cycle."

Closely related to the issue of economic growth is the problem of the business cycle and a related stock market cycle. The term "business cycle" refers to the recurrent ups and downs in the gross domestic product over several years. While individual business cycles vary substantially in length and intensity, *all* display common phases, as illustrated in Fig. 1-1.

You can see that the business cycle looks like a roller coaster. There is a *peak* where business activity reaches a maximum, a *trough* which is brought about by a recessionary downturn in total output, and a *recovery* or upturn in which the economy expands towards full employment. Note that each of these phases of the cycle oscillates around a *growth trend* line.

Now here's why the business cycle is so important. There is also a fairly predictable *stock market cycle* that goes right along with it. This was alluded to in the excerpt from the *Houston Chronicle* above. It is further illustrated in Fig. 1-2, which shows the typical relationship between the business cycle and the stock market cycle.

Now, to carefully study this figure is to observe at least three important things. First, there are very distinct phases of the stock market cycle that

FIGURE 1-1   The roller coaster ride of the business cycle.

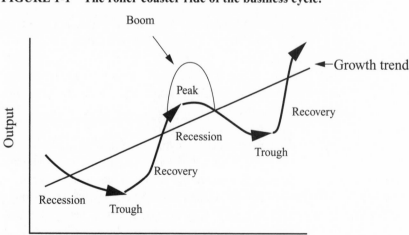

FIGURE 1-2   The business cycle and the stock market cycle.

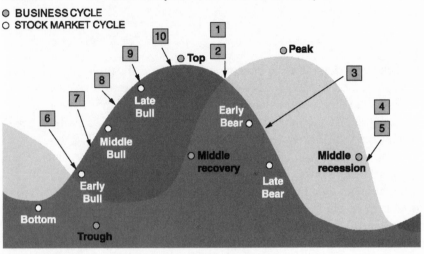

1. Consumer Noncyclicals (e.g., food, drugs, cosmetics)
2. Health Care
3. Utilities
4. Consumer Cyclicals (e.g., autos, housing)
5. Financials
6. Transportation
7. Technology
8. Capital Goods
9. Basic Industry (e.g., aluminum, chemicals, paper, steel)
10. Energy

move in tandem with different phases of the business cycle. For example, in the business cycle, we can see a peak at the top of the economic expansion and a trough at its bottom along with a *middle recession* phase between peak and trough and a *middle recovery* phase between trough and peak. By the same token, in the stock market cycle, there are both *early bear* and *late bear* phases on the downswing just as there are *early bull, middle bull,* and *late bull* phases on the upswing.

Second, not only do the stock market cycle and business cycle move in tandem, the stock market cycle is actually a *leading indicator* of movements in the business cycle! To see this, look at the bottom of the stock market cycle at the late bear stage. Its trough typically well precedes the recessionary trough of the business cycle. Similarly, you can see quite clearly that even before the economy reaches its expansionary peak, the stock market cycle has already entered its early bear phase. Now the trick in all of this is to clearly understand which sectors are strongest and which are weakest at different points in these two cycles. Indeed, to understand this market dynamic is to cut to the very heart of the matter of *sector rotation* and effective macrowave investing. That is where our third observation from the figure comes in.

In the figure, you can see a clear progression through nine different categories of industries beginning with the transportation and technology categories in the early bull phase of the market and ending with the financial and consumer cyclical categories in the late bear phase. In fact, this figure marks the points at which it becomes most profitable for investors to *rotate* out of stocks in certain sectors of the economy like energy or financials and into other sectors of the stock market like technology or health care.

For example, we see in the figure that technology and transportation stocks typically outperform the market in the early bull phase of the market while capital goods and basic industries stocks don't hit their stride until the middle to late bull phases. In contrast, once the business cycle has hit its peak and the stock market cycle moves into early bear territory, it's usually time for investors to rotate into defensive stocks, which include consumer staples like food and beverages as well as drugs and health care.

Of course, you can see why this information and the whole concept of sector rotation are so very valuable to the savvy macrowave investor. That's why we will talk about this in a lot more detail in Part Three of this book.

THE ARCHANGEL OF PRODUCTIVITY

> Federal Reserve Chairman Alan Greenspan did not even say the words "stock market," but his proclamation Thursday that new technology is making the U.S. economy more productive helped Wall Street register its strongest two-week rally in 12 years and sent the Nasdaq market to a new high yesterday.
>
> *THE WASHINGTON POST*

The rate of productivity measures the increase in output per worker, and nothing soothes the Wall Street soul so much as good news on the productivity front. In fact, the rate of productivity is one of the most important economic indicators that the macrowave investor can track for at least two reasons.

First, rising productivity is the best antidote for wage inflation. Think of it this way. If productivity is rising annually at a 3 percent rate, wages can rise by 3 percent without any inflationary effect. But what if productivity is less than 1 percent annually and wages are rising 3 percent? That's wage inflation, and it is sure to draw both the attention and wrath of the Federal Reserve.

This leads us to the second reason why the rate of productivity is so important. Over the longer term, our wages simply cannot rise in real, inflation-adjusted terms unless we produce more per hour of work. It's a simple, ironclad equation, and it is one quite evident in these statistics: Between 1948 and 1973, labor productivity grew at 3 percent annually while real wages grew at almost exactly the same pace. These were great years for the American worker—years when millions of blue-collar workers in our nation's factories were lifted by the archangel of productivity into the afflu-ent ranks of the middle class.

But all of this progress on the prosperity front came crashing down in the 1970s amid an energy crisis, a currency devaluation, stagflation, peri-odic droughts, and political upheaval. That's when productivity fell to less than 1 percent annually—and it stayed right there through 1996. Now here's what's important about this: As a result of this so-called "productiv-ity slowdown," the growth in real wages fell almost in lockstep with the productivity rate—to less than 1 percent annually.

As a practical matter, this meant that millions of Americans saw little or no improvement in their standard of living for more than 20 years. More-over, many American workers who were caught in the crossfire of a shrink-ing defense sector, the export of American factory jobs abroad, and more broad-based technological changes actually saw their real wages and stan-dard of living fall dramatically.

Fortunately, since 1997, productivity has jumped back up to more than 2 percent annually. As Fed Chairman Greenspan has said repeatedly, this rise in productivity has kept the inflationary tiger at bay and allowed us to prosper. Indeed, high productivity driven by rapid technological change is one of the major reasons why the Fed has exercised so much restraint over the last few years. It is also why many of us have seen a resumption of a healthy upward march of our paychecks.

THE BUDGET DEFICIT DRAGON

This is the day many budget experts thought might never come. The fis-cal year that ended Wednesday night at midnight was the first since

1969—the year Neil Armstrong walked on the moon and 400,000 rock fans spent a weekend at Woodstock—that the nation has recorded a federal budget surplus....

THE VIRGINIAN-PILOT

Between the end of World War II and the end of the 1990s, budget surpluses were few and far between even as chronic deficits swelled America's accumulated national debt to over $5 trillion.

At least for now, the times are happily a-changin'. For the past several years, the U.S. has been running large budget surpluses. The irony, of course, is that both budget deficits and surpluses can create headaches for Wall Street investors, and it pays for the savvy macrowave investor to understand why.

The deficit problem is the easier one to grasp. When the government incurs a budget deficit, it must borrow from the public to pay its bills. To do so, it issues bonds and sells them in the marketplace. As it does so, the government is forced to compete with corporate bonds and other financial instruments—and it is this competition for scarce funds that drives interest rates up. Wall Street, of course, hates this because higher interest rates mean less corporate investment, slower growth, and lower corporate earnings. That's why chronic budget deficits can drag an economy down—and bring both the stock and bond markets down with it.

As for the problems associated with budget *surpluses,* the competing goals of the different branches of government can often create interesting crosscurrents in the financial markets. A compelling case in point occurred in the first half of the year 2000. On the one hand, the Federal Reserve was steadily *raising* interest rates to contract an overheated economy and fight inflation. At the same time, the U.S. Treasury was engaged in large bond buybacks because the budget surplus allowed it to use the surplus funds to shrink the public debt. But this action *lowered* interest rates and appeared to work at cross-purposes to the Fed.

THE TRADE DEFICIT TRAP

The tiny threads of confidence that were pulling stock prices steadily higher suddenly snapped yesterday, sending the Dow Jones industrial average plunging 101.46 points. Traders, shocked by the unexpected bulge in the nation's trade deficit, unceremoniously dumped stocks across the board.... The unfavorable trade figures also clobbered the dollar in foreign exchange markets and sent interest rates higher as bond prices fell sharply.

THE WASHINGTON POST

When the trade deficit trap is sprung, it can ensnare everyone on Wall Street—from stock and bond traders to the biggest guns of currency speculation. To understand why, consider this deficit disaster scenario.

A sharp spike in the trade deficit signals to foreign investors that the dollar may begin to weaken. Since these investors don't want to be caught holding stocks denominated in a possibly weakening dollar, they begin to pull their money out of the U.S. market. This puts downward pressure on both the Dow and the Nasdaq indices and even more downward pressure on the dollar. As the stock market begins a sharp slide, more foreign investors together with a growing number of domestic investors join the now panic selling. At this point, the Fed panics, too. It raises interest rates to help prop up the dollar by attracting more foreign investment. But the move backfires as these higher interests rates trigger a slowdown in the economy and a further drop in the stock market.

Meanwhile, with the market dropping precipitously, investors suddenly find themselves feeling much less wealthy. After all, they have just seen their stock portfolios fall by more than 30 percent. In response to this loss of wealth, these investors begin to spend much less money on big-ticket items like cars and homes and computers and even cut back on smaller expenditures on things like entertainment and travel. This reduced consumption contributes further to the recessionary pressures created by the Fed, and the next thing anyone knows, the U.S. economy is falling in a steep downward spiral—and taking both the global economy and stock market down with it.

THE FOUR HORSEMEN OF THE APOCALYPSE

When a 7.6-magnitude earthquake hit the island [of Taiwan]...analysts worldwide warned of major chip shortages.... Prices for the benchmark 64-megabit dynamic random access memory (DRAM) chip rose from $14 to $21, just as manufacturers worldwide were working at full speed to meet anticipated Christmas demands.

THE KNIGHT RIDDER/TRIBUNE SYNDICATE

The eminent financial authority Jeremy Siegel has written that "the word 'crisis' in Chinese is composed of two characters: the first, the symbol of danger...the second, of opportunity." And Professor Siegel is right. From the savvy macrowave investor's point of view, every natural disaster or war should be viewed as a macroplay opportunity—morbid as that may sound. This will be true, however, only if the impact of the disaster on the financial markets can be accurately interpreted and anticipated. That's why it's important to understand how various shocks can differentially affect different industries and market sectors.

For example, when a mammoth earthquake in Taiwan shut down production at many factories for personal computers and semiconductor chips, both Apple and Dell would turn out to be excellent shorting opportunities whereas Korean chip producers like Samsung and Hyundai would be great stocks to buy. Why? Because both Dell and Apple rely heavily on Taiwanese production for their computer boxes and would be severely hurt by Taiwan's loss of production capacity. In contrast, both Samsung and Hyundai benefited the most from the inevitable spike in chip prices from the loss of Taiwanese production because their production facilities were unaffected.

Similarly, an outbreak of war in the Balkans and a collateral fear of U.S. military intervention might depress the overall stock market; but such a war might also boost stocks in the defense sector. On the other hand, a debt crisis in Mexico might not have much of an effect on the overall market; nonetheless, it may take a very big toll on banking sector stocks like Chase Manhattan and Citibank that are holding much of the Mexican paper. Finally, as the title of this book suggests, if it rains in Brazil to break a drought, it may be a great time to buy Starbucks stock.

And so it is that traditional Horsemen of the Apocalypse such as war and pestilence are regularly joined by a myriad of other episodic and unpredictable events like hurricanes, oil price shocks, and computer viruses. Understanding how these kinds of unpredictable shocks may filter through the financial markets is one of the most important arrows in the macrowave investor's quiver.

BIG BROTHER AND YOUR PORTFOLIO

Never quite understanding where they were stepping, President Clinton and British Prime Minister Tony Blair rudely popped the biotech stock bubble last week. On March 14, they jointly declared that rivals in the race to discover new genes should share their results.... Wall Street misinterpreted that pronouncement as an attack on patent rights—and investors well beyond biotech quickly paid the price. Biotech shares tumbled almost 13 percent in a day, taking the entire Nasdaq index down 200 points with them.

BUSINESS WEEK

Make no mistake about it. Deeds by government officials—and as the news story above indicates, sometimes even just words—can kill a stock, an industry sector, or even the entire market faster than an Uzi. If Congress threatens price controls on prescription drugs as part of a broader Medicare reform, you can bank on the share prices of Lilly and Pfizer and Merck taking a plunge. Or if gas pump prices soar on OPEC production cutbacks and the Speaker of the House of Representatives proposes a windfall profits tax on Big Oil, get out of the way as the share prices of Exxon and Chevron drop double digits.

But it's not just bad things that can happen to good stocks. Actions by the government can often have a very favorable impact on the market as well. If a U.S. appeals court grants Eli Lilly a broader patent on its antidepressant drug Prozac, watch for its stock to soar. If the FDA accelerates the approval of a clinical study for a new blood substitute by Alliance Pharmaceuticals, guess which way its stock is heading.

The broader point here is that if you ignore the impacts of Big Brother on the stock market, you do so at your own peril. In this regard, regularly reading daily publications such as the *Los Angeles Times* or *New York Times,* the *Wall Street Journal,* and *Investor's Business Daily,* as well as magazines like *Barron's, Business Week, Forbes, Fortune, Money, Newsweek, Time,* and *Worth,* will keep you well ahead of the government's regulatory curve—and keep you out of harm's way from its many curveballs.

THE WHIP OF TECHNOLOGICAL CHANGE

Like rotary telephones and eight-track tapes, the typewriter has lost its battle against technological obsolescence. Yesterday Smith Corona Corp., one of the last American typewriter makers and on whose machines countless term papers, business plans and Dear John letters were hammered out, filed for bankruptcy protection.

THE BOSTON GLOBE

Let me understate the case here: Technological change is the single most important determinant of stock prices over the longer term. Such change can bring untold new wealth to shareholders in new companies like Apple, which commercialized the computer, Celera Genomics, which is one of the leaders in the race to chart the human genome, Cisco, which took the lead in Internet infrastructure, and VISX, which holds some of the most valuable patents in laser eye surgery.

Note, however, that such change can also decimate or destroy companies, as well, and leave investors holding fistfuls of worthless stock certificates. Don't believe me? Just ask the shareholders of the typewriter dinosaur, Smith-Corona.

And what about the venerable AT&T? While this giant once ruled the long-distance phone market roost, it has seen a steady erosion of its market share under the onslaught of new cell phone and wireless technologies.

The important point here is that the savvy macrowave investor—particularly traders who focus on the technology sector—will want to closely follow announcements of new technological breakthroughs and the patents that may be granted on these breakthroughs. In this regard, let me happily recommend visiting web sites like Changewave.com, Individualinvestor.com, and Redherring.com. Each of these web sites—as well as their print media incarnations—has a very sophisticated take on how to profit from technological change.

C H A P T E R

THE WARRING SCHOOLS

*A*t the not so tender age of 91, retired economics professor Herb
Hoover still loves to rage against the stock market machine.
You see, throughout his stock picking life, Professor Hoover has
always managed to be at exactly the wrong place at the worst
possible time.

It started in 1931 when Herb's namesake President Hoover
raised interest rates to protect the gold standard. Just the right
classical economic medicine, thought graduate student Herb at the
time. So he bought his first 100 shares of stock and then watched
his certificates turn worthless as President Hoover's tight money
policies shoved the country off the precipice of recession into the
Great Depression.

Nor did Herb do any better on his next market foray. That was
a few years later after Franklin Roosevelt had replaced Hoover
and started listening to that radical English economist John
Maynard Keynes. It just made no sense to run a huge budget deficit
to save the country—or so his professors at Harvard told him. So
this time, Herb plunged. He shorted 1000 shares of General

21

Motors—and then watched in dismay as the economy recovered and the stock zoomed in price.

These two stock market experiences pretty much cured Herb of wanting to take any more risks for the next 40 years. So Herb stayed out of the market until 1979. That's when the Federal Reserve embraced the philosophy of one of Herb's great idols in life, the monetarist guru Milton Friedman. Herb was so sure that the economy would boom under the Fed's newfound monetarism that he took all his retirement money out of bonds and put the cash into a high-growth mutual fund. Three years later, after the Fed's monetarist experiment had caused the worst recession since the Great Depression, the fund was as broke as Herb.

Too bad, because Herb missed out on the great bull market that took off when Ronald Reagan started all that supply side nonsense. Cut taxes to increase budget revenues? Herb knew that was smoke and mirrors. But boy did the stock market love it.

For Herb, the last straw came in the early 1990s. Herb was sure there would be a presidential election stock market rally because there always had been. So he tried the market one last time—this time with some very heavy margin buying. He was going for broke— and he got just that. But how was Herb to know that some new branch of economists calling themselves "new classicals" had taken over the George Bush White House and were refusing to prime the economic pump. The resulting economic slump not only cost Bush the election, it wiped Herb out for the fourth and final time.

A s Herb Hoover learned the very hardest of ways, if you are going to trade or invest successfully, it is essential that you understand the basic differences between the warring schools of macroeconomics. These five schools include: *classical economics, Keynesianism, monetarism, supply side economics,* and *new classical economics.* Understanding the differences between these schools of thought is essential for at least two reasons.

First, each school has important insights that the macrowave investor can use to sharpen his or her perspective on the financial markets. For example, classical economics teaches us about how economies and markets naturally adjust, while Keynesian economics explains the conditions under which those adjustments are unlikely to take place. Similarly, monetarism reveals the all-important link between money and prices, while supply side economics explains how an economy can use tools such as tax cuts and deregulation to grow without worry of inflation. And, of course, new classical economics shines an absolutely brilliant light on the role of expectations in the stock market and the broader macroeconomy.

Second, and more important, each of the different schools of macroeconomics will prescribe a very different policy cure for whatever macro ills may be ailing us. This is of a very real practical importance because, at any given time, one of these schools of macroeconomics may have the ear of the President or the Congress or even the Federal Reserve. For example, both Presidents Herbert Hoover in the 1920s and Dwight Eisenhower in the 1950s were strongly influenced by classical economics, while Presidents Franklin Roosevelt in the 1930s and John F. Kennedy in the 1960s were surrounded by Keynesian advisors.

In contrast, during the late 1970s when stagflation was raging, monetarists quite literally took over the Federal Reserve, and the Fed under Chairman Paul Volcker stopped trying to control interest rates and instead established monetary growth targets. The result was a sharp spike in interest rates that wreaked havoc with the bond and currency markets and sent interest-sensitive stocks reeling.

The broader point here is that it is not just the macroeconomic problems that we discussed in the first chapter that the macrowave investor has to worry about. It's also how Congress and the President and the Federal Reserve are likely to react to the problems. Will Congress cut taxes? Will the Fed raise interest rates? Will the President support an increase in government spending? And the punch line here is that the answers to all of these questions will be very dependent on which political party is in control of the White House and Congress and which of the warring schools of macroeconomics that party is currently listening to.

In this regard, it is fair to say that the Democrats are generally Keynesians who favor an activist fiscal and monetary policy. In contrast, the Republicans are generally divided among the monetarist, supply side, new classical, and even classical camps—all of which discourage an activist fiscal and monetary policy in some degree.

With this, then, as background, let's dive into a quick, capsule history of the warring schools. This history begins with classical economics and moves, during the Great Depression, to Keynesian economics. Then, during the 1970s era of stagflation, we witness the triumph of monetarism, which is then quickly eclipsed in the 1980s by supply side economics. However, after a brief reign of the new classical economists in the 1990s, the nation's policymakers like Alan Greenspan return in the 2000s to an eclectic form of Keynesian macroeconomic policy which appears to incorporate, in some small or large way, the wisdom of *all* of the schools.

A NOT SO CLASSICAL GAS

"The truly savage and frenetic part of New York is not Harlem," the Spanish poet [Federico] Garcia Lorca told a Madrid lecture audience in 1932. "In Harlem, there is human warmth and the noise of children, and there are homes and grass, and sorrow finds consolation and the wound finds its sweet bandage." "The terrible, cold, cruel part," he declared, "is Wall Street." Wandering through its "limestone canyons" in October, 1929, Lorca observed the great stock-market crash that would help usher in the Great Depression. "A rabble of dead money went sliding off into the sea. Ambulances collected suicides whose hands were full of rings."

THE NATIONAL POST

The irony of the Great Depression is that Herbert Hoover was one of the brightest men to ever occupy the White House. His problem, however, is that he had become a pitiful and much ridiculed prisoner of the prevailing economic doctrine of his time—classical economics.

Classical economics dates back to the late 1700s and has its roots in the *laissez faire* writings of free market economists like Adam Smith, David Ricardo, and Jean-Baptiste Say. These classical economists believed that the problem of unemployment was a natural part of the business cycle, that it was self-correcting, and, most important, that there was no need for the government to intervene in the free market to correct it.

Between the Civil War and the Roaring Twenties, America sustained periodic booms and busts—recording no less than five official depressions. However, after every bust, the economy always bounced back—exactly as the classical economists predicted. That was true until these classical economists met their match in the Great Depression of the 1930s. With the stock market crash of 1929, the economy fell into first a recession and then a deep depression. The gross domestic product fell by almost a third and by 1933, 25 percent of the work force was unemployed. At the same time, business investment virtually disappeared, from about $16 billion in 1929 to $1 billion by 1933.

While President Herbert Hoover kept promising that "the worst is over" and "prosperity is just around the corner," and the classical economists kept waiting for what they viewed as the inevitable recovery, two key figures walked onto the macroeconomic stage—economist John Maynard Keynes and Hoover's presidential successor, Franklin Roosevelt.

LORD KEYNES TO THE RESCUE

We have involved ourselves in a colossal muddle, having blundered in the control of a delicate machine, the working of which we do not understand.

JOHN MAYNARD KEYNES

John Maynard Keynes flatly rejected the classical notion of a self-correcting economy. He warned that patiently waiting for the eventual recovery was fruitless because, as his most famous utterance informs us, "in the long run, we're all dead."

Keynes believed that under certain circumstances, the economy would not naturally rebound but simply stagnate or, even worse, fall into a death spiral. To Keynes, the only way to get the economy moving again was to prime the economic pump with increased government expenditures. Thus, fiscal policy was born and the Keynesian prescription became the underlying, if unstated philosophy, of Franklin Roosevelt's New Deal. *Fiscal policy* uses increased government expenditures or, alternatively, tax cuts to stimulate or expand the economy. Fiscal policy can also be used to contract the economy and fight inflation by reducing government expenditures or raising taxes.

Roosevelt's ambitious public works programs in the 1930s, together with the 1940s boom of World War II, were enough to lift the American economy—and the stock market—out of the Great Depression and up to unparalleled heights. In the early 1950s, the Keynesian prescription of large-scale government expenditures worked again—this time when the heavy spending associated with the Korean War helped pull the economy out of a slump. A decade later, pure Keynesianism reached its zenith with the much heralded Kennedy tax cut of 1964 passed in honor of the slain president.

In President John F. Kennedy's Camelot, the Council of Economic Advisors Chairman Walter Heller popularized the term "fine tuning," and Heller firmly believed that through the careful mechanistic application of Keynesian principles, the nation's macroeconomy could be held very close to full employment with minimal inflation. In 1962, Heller recommended to Kennedy that the President advocate a large tax cut to stimulate the sluggish economy. The Congress eventually agreed, and this Keynesian tax cut helped make the 1960s one of the most prosperous decades in America. However, this fiscal stimulus also laid the foundation for the emergence of a new and ugly macroeconomic phenomenon known as stagflation—simultaneous high inflation and high unemployment.

OF NAPALM AND MONETARISM

> I knew from the start that if I left a woman I really loved—the Great Society—in order to fight that bitch of a [Vietnam] war...then I would lose everything at home. My hopes...[and] my dreams.
>
> LYNDON B. JOHNSON

The stagflation problem had its roots in President Lyndon Johnson's stubbornness. In the late 1960s, against the strong advice of his economic advisors, Johnson increased expenditures on the Vietnam War but refused to cut spending on his Great Society social welfare programs. This refusal helped spawn a virulent demand-pull inflation.

The essence of demand-pull inflation is too much money chasing too few goods, and that's exactly what happened when the U.S. tried to finance both guns and butter—both the Vietnam War and the Great Society. The result not only was a roaring economy and a very low unemployment rate, but rapidly increasing inflation as well. In this sense, demand-pull inflation is a very *bullish* phenomenon in that it emerges when times are *too* good.

In 1972, President Richard Nixon imposed price and wage controls and gained the nation a brief respite from the Johnson-era demand-pull inflation. However, once the controls were lifted in 1973, inflation jumped back up to double digits—helped in large part by a different, much more bearish kind of inflation then emerging. This inflation was known as *cost-push* inflation.

Cost-push inflation occurs as a result of so-called "supply shocks" such as those experienced in the early 1970s. During this period, such shocks included crop failures, a worldwide drought, and a quadrupling of the world price of crude oil. Over time, cost-push inflation can lead to a longer-term *stagflation*. This is simply recession or economic stagnation combined with inflation. In this situation, and unlike with demand-pull inflation, the economy suffers the double whammy of both higher unemployment *and* higher prices.

What's most interesting about stagflation is that prior to the 1970s, economists didn't believe you could even have both high inflation and high unemployment at the same time. If one went up, the other had to go down. But the 1970s proved economists wrong on this point and likewise exposed Keynesian economics as being incapable of solving the new stagnation problem. The Keynesian dilemma was simply this: Using expansionary policies to reduce unemployment simply created more inflation, while using contractionary policies to curb inflation only deepened the recession. That meant that the traditional Keynesian tools that worked so well getting the nation out of the Great Depression could solve only half of the stagflation problem at any one time—and only by making the other half worse.

It was this inability of Keynesian economics to cope with stagflation that set the stage for Professor Milton Friedman's monetarist challenge to what had become the Keynesian orthodoxy.

A SPOONFUL OF RECESSION MAKES THE INFLATION GO DOWN

Federal Reserve Chairman Paul Volcker's war on inflation strangled the economy—and the stock market.

USA TODAY

Milton Friedman's monetarist school argues that the problems of both inflation and recession may be traced to one thing—the rate of growth of the money supply. To the monetarists, inflation happens when the government prints too much money, and recessions happen when it prints too little.

From this monetarist perspective, stagflation is the inevitable result of government mischief—namely, the repeated use of activist fiscal and monetary policies to try to push the economy beyond its growth limits. In the somewhat tortured parlance of monetarism, these limits are referred to as the economy's "natural rate of unemployment"—although most of us probably believe that there is nothing natural about unemployment.

Be that as it may, according to the monetarists, expansionary attempts to exceed the economy's natural limits may result in short-run spurts of growth. However, after each growth spurt, prices and wages inevitably rise and drag the economy back to its natural rate of unemployment—albeit at a higher rate of inflation.

Over time, these repeated and futile attempts to push the economy beyond its limits eventually lead to an ugly upward inflationary spiral. In this situation, monetarists believe that the only way to wring inflation and inflationary expectations out of the economy is to have the actual unemployment rate rise above the natural rate and that means only one thing: inducing a recession.

This is at least one interpretation of what the Federal Reserve did beginning in 1979 under the monetarist banner of setting monetary growth targets. Under Chairman Paul Volcker, the Fed adopted a sharply contractionary monetary policy and interest rates soared to over 20 percent. Particularly hard-hit were the bond and currency markets, along with interest-sensitive sectors of the economy like housing construction, automobile purchases, and business investment.

While the Fed's bitter medicine worked, three years of hard economic times left a bad taste in the mouths of the American people now hungry for a sweeter macroeconomic cure than either the Keynesians or monetarists could offer. Enter stage right: supply side economics.

VOODOO BULLS AND DEFICIT BEARS

They say the U.S. has had its day in the sun; that our nation has passed its zenith. They expect you to tell your children…that the future will be one of sacrifice and few opportunities. My fellow Americans, I utterly reject that view.

RONALD REAGAN

In the 1980 presidential election, Ronald Reagan ran on a supply side platform that his then-rival George Bush branded as "voodoo economics." Voodoo or not, Reagan cast a wonderful spell over both the general public and the stock market as he promised to simultaneously cut taxes, increase government tax revenues, and accelerate the rate of economic growth without inducing inflation. This was a promise of a very sweet macroeconomic cure indeed.

On the surface, the supply side approach looks very similar to the kind of Keynesian tax cut prescribed in the 1960s to stimulate a sluggish economy. However, the supply-siders of Reagan's time viewed such tax cuts from a very different behavioral perspective. Unlike the Keynesians, they did not agree that such a tax cut would necessarily cause inflation. Instead, the supply-siders believed that the American people would actually work much harder and invest much more if they were allowed to keep more of the fruits of their labor. The end result would be to increase the amount of goods and services our economy could actually produce by pushing out the economy's supply curve—hence, "supply side" economics.

Most important, the supply-siders promised that by cutting taxes and thereby spurring rapid growth, the loss in tax revenues from the tax cut would be more than offset by the increase in tax revenues from increased economic growth. Thus, under supply side economics, the budget deficit would actually be reduced.

Unfortunately, that didn't happen. While the economy and stock market boomed, so too did America's budget deficit. And as the budget deficit soared, America's trade deficit soared with it.

A CASUALTY OF ECONOMIC WAR

> President Bush, thrown on the defensive by continued national economic problems…, plans to try to regain political momentum by accelerating the formation of his official reelection campaign…. "It's falling apart," one GOP activist said of the once well-oiled White House political and message machinery…. "We're getting the crap beat out of us. The Democrats have pulled George Bush right into their playing field and they're punching him out."
>
> *THE WASHINGTON POST*

How a president with a sky-high approval rating right after winning the war with Iraq fell so far and so fast in the polls is one of the great political stories of all time. But it is a story that hinges purely on economics.

At the time of the Gulf War, President George Bush was deeply concerned about a lot more than Saddam Hussein. Indeed, the budget deficit had already jumped to over $200 billion, and the economy was sliding into a serious recession. To any red-blooded Keynesian, this onset of recession would have been a clear signal to engage in expansionary policy. However, in the Bush White House, Ronald Reagan's supply side advisors had been supplanted not by Keynesians but rather by a new breed of macroeconomic thinkers—the so-called "new classicals."

New classical economics is based on the theory of *rational expectations*. This theory says that if you form your expectations *rationally,* you will take into account all available information including the future effects of activist fiscal and monetary policies.

The idea behind rational expectations is that activist policies might be able to fool people for a while. However, after a while, people will learn from their experiences, and then you can't fool them at all. The central policy implication of this idea is, of course, profound: Rational expectations render activist fiscal and monetary policies completely ineffective, so they should be abandoned.

For example, suppose the Federal Reserve undertakes an expansionary monetary policy to close a recessionary gap. Repeated experiences with such activist policy have taught people that increases in the money supply fuel inflation. To protect themselves in a world of rational expectations, businesses will immediately respond to the Fed's expansion by raising prices, workers will demand higher wages, and the attempted stimulus will be completely offset by the contractionary effects of inflation.

In fact, we observe global financial markets acting with such rational expectations all the time, and it is precisely this kind of forward thinking that this book is trying to cultivate. One small example is offered up by how the financial markets reacted in the first part of the year 2000. During that turbulent time, as demand-pull inflationary pressures continued to mount, the Federal Reserve steadily raised interest rates—six times over an 11-month period. However, the financial markets never waited for the Fed to actually raise the rates. Instead, adjustments took place well prior to the events on the expectation that the Fed would do what it actually did. Bond yields rose while bond prices fell; the dollar strengthened; the commodity market emerged as an inflation hedge; and the stock market reversed into bear territory. Of course, any microtrader who ignored all of these macrowave signals consistently wound up on the wrong side of any trade.

But let's get back to President Bush's plight back in the early 1990s. While Bush's new classical advisors may have been giving him some very good economic advice, it was absolutely horrible political advice. Indeed, these new classical advisors flatly rejected any Keynesian quick fix to the deepening recession. Instead, they called for more stable and systematic policies based on long-term goals instead of continuing to rely on short-sighted discretionary reactions.

Bush took this new classical advice to heart, the economy limped into the 1992 presidential election and, like Richard Nixon in 1960, Bush lost to a Democrat promising to get the economy moving again. What is perhaps most interesting about this transition of power is that Bill Clinton actually did very little to stimulate the economy. The mere fact, however, that Clinton promised a more activist approach helped restore business and consumer confidence.

ONE PICTURE IS WORTH 10,000 POINTS ON THE DOW

Today, the nation's macroeconomic magicians appear to be able to keep severe recessions and depressions at bay. This is the real triumph of modern macroeconomics; it is great news for investors and is illustrated in Fig. 2-1. Note how the amplitude of the business cycle has been considerably reduced since the wide-scale application of macroeconomic policies after World War II.

This figure would appear to provide strong testimony to the argument that activist fiscal and monetary policies can reduce the volatility of the business cycle and, by implication, the volatility of the stock market cycle. In the next two chapters, we will delve more deeply into the mysteries of fiscal and monetary policy. In the meantime, however, the broader points we want to take away from this chapter are simply these:

- The warring schools of macroeconomics will always disagree about how to fight the problems of recession, inflation, and stagflation.

- At any given point in time, the Federal government's solutions to these problems will be shaped by whichever of the warring schools has the ear of the President and the Congress and the Federal Reserve.

- Depending on which solutions are adopted, the stock market will react in different ways and in different degrees.

For example, in the event of a recession, a Keynesian president may opt for an increase in government spending to stimulate the economy. This may provide a short-run boost to the stock market as well as a stimulus to specific sectors of the market like defense and housing that rely heavily on the government for business. But the bond market may react negatively for fear that the resultant budget deficits will drive up interest rates.

In contrast, a supply side president may favor a large tax cut for consumers coupled with a cutback in the regulation of certain businesses to jump-start the recessionary economy. This, too, may boost the stock market. But the consumer tax cut may also give a particular boost to the stock prices of companies in consumer-dependent sectors like retailing and automobiles. In addition, the companies in those industries most likely to benefit from the deregulation—perhaps chemicals or telecommunications—may likewise get a share price boost.

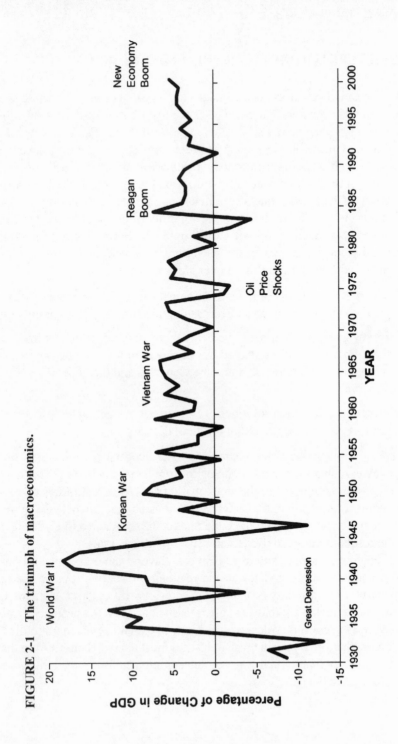

FIGURE 2-1 The triumph of macroeconomics.

3

UNCLE SAM'S
TOOLBOX

- *In 1933, President Franklin Roosevelt began to dramatically increase government expenditures on a whole slew of Keynesian-inspired New Deal programs, and the U.S. economy began what would be its very long journey out of the depths of the Great Depression. Over the next four years, the Dow Jones stock market average would rise by 240 percent.*

- *In 1954, the U.S. economy fell into its deepest recession since the Great Depression. President Dwight D. Eisenhower responded with a call for major tax cuts and increased public spending, bears turned to bulls, and the stock market rallied more than 80 percent over the next 15 months.*

- *In 1964, Congress passed the famous Kennedy Tax Cut in honor of the slain president. This textbook Keynesian remedy shook the U.S. economy out of its doldrums, and the Dow Jones Industrial Average raced up over 40 percent over the next two and a half years.*

- *In 1982, President Ronald Reagan dramatically cut taxes, the economy broke free of its chains of monetarist restraint, and the stock market took off on a five-year bull run, rising over*

200 percent. This would not be the longest bull run in history, however. That happened during the long and often tumultuous reign of William Jefferson Clinton.

- *At the beginning of his first term in the 1990s, Bill Clinton raised taxes and cut spending to help balance the Federal budget. This calmed Wall Street's fears over the burgeoning budget deficit, the economy prospered, and the bulls on Wall Street went on rampaging right into the new century.*

- *At the beginning of his term in 2001, President George W. Bush engaged in a very subtle war with Fed Chairman Alan Greenspan over whether a flagging economy should be revived by Bush's tax cut or Greenspan's interest rate cuts. The ensuing uncertainty heightened inflationary concerns, while a policy gridlock made it much more difficult for either Bush or Greenspan to take the appropriate steps needed to restore the nation's economic health. In the process, the stock market's recovery was stalled.*

A ll of these examples illustrate how *fiscal policy* can have a profound effect on the movements of the stock market—where fiscal policy is simply increasing government spending or cutting taxes to stimulate the economy, or decreasing government expenditures or raising taxes to contract an overheated economy. What we want to do in this chapter is to first understand how fiscal policy works and then use our macrowave logic to figure out how the effects of fiscal policy are likely to ripple through the stock and bond markets.

KEEPING THE ECONOMIC SCORE

To really understand the essence of fiscal policy, we need to start with a little national income accounting. To total a nation's gross domestic product (GDP), all we have to do is add up consumption spending, investment spending, government spending, and net exports, where net exports are simply exports minus imports. In terms of understanding fiscal policy, this GDP calculation is important for two reasons.

First, it gives us an idea of the *relative importance* of each of the components that make up the GDP. For example, consumption represents almost 70 percent of the GDP. That's why the savvy macrowave investor will pay particular attention to consumption indicators like consumer confidence, retail sales, and personal income. Changes in these major indicators can all be early warning signs that the largest component of the GDP is about to tank and trigger a recession—or perhaps overheat and ignite inflation.

The second and perhaps even more important reason that the GDP formula is important is that it helps us work through the macrowave logic that motivates discretionary fiscal policy actions to begin with. For example, suppose the macroeconomy suffers some kind of negative shock like a war in the Middle East or a worldwide drought triggered by an El Niño condition. This might cause consumers to save more out of worry and therefore consume less. While consumption starts to go down in our GDP formula, this is just the beginning of the story.

The next thing that happens is that inventories begin to pile up at businesses because consumers are spending less. Businesses not only respond by reducing their investment, they also begin to lay people off. And what do you think the newly laid off people do—or don't do, as the case may be? That's right. They spend less, so consumption falls some more. This leads to more inventory accumulations, even less investment, and more layoffs. And so the downward recessionary spiral goes until it reaches some kind of bottom.

Now, the whole idea behind fiscal policy is to first stop, and then reverse, this recessionary slide. It does so by offsetting the declines in consumption and investment in one of two ways.

INSIDE UNCLE SAM'S TOOLBOX

The first Keynesian option is to simply increase government spending. In fact, this is exactly what the government did to get us out of the Great Depression in the 1930s, as it spent large sums on New Deal public works projects to offset the massive declines in consumption and investment brought about by the 1929 stock market crash. Such a Keynesian stimulus was also used very successfully in the 1950s to pull the economy out of a recession. However, since that time—more than 50 years ago—this kind of fiscal policy has rarely been used as an antirecessionary tool.

Not so for the second fiscal policy option. This second Keynesian option, which has obvious political appeal, involves cutting taxes to stimulate economic growth. For example, the most famous Keynesian tax cut ever administered was in 1964 during Lyndon Johnson's presidency. This was the broad-based tax cut noted earlier that was passed in honor of the recently assassinated President Kennedy, who had originally proposed it. This tax cut helped drive the Dow Jones Industrial Average up by more than 40 percent over two and half years. The irony of this tax cut, of course, is that just five years later, the Johnson Administration had to impose a tax *increase* to cool down an economy overheated by a combination of the original Kennedy tax cut, the war in Vietnam, and expenditures on President Johnson's Great Society programs. Essentially, this tax hike was fiscal policy in reverse.

A second historic example of a tax cut which stimulated the economy occurred in the Reagan years in the 1980s. While this cut was marketed as a supply side tax cut by the Republican president, at least some have argued that the effects of the Reagan tax cuts were primarily on aggregate demand and that it really was a classic Keynesian example of fiscal policy rather than true supply side economics. Here is how *Business Week* put it:

> The Reagan Administration was launched with a flurry of economic experimentation. Citing supply-side economics, the President proposed to cut taxes, boost defense spending, and still balance the budget. But the 1981 tax cut failed to produce a surge in revenues. Many economists now believe that growth under Reagan was stimulated by deficits and that supply side [economics] is nothing more than Keynesianism on steroids.

That assessment is a harsh one—and perhaps inaccurate. But regardless of who is right about whether the Reagan tax cuts were new-fangled supply-side or old-style Keynesianism, the effects of these cuts on both the economy and the stock market were dramatic.

As for how and why the effects of fiscal policy are likely to ripple through the stock market, this is where fiscal policy really gets interesting from the macrowave investor's point of view. This is because to increase government expenditures or cut taxes, the government typically has to increase the budget deficit. The important question for the macrowave investor to ask here, then, is this: *How will the government finance a budget deficit that results from expansionary fiscal policy?*

As a practical matter, there are two ways to finance a deficit. The government can either sell bonds or print money. And the point we want to make here is that these two options present both very different dangers and very different profit-making opportunities for the macrowave investor.

DON'T CROWD ME OUT!

As an undergraduate in the 1970s, I was taught that...one of the important features of a successful economy was the use of budget deficits as a stimulus to economic growth. This idea, which had its roots in Keynes's writings…still captures a very important truth about certain economies at certain times.… Since the time when I studied these theories, however, …we have come to understand that we must place much greater emphasis on the importance of supply factors for long-term growth and be much more cognizant of the danger that by crowding out investments, budget deficits can slow productivity growth and lead to a vicious cycle of higher public borrowing at higher interest rates, leading to still lower investment and economic growth, which in turn leads to even larger budget deficits.

TREASURY SECRETARY LAWRENCE SUMMERS

With bond financing, the U.S. Treasury goes directly to the private financial markets and sells the bonds it needs to finance its deficit. The big danger of this option is that the sale of these government bonds will raise interest rates and thereby crowd out private investment—as former Treasury Secretary Larry Summers eloquently warns above. This crowding out can happen because in order to sell its bonds, the Treasury may have to raise interest rates. But higher rates will make corporate bonds less attractive, and the result will be a lower level of private investment. You can see, then, why budget deficits make both the stock and bond markets very, very nervous.

And note the irony here. The government is increasing government spending to offset declines of consumption and investment during a recession. However, when the government sells bonds to finance its expenditures, this can raise interest rates, and that, in turn, can drive down investment in the GDP formula even further. To the extent, then, that private investment falls as government spending rises, there is crowding out of the private sector even as fiscal policy becomes a much less effective tool.

THE GOVERNMENT PRINTING PRESS

At the beginning of 1970, [President Richard] Nixon had installed his old friend Arthur Burns as chairman of the Federal Reserve.… Burns had more or less promised Nixon that he would, if appointed, flood the economy with whatever liquidity it took to elect Republicans in 1970 and '72. Once he got the job, however, he hesitated. Burns understood perfectly well how inflationary Nixon's monetary policy would be. He would only proceed, he decided, if Nixon restrained prices directly.… On August 15, 1971, Nixon announced the most stunning turnabout in American economic policy since 1933. He froze wages and prices for ninety days, imposed a 10 percent surcharge on all imports, and refused any longer to exchange gold for dollars at the $35 rate.

In the short term, the plan worked. A delighted Arthur Burns started the printing presses rolling at the Mint, and Nixon got his 1972 boom—and 61 percent of the vote. What he also got, however, was double-digit inflation in 1973–74, an energy shortage, the collapse of the international monetary system, and the worst economic slump since 1940.

THE WEEKLY STANDARD

Here, I might add one important item to the *Weekly Standard*'s list of financial disasters wrought by the Fed's unrestrained printing of money in the Arthur Burns era. That item, of course, was the second worst bear market in American history. In 1973 and 1974, this bear market ripped the Dow Jones Industrial Average almost in half. Only the bear market of the Great Depression, which saw the Dow drop by 89 percent, was worse.

Clearly, then, the government's printing press can pose a grave threat to your portfolio—or perhaps a wonderful shorting opportunity. But how, you may ask, does the Federal Reserve actually print money to finance a budget deficit?

Well, this happens when the Fed purchases the U.S. Treasury bonds before they hit the open market. In this case, the Fed is said to be "accommodating" the government's fiscal policy because it is buying the bonds rather than letting those bonds go out on the open market to compete with corporate bonds. And that's why this method of financing the budget deficit is equivalent to "printing money." The Fed simply pays for the Treasury bonds with a check that increases bank reserves.

Historically, there have been some very interesting battles over the Fed's accommodation, or lack thereof, of discretionary fiscal policy. For example, during the Vietnam War, Federal Reserve Chairman William McChesney Martin steadfastly refused to accommodate the budget deficit being run by the Johnson Administration to finance the Vietnam War and Great Society, and the result was a double-digit spike in interest rates. On the other hand, as our news clip from the *Weekly Standard* notes above, the Fed under Arthur Burns accommodated the Treasury when the U.S. tried to use fiscal policy to get out of the recession. However, the result of this easy money policy was a disaster as well.

More broadly, the savvy macrowave investor should clearly understand that the two different ways of financing a budget deficit—bond financing and printing money—can have very different impacts on the financial markets. In the case of bond financing, higher interest rates are likely to drive the stock and bond markets down and the value of the dollar up. This is a recipe for short selling and currency speculation. In contrast, with the print money option and lower interest rates, bond prices will tend to fall along with the value of the currency while the stock market will tend to rise; that's very bullish for stocks—at least in the short run. However, if the easy money policy ignites inflation, as it did in the Arthur Burns era, just about everyone on Wall Street will be running for the exits. In this kind of situation, only the bears and nimble short sellers are going to be making a buck.

You can see, then, how complicated the impact of an application of fiscal policy is on the financial markets. In the next chapter, we will see that the same is true for monetary policy.

ALAN GREENSPAN'S BRIEFCASE

When we moved on February 4th [to raise interest rates], I think our expectation was that we would prick the [speculative] bubble in the equity markets.

FEDERAL RESERVE CHAIRMAN ALAN GREENSPAN

Now *that* is a truly scary quote. Here we have the Federal Reserve Chairman openly admitting that he purposely used monetary policy to bring the stock market crashing down from its "irrationally exuberant" speculative heights. And what about this quote from one of the most eloquent economists of our time, Paul Krugman:

You may quarrel with the Fed chairman's judgment—you may think that he should keep the economy on a looser rein—but you can hardly dispute his power. Indeed, if you want a simple model for predicting the unemployment rate in the United States over the next few years, here it is: It will be what Greenspan wants it to be, plus or minus a random error reflecting the fact that he is not quite God.

Get the picture? Now do you see why "Don't fight the Fed!" is one of the most important maxims among professional traders on Wall Street—one which speaks directly to the overriding importance of the Federal Reserve and monetary policy. Indeed, any investor or trader who has tried to fight the Fed knows from bloody experience just what kind of havoc and uncertainty monetary policy can create on the financial markets.

THE MYSTERIES OF MONETARY POLICY

Monetary policy involves expanding the money supply to stimulate a recessionary economy or shrinking the money supply to contract an overheated and inflationary economy. As for how the Federal Reserve conducts monetary policy, it uses two primary tools.

The first is *open market operations.* In a nutshell, the Fed buys government securities when it wants to expand the money supply and lower interest rates, and it sells government securities when it wants to contract the money supply and increase interest rates.

While open market operations used to be the most important of the Fed's weapons, its second policy tool has emerged as the lever of choice, at least in the era of Alan Greenspan. This tool involves the setting of the so-called *discount rate* and *Federal funds rate.* The discount rate is the interest rate that the Fed charges banks when they borrow money from the Fed while the Federal funds rate is the rate that banks charge each other for making loans. Lowering these rates makes it cheaper for banks to borrow money and expand the money supply. In contrast, raising the discount and Federal funds rates makes it more expensive for banks to borrow from the Fed and is contractionary.

A MACROWAVE CHAIN REACTION

Sales of new homes in June fell 3.7 percent from May to the slowest pace in more than two years as rising mortgage rates took another bite out of the booming housing market.... Slower new-home sales could mean slowing consumer spending.... New homes need new appliances—washers and dryers, dishwashers, refrigerators, and similar items. Demand for carpeting and other home-improvement or remodeling outlays also is affected. Moreover, when people avoid big-ticket purchases, they tend to cut back on smaller ones.

INVESTOR'S BUSINESS DAILY

The chain of events explained in this news excerpt is just one of the ways a small Fed rate hike winds up rippling through the economy in a big way. In this case, as new home sales fall, a host of other housing-related sectors take a very big hit.

At the heart of these kinds of adjustments is something we need to know about. It's called the *monetary transmission mechanism,* and it tells us more precisely how and why a change in interest rates by the Fed can contract or expand the economy. Here is how this mechanism works in the case of rising inflation due to an overheated economy.

First, the Fed increases interest rates either through open market operations or by raising the discount rate. This rise in interest rates, in turn, not only reduces business investment, it also reduces consumption expenditures as well as our exports. For example, consumers may respond to higher mortgage interest rates by buying a smaller home or renovating their old home rather than purchasing a new one. Similarly, in an economy open to international trade, higher interest rates will raise the value of the dollar and this stronger dollar will, in turn, reduce our ability to sell exports. The total effect of a fall in consumption, investment, and exports is to push both the gross domestic product and the rate of inflation down, thereby achieving the desired policy goal.

In the case of recession, one might think that the policy works exactly in reverse to stimulate the economy back to full employment. But does it? That question is our cue to discuss the important question of when monetary policy is likely to be most—and least—effective, as well as when fiscal policy might be the preferred policy option.

YOU CAN PULL ON A STRING BUT YOU CAN'T PUSH ON A STRING

In the 1930s, the Fed flooded the banking system with reserves, but the bankers refused to lend, and their customers were reluctant to borrow. That led financial journalists to coin the expression, "You can't push on a string." You still can't.

FORBES

In general, fiscal policy is the policy instrument of choice when the economy has fallen into a relatively deep recession or depression. In contrast, monetary policy is the preferred policy option when the government is fighting inflation or simply trying to cure a minor recession. To understand why, it is useful to introduce this well-known aphorism: You can pull on a string but you can't push on a string.

Here's the pull-on-the-string scenario. The economy is at or near full employment and in danger of overheating and causing inflation. In this case, all the Fed has to do is start to slowly raise interest rates. In response, consumers will begin to cut back on the credit they will shoulder. That is likely to mean reduced expenditures on home and auto purchases as well as other consumer durables like refrigerators and washing machines. These consumption cutbacks, in turn, ripple through the sectors that manufacture these goods and the rest of the economy. At the same time, businesses are likely to start cutting back on their investment levels. Some businesses in interest-sensitive sectors like retail and financial will do so on the expectation of reduced sales and revenues. Others in less interest-sensitive sectors will cut back simply because the price of money—the interest rate—has risen. The result will be a contraction in the economy and a reduction in inflationary pressures—even though the result may take three to six months or more to be observed. In such a case, the Fed has successfully pulled on the string and brought the economy back from the inflation precipice.

Now contrast this situation with the push-on-the-string scenario. Here, the economy is falling into a deepening recession. In this case, the Fed may well adopt an easy money policy to try and stimulate the economy back to full employment. However, in this case, there is no guarantee that either consumers or businesses will respond to the interest rate reductions. In the case of consumers, worries about the deepening recession may motivate a more cautious approach to buying new cars or refrigerators—even if interest rates drop lower. At the same time, businesses that are looking at idle production capacity and inventories piling up in their warehouses may not want to increase their investment even if interest rates are falling. This is the can't-push-on-a-string problem and it is just as easily framed as a paraphrase of the old horse-and-water cliché: You can lead a business to lower interest rates but you can't make it invest. In such a case, the government will likely have to turn to expansionary fiscal policy to stimulate the economy out of its recessionary funk.

The broader point for the macrowave investor is this: *Look for fiscal policy fixes when the economy is in recession and monetary policy fixes when the economy is at or near full employment.*

Of course, we have already talked about how the markets react differently to these two kinds of policies. Now to finish our story, let's talk about how the conduct of *domestic* monetary policy by the Federal Reserve can have a profound effect on *foreign* economies and their stock markets—from Europe and Asia to Latin America.

WHEN ALAN GREENSPAN SNEEZES, EUROPE GETS PNEUMONIA

> Gillette...fingered the impact of the weak euro as the culprit for recently reported disappointing earnings and its not so great expectations; its stock, as any unfortunate who owns it knows, swiftly took gas. Gillette's plaint is that something—quite a bit, actually—got lost in the translation from euros into dollars. A growing chorus is likely to be intoning that same sad refrain in the weeks and months ahead.
>
> ALAN ABELSON, *BARRON'S*

In thinking about how Fed policy spills over U.S. borders, the important link to understand is the one between interest rates and exchange rates, where an exchange rate is simply the rate at which one currency trades for another. For example, if the exchange rate between the dollar and the yen is 110, that means you can purchase 110 yen with 1 dollar.

Now here's the deal. When the Fed raises interest rates to fight domestic inflation, foreigners see an improved opportunity to invest in the U.S. However, to do so, they must convert their foreign currency into dollars before they can acquire U.S. assets like Treasury bonds or stocks. This currency conversion increases the demand for dollars and drives the value of the dollar up relative to other currencies. What is most interesting about all of this is that, under certain circumstances, the Fed's decision to raise interest rates can wreak absolute havoc with the U.S.'s major trading partners. To illustrate why, consider the dilemma the Fed's rate hikes can pose for the nations of Europe.

Suppose, then, that the U.S. economy is overheating and that the Fed is going to try and pull on the economy's string by raising interest rates. Now further suppose that both Germany and France are growing at a much slower pace than the U.S., while other countries in the European Monetary Union like Belgium, Italy, and Spain are actually facing double-digit unemployment.

Now, here is the European dilemma. As the Fed steadily raises interest rates in the U.S., the value of the dollar steadily increases relative to the weakening euro—the common currency of the European Monetary Union.

Because of these higher U.S. interest rates, European investment capital flees Europe for the more lucrative pastures of the U.S. financial markets. This flight of capital, in turn, causes the European economy to sputter further even as stock prices on the London and Paris exchanges continue to slide into a bearish oblivion.

So what are the Europeans to do? In fact, they have two options—but *neither* option is particularly attractive. Indeed, for the Europeans, the American Federal Reserve is presenting them with a lose-lose situation—a proverbial Hobson's choice.

Option One is for the Europeans to do nothing and let their currency continue to devalue even as investment capital flees. The main benefit from this option is that the strengthening dollar and weakening euro will increase European exports to the U.S. Eventually, this will help stimulate the European economy along with Europe's export industries. On the other hand, with this do-nothing option, imports from the U.S. will become more expensive because of the weak euro and this will be inflationary for the European economies. The reduction in purchasing power for the European consumer will also create increased political pressures on the European democracies to fight back against the "imperialistic American Fed," and angry European citizens just might vote to throw their leaders out. So Option One doesn't look very good.

So what about Option Two? It might be even worse. In this option, the European Central Bank can match the Fed's rate hikes basis point for basis point and thereby stem the flow of European capital to the U.S.; but this option creates a huge downside risk for the European economies. Indeed, if the Europeans adopt this option, they, like the U.S. Fed, will be adopting a contractionary monetary policy. Of course, the big difference in this situation is that while the U.S. is already at full employment in an inflationary range of its economy, the Europeans are stuck in a recession and a tight monetary policy will only make things worse—a whole lot worse. So what's a prime minister to do?

The broader point, of course, is that the conduct of U.S. domestic monetary policy will inevitably spill over into the financial markets around the globe. When Alan Greenspan sneezes, Europe does indeed catch pneumonia. That means both danger and opportunity for the macrowave investor.

In this particular example, a trader who closely watches these events unfold might speculate in the U.S. bond market or short the euro. Alternatively, he might invest in the stocks of export-oriented European companies, or short U.S. cyclical stocks. Of course, in Part Three of this book, we will talk more about the trading opportunities that the conduct of U.S. monetary policy can create. Now, however, it's time to turn to Part Two and the nuts and bolts of macrowave investing.

The Nuts and Bolts of Macrowave Investing

5

THE EIGHT PRINCIPLES OF MACROWAVE INVESTING

---

*R*obert Fisher has two passions: chess and stock trading. *Because he's good at one, he's also good at the other, and today, he's about to make a lot of money because he sees the whole stock market chessboard and thinks many moves ahead.*

Robert's gambit will be to buy a thousand shares of Northwest Airlines. Why? Because minutes ago, the King of the Friendly Skies, United Airlines, announced that it would purchase a very valuable pawn, U.S. Air. This will make United the largest air carrier in the world—and truly a King.

Upon the news, traders immediately begin scrambling to buy shares of U.S. Air, but Robert knows that most of these "checker players" will wind up paying far too much for their shares in the resultant speculative bubble—and many will lose money.

Meanwhile, Robert immediately understands that such a strategic move by United is a clear attempt at a monopolistic checkmate of rivals like Delta and American. Robert also knows that as a purely defensive response, Delta and American will now be forced to quickly look for acquisition targets of their own. That's why Robert immediately buys 2000 shares of Northwest Airlines, the likeliest purchase target.

Over the next two weeks, Northwest's stock jumps first from $24 to $28 and then to $35 as American Airlines does indeed make a fat offer. That's when Robert exits the trade. He walks away with a lovely macrowave windfall of $22,000. Meanwhile, the U.S. Air speculators who only got in after U.S. Air stock had gapped up from $25 to $49 are now getting clobbered as the price sinks back from its $49 peak to $40. God, Robert loves this game!

T he goal of macrowave investing is to maximize gains for a given risk level while minimizing losses and preserving capital. To achieve this goal, the macrowave investor must understand these eight principles, which are the foundations of macrowave investing.

---

1. *Speculate but never gamble.*

2. *Distinguish clearly between market risk, sector risk, and company risk. Use the principles of macrowave investing to diversify and minimize these risks.*

3. *Ride the train in the direction it is going. Go long, short, or flat as the situation demands.*

4. *Ride the appropriate train. Don't limit your perspective to the stock market. Learn to observe, and perhaps even trade in, the bond and currency markets as well.*

5. *Macroeconomics is the most important determinant of a bullish or bearish market trend, and the trend is your friend. Never buck the trend.*

6. *Within the stock market, different industry sectors react very differently to good and bad macroeconomic news. The*

macrowave investor buys strong stocks in strong sectors in up trends and shorts weak stocks in weak sectors in down trends.

7. *The stock, bond, and currency markets likewise react very differently to macroeconomic news. The macrowave investor knows that movements in one market can often presage movements in others and watches each of these markets carefully.*

8. *Don't play checkers in a chess world. Macroeconomic events affecting one particular company or sector invariably have spillover effects that wash over other companies, sectors, or markets. To see these effects, the macrowave investor must become a chess player, looking as many moves ahead as possible.*

Let's look now at each of these eight principles from the macrowave investor's point of view.

1. SPECULATE—BUT NEVER GAMBLE

Do you wish to gamble blindly in the hope of getting a great big profit or do you wish to speculate intelligently and get a smaller but much more probable profit?

JESSE LIVERMORE, *REMINISCENCES OF A STOCK OPERATOR*

The macrowave investor speculates but never gambles. The distinction between speculation and gambling is a very important one because over time it clearly draws the line between consistent winners and inevitable losers.

The gambler inevitably loses because he takes risks when the odds are against him. Buying a lottery ticket or playing roulette or dropping coin after coin into a slot machine are all forms of gambling. To take these kinds of risks is to bet against the House.

The gambler keeps taking such risks because of the occasional exhilarating big wins that buck the odds. However, the laws of probability eventually must catch up with him—no matter how lucky he may be on any given day. This is because, over time, the House never loses. This is the "gambler's ruin."

In contrast, the speculator only takes a risk when the odds are in his favor. That means the speculator only plays on a field that is tilted in his favor—not the House's favor. Moreover, he never risks more than he can gain, and he never risks it all on one bet.

Poker is one form of speculation. Trading in the stock market is another. Gary Bielfeldt beautifully explains the relationship between these two speculative pursuits in the classic book *Market Wizards*.

I learned how to play poker at a very young age. My father taught me the concept of playing the percentage hands. You don't just play every hand and stay through every card, because if you do, you will have a much higher probability of losing. You should play the good hands, and drop out of the poor hands, forfeiting the ante. When more of the cards are on the table and you have a very strong hand—in other words, when you feel the percentages are skewed in your favor—you raise and play that hand to the hilt.

If you apply the same principles of poker strategy to trading, it increases your odds of winning significantly. I have always tried to keep the concept of patience in mind by waiting for the right trade, just like you wait for the percentage hand in poker. If a trade doesn't look right, you get out and take a small loss; it's precisely equivalent to forfeiting the ante by dropping out of a poor hand in poker.

The remaining seven principles of macrowave investing are essential in helping you distinguish between profitable speculation and gambler's ruin.

2. MINIMIZE AND DIVERSIFY MARKET, SECTOR, AND COMPANY RISK

Not diversifying is like throwing your lunch out the window. If you have a portfolio and are not diversifying, you're incinerating money every year.

VICTOR NIEDERHOFFER

The macrowave investor knows the critical differences between market risk, sector risk, and company risk. By a careful adherence to the principles of macrowave investing, she knows how to diversify and minimize these risks.

Market risk revolves around the basic question: Is the stock market going up, down, or sideways? In this regard, market risk involves the purest kind of macroeconomic risk. This is because market trends are, by and large, determined by emerging macroeconomic news and conditions. A broad case in point is the Asian financial crisis of 1997–98. When it first hit, virtually every stock market around the world suffered a meltdown. Similarly, when the U.S. Federal Reserve announced a large increase in interest rates in the year 2000, both the Dow and Nasdaq markets fell precipitously on the news.

The macrowave investor knows that the best way to minimize market risk is to adhere to macrowave investing principles 3, 4, 5, and 8. Principle 3, being able to go long, short, or flat, and principle 5, never bucking the trend, allow the macrowave investor to constantly turn market risk in the direction of a reward. Principle 4, being able to trade in all markets—stocks, bonds, and currencies—provides the opportunity to further diversify across different broad markets. Finally, by anticipating spillover effects into other markets according to principle 8, the macrowave investor is always seeking to stay one step ahead of any indirect market risk—she does not play checkers in a chess world.

As for *sector risk,* it is any kind of event that affects a specific industry or sector. For example, when the American president and British prime minister jointly declared that rivals in the race to discover new genes should share their results, the biotech sector plunged dramatically. The clear regulatory risk was an implied threat of some future restrictions on patent rights for those companies charting the human genome. Similarly, any time the OPEC oil cartel announces an increase in oil prices and a cutback in production quotas, fuel-intensive sectors like the airlines, autos, and utilities are all exposed to increased energy cost risk that can translate into lower profits and stock prices. Or when Cisco warns of dropping sales, every company that would be considered a supplier or beneficiary of Cisco begins to fall as a result. Or when a new technology comes out for broadband communications, such as wireless high speed or DSL, then cable modem providers fall off sharply.

Now here's the larger point, and it is one of the most important ones we will share in this book: Sector risk typically accounts for at least 50 percent and perhaps as much as 80 percent of an individual stock price's movement. That means that when a semiconductor stock like Applied Materials or Intel goes up or down, much of the movement results *not* so much because fortune and fate are smiling or frowning on the particular companies; rather, these movements are largely attributable to what kinds of macroeconomic and microeconomic forces are bearing down on the semiconductor sector as a whole.

It follows that when the macrowave investor buys individual stocks, he is always aware of sector-level risk. For example, a portfolio consisting of Ivax, a drug stock, Cisco, an Internet infrastructure stock, Schwab, a financial sector stock, and Enron, an energy sector stock, is a portfolio that clearly diversifies sector risk. However, a portfolio featuring Motorola,

Nokia, Qualcomm, and Vodaphone—all of which operate in the same wire-less telecommunications industry—does not diversify sector risk but merely company risk. In essence, you are not holding four positions but merely one. And what is the nature of *company risk?* It may involve management risk—the chief operating officer of Ask Jeeves unexpectedly resigns and throws the company into turmoil. It might involve regulatory risk—a Microsoft finds itself in the gun sights of a trust-busting Department of Justice and its stock value is slashed in half. It might involve a natural disaster—a severe blizzard disrupts the flow of raw materials to a General Motors factory. Or it might involve unfavorable news coverage—*Barron's* publishes an article questioning the valuation of Cisco, and its stock plunges.

As a rule, the macrowave investor prefers to minimize company risk in one of several ways. One option is to trade at the sector level. For example, instead of buying Linear Technologies, which is a semiconductor stock, he might buy an index share stock like SMH that represents the semiconductor sector. Better yet, he might *basket trade.* That is, if he wants to open a position in semiconductors, he might buy three or four leading semiconductor stocks like Intel, Broadcom, Micron, and Xilinx, and then exit one or more of the stocks that perform least well over time while maintaining his positions in the others.

In this regard, when the macrowave investor does trade or invest in a specific company, he will carefully look at fundamentals such as earnings-per-share growth, the price-to-earnings ratio, and market capitalization. He will also look at the technical characteristics—is it overbought or oversold? Is it near a key support or resistance level? Has it just hit a "double top breakout"? Most importantly, he will never speculate in a stock without first carefully checking the latest news on the wire services about the company as well as its earnings announcement calendar.

3. RIDE THE TRAIN IN THE DIRECTION IT IS GOING

What is the biggest misconception the public has about the marketplace? The idea that the market has to go up for them to make money. You can make money in any kind of market if you use the right strategies.

TONY SALIBA

Except within the professional trading elite, virtually all traders and investors favor the *long* side of the market. That is, most traders and investors limit their bets to buying stocks in the hope that the stocks will rise. The macrowave investor, however, is just as likely to go *short* or *flat* when the situation demands it.

To sell short is to bet that a stock, a market sector, or a broad market index is going to fall in value. Mechanically, selling short involves selling a stock that you do not own. How can you do this? Well, all major stock brokerage firms maintain an inventory of stocks that you can effectively borrow to offer for sale. Thus, if Cisco is selling at $100 a share and you believe that it is going to fall, you can short-sell it at $100. Then, if the stock falls to, say, $95, you can *cover your short* by buying the stock in the market at $95 and putting it back in the brokerage firm's inventory. In the process, you've made $5 a share.

As for going *flat,* that can simply mean moving out of the market into cash. Alternatively, it can mean neutralizing your position with an offsetting transaction that doesn't necessarily take you out of the market, but effectively takes you to net neutral until conditions once again dictate net exposure in one direction. For example, you can hold 1000 shares of the same stock both long and short. Then, when you feel like you know which direction the market is trending, can close out one of those positions. During this time, you would be flat, even though you were not holding an all-cash position. Going flat typically is the best strategy when the markets are trading sideways and the macrowave investor can read no clear signals as to which way the market is likely to turn. In such a case, going either long or short in the market would simply be gambling, which would be a violation of our first macrowave investing principle.

In this regard, you can take this idea to the next level by discussing strategies involving the writing of options in order to exploit a sideways market for the purpose of capturing time premium. There are several tax strategies that also come into play here. For example, suppose you've been holding a stock long for seven months, it's up 45 percent, but if you sell it, you have a big tax hit. At the same time, however, you don't want to hold the stock while it moves against you 15 percent. In such a case, you can write some *covered calls,* then close the options position out when the pullback is over, and use the profits earned from the options transaction to immediately roll into additional shares of the underlying position.

4.   RIDE THE APPROPRIATE TRAIN

Almost without exception, the stock market turns down prior to recessions and rises before economic recoveries.... Since stocks fall prior to a recession, investors want to switch out of stocks into Treasury bills, returning to stocks when prospects for economic recovery look good.

JEREMY SIEGEL

Just as most nonprofessional traders and investors typically go long, the vast majority also focuses singularly on the stock market. However, in at least some circumstances, this isn't always the appropriate train to ride. Indeed, under certain circumstances, the bullet express train to Profit Land might be the bond or currency markets.

One such timely circumstance for moving into bonds from stocks is offered up by the quotation leading off this principle by the esteemed Wharton professor, Jeremy Siegel. But it is not just these broad cyclical turning points that the macrowave investor can exploit.

To see this, suppose the Federal Reserve uses a series of interest rate hikes to aggressively fight inflation. This is likely to drive stock prices down. In this case, a macrowave investor might want go short in the stock market. However, there is a catch here known as the *up-tick rule* which can make going short with individual stocks very difficult. (Note here, that I will talk about the benefits of using so-called "exchange-traded funds" to get around the up-tick rule in a later chapter.)

The up-tick rule was instituted by the Securities and Exchange Commission to promote stability in the markets. It dates back to the days of the Great Depression and the stock market crash of 1929. It basically says that you can't short a stock that is falling in price; the clear intent of this up-tick rule is to prevent short selling from driving a stock into a death spiral. Because of the up-tick rule and because, as we will discuss further in principle 7 below, the bond, stock, and currency markets sometimes move in opposing directions, it is important for the macrowave investor to be able to ride the appropriate train when the situation warrants.

For example, an easy money policy by the Fed might buoy stocks, but such a policy can also send ripples of inflationary fears through the bond market and knock prices down. Similarly, while stock prices typically fall on the expectation of higher interest rates, the value of the dollar may well rise. That's why a very experienced macrowave investor can often realize a much greater profit on inflation news by placing a *futures bet* in the currency market. But be very careful here about an important market misconception.

Although technically the dollar is supposed to rise with rising interest rates, the prospects of a slowing economy sometimes can far outweigh the increase in demand caused by marginally higher rates. As a result, investors may begin to switch out of dollar-denominated assets when expectations are for a recession. And once interest rates start to come back down, the dollar begins to rise because of capital inflows to dollar-denominated assets, even though technically the dollar should fall with falling rates.

The broader point is that just as the macrowave investor must be able to go short and flat as well as long, he should also be able to trade in markets other than the stock market, for this will prove to be a valuable skill at key times. However, even if you prefer not to trade in the bond and currency markets—it is complicated, risky, and time-consuming—it is still very important to observe the behavior of these markets because movements in one market can often presage movements in others. This is a point we shall return to discussing principle 7 below. But first, let's see why the trend is your friend.

5. NEVER BUCK THE TREND

Even turkeys fly in hurricanes. As the wind subsides, the turkeys stay on the ground.

KEVIN MARONI

If you stick around when the market is severely against you, sooner or later they're going to carry you out.

RANDY MCKAY

On any given day, the stock market can only go in three directions: up, down, or sideways. Over time, these daily movements help define a trend. For example, the chart (see Fig. 5-1) of the Nasdaq Composite Index shows various different trends over a 12-month period.

For example, in September and October, the Nasdaq basically traded sideways, moving up some days and down some days but always staying within a clearly defined trading range. But then, between November and March, the Nasdaq rode a sustained and very bullish trend upward. For most investors, this was a great ride while it lasted. Indeed, even weaker stocks were buoyed by the updraft because, as Kevin Maroni's trenchant quote tells us, "Even turkeys fly in hurricanes." Note, however, that things turned very choppy in March. Then, from the end of March until the end of

FIGURE 5-1   Bullish, bearish, and sideways markets.

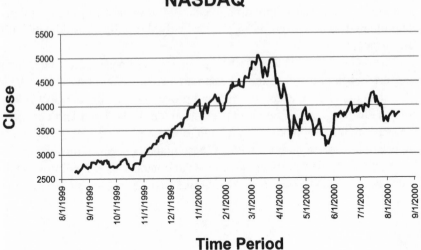

May, the trend was clearly down and bearish. At that point, the market trend went back into a mostly sideways pattern.

Now, it should be obvious just from looking at the chart why it's so risky to short stocks during a bullish up trend or to buy stocks in a bearish downdraft. Indeed, to do so is to engage in gambling against the odds, and it is a violation of our first macrowave investing principle. As to precisely why the odds are against you when you try and buck the trend, consider this: In an upward-trending market, stock price advances typically lead stock price declines. In other words, the prices of more stocks are going up than down. In contrast, in a downward trending market, declines typically lead advances.

Knowing this, let's get out our stock market dartboard and play a little game. The game is to throw a dart at a list of the Nasdaq 100 each day and then make a trade on the result. If the *advance-decline line* and trend are up and you are buying, you've got a better than 50–50 chance of making money. Perhaps this is why even the most inept of investors can make money in a rising market and perhaps also why numerous Wall Street wags have observed: Never confuse brains with a bull market.

But wait. Let's introduce one more subtlety here regarding our dart board analogy. Specifically, let's talk about the relationship of market breadth to the market trend. There are times, quite often in fact, when the market is advancing, but breadth remains negative. In other words, even though the broad indices are moving up, there may be more declines than advances. In this case, you would lose at the dart game. Accordingly, looking closely at the degree of market breadth is critical to accurately measuring the health of any advance. For example, several times in the early months of 2000, the market was surging but breadth was very poor. This negative breadth kept the bullish macrowave investor on guard and protected.

Now, having convinced you to never buck the trend, let me also suggest that the only time you should break this ironclad rule is when the macro-economic signals are clearly telling you that the trend is about to reverse. But be very, very careful here. One of the few things that virtually all pro-fessional traders seem to agree on is that only the luckiest and smartest are able to catch a trend change right at its beginning. My favorite quote on this subject comes from the classic *Reminiscences of a Stock Operator.* So take these words of the legendary Jesse Livermore to heart:

> One of the most helpful things that anybody can learn is to give up trying to catch the last eighth—or the first. These two are the most expensive eighths in the world. They have cost stock traders, in the aggregate, enough millions of dollars to build a concrete highway across the continent.

6. DIFFERENT STOCK MARKET SECTORS REACT IN DIFFERENT DEGREES AND DIRECTIONS

> The early investment birds who were buying interest-sensitive sectors such as the utilities four months ago and the technology stocks a month or two ago have already been switching to sectors that should be early bene-ficiaries of recovery. They have been buying the automakers, even as those behemoths have been slashing their payrolls and their dividends.

> *THE FINANCIAL POST*

Within the stock market, different industry sectors react in different degrees—and in some cases in different directions—to good or bad macro-economic news. While technically, this is macrowave investing principle number 6, it really is, in many ways, principle *numero uno.* This is because by thinking about the market in terms of its individual sectors, the macrowave investor is able to exploit his or her greatest opportunities for profit making and profit taking.

Perhaps the best way to see this is by example. Let's go back in time, then, to April 13, 2000, the day before the latest data on the Consumer Price Index are about to come out. Because you've done your research, you know this will be a key report: If the report shows any signs of significant inflation, the Federal Reserve will almost certainly hike interest rates by another 25 basis points—and perhaps even 50 points. Because you've done your research, you also know that the market is expecting a mild CPI number. However, you believe that the market is overly optimistic and is refusing to acknowledge increasing signs of inflation that are quite visible in the economy. At that point, you decide to make a trade on an unexpected inflationary spike. But what trade would you place?

Table 5-1 provides one possible answer to that question. It shows several stock market sectors that have typically reacted most sharply to unexpected changes in the Consumer Price Index. In the case of an unexpected rise in the CPI, these sectors fall sharply and vice versa. But exactly why is it that these particular sectors are so reactive? The quite intuitive answer is that all of these sectors are very interest rate–sensitive. Indeed, for each of these sectors, higher interest rates directly raise the price of industry products such as mortgages, loans, and margin interest. And of course, when a product's price rises, fewer products are sold. That means lower profits and when profits fall in a sector, stock prices can't be far behind.

More broadly, the kind of sector information in Table 5-1 provides macrowave investors with a very clear strategic direction. In this particular case, the macrowave investor could have made any one of a number of trades in anticipation of unexpectedly bad CPI news. For example, she might have shorted a weak stock in the banking or brokerage sectors. Alternatively, a more defensive play might have been to simply go flat. That is, she could have simply closed out positions in any stocks in any sectors most vulnerable to a large price drop on bad CPI news.

**TABLE 5-1. Some Sectors
That React Strongly to CPI
News**

- Banking
- Brokerage and investment
- Construction and housing
- Financial services
- Home finance
- Leisure
- Multimedia

7. THE STOCK, BOND, AND CURRENCY MARKETS REACT DIFFERENTLY TO GOOD AND BAD MACROECONOMIC NEWS

A typical move in U.S. stocks might start like this. The U.S. bond market goes up.... The dollar follows. The U.S. stock market immediately rises because of the increased value of U.S. earnings with the lower interest rates. Then high-grade copper, a primary industrial metal, moves up in anticipation of greater investment spending. The Japanese stock market drops because U.S. assets are now becoming more attractive to foreigners. But this makes gold decline because inflation is likely to be lower with a strong dollar. With inflation down, something has to be less attractive. It is time for meats, grains, and soft commodities to recede because there will be less purchasing power left for them. But if European and Japanese assets are going to decline, soon they will pull down the U.S. stock market. And the cycle will be ready to reverse. All this in a minute or two, 10 or 12 times a day.

VICTOR NIEDERHOFFER

You can't help but love Victor Niederhoffer. He's the Crown Prince—and sometimes Clown Prince—of macrowave thinking. In this regard, he can also be spectacularly wrong. For example, in 1997, Niederhoffer suffered a legendary blow-up when he bet against George Soros in the Thai baht. His guess was that the U.S. markets would bounce back from the Asian crisis, but he was dead wrong. Nonetheless, the underlying point of his quote is an important one. The stock, bond, and currency markets—as well as commodity markets and financial markets all around the world—react in different degrees to good and bad macroeconomic news and can move in different directions from one another. Table 5-2 illustrates this point once again for the stock and bond markets using the case of the unexpected spike in the Consumer Price Index that occurred on April 14, 2000.

From the table, we see that from the close of the markets on the day before the CPI news was released to the close of the markets on the day of the release, the Dow fell by almost 6 percent while the Nasdaq composite fell by almost 10 percent. Of course, this drop is very intuitive—bad news moves the stock market down.

But what about the bond market? Here we see that yields on the 30-year, 10-year, and 5-year instruments all went down. This means that bond prices actually went *up* on the inflation news because bond yields are inversely related to bond prices. This actually seems like a very counterintuitive result. After all, if there is an unexpected spike in inflation, this must raise

TABLE 5-2.   How the Stock and Bond Markets React to Inflation

Stock Market Indexes	Close— April 13, 2000	Close— April 14, 2000	Percent change
• Dow Jones Industrial Average	10923.55	10305.77	−5.66%
• Nadsdaq Composite	3676.78	3321.29	−9.67%
Bond Market Indexes	**Close— April 13, 2000**	**Close— April 14, 2000**	**Percent change**
• 30-year bond	5.803	5.782	−0.36%
• 10-year note	5.914	5.885	−0.49%
• 5-year note	6.207	6.167	−0.64%

the probability that the Federal Reserve will raise interest rates. And when the Fed does this, bond prices must fall. But at least on April 14, they didn't.

So what exactly is going on here? Well, if we look at the actual intraday movements of bond prices on April 14, our counterintuitive paradox is easily resolved. In fact, bond prices did fall sharply on the morning of April 14 on news of the inflationary spike—just as one would predict. However, as this news also began to pummel the stock market, investors began to stampede out of equities into the safer haven of bonds. This flight to quality dramatically increased demand for bonds and bond prices began to move back up. And by the time the market closed, bond prices were indeed up for the day while bond yields were down.

In this case, then, there were two competing effects for the macrowave investor to sort out. One was an *interest rate effect* pushing bond prices down; the other was an *equity effect* pushing bond prices up. At least in this case, the net effect on bond prices was positive.

This example not only illustrates how complex macrowave logic can be, it also illustrates why the Wall Street game is much more one of chess than checkers—which leads us to our last principle.

8. DON'T PLAY CHECKERS IN A CHESS WORLD

A good speculator builds his position from a single base linked to a long, flexible chain of trades. Here's a hoary old favorite that emerges once or twice a year and is good for a trillion or so of outright trading on each round. The dollar's going to be weak because the government's going to keep interest rates down so jobs will be good when the election comes. The mark will be the chief beneficiary, so let's buy it. Strong markets will create demand for German bonds and stocks. Let's buy some of those also. Pressure will be put on the pound and the lira to keep pace. Sell them and their stock and bond markets. The whole support system might entangle, which will be bad for Mexico. Sell the peso and, while you're at it, sell the Indian global depository receipts short and calls on Telemex on the CBOE.

VICTOR NIEDERHOFFER

Behind Niederhoffer's humor, there is again an enduring truth: Macroeconomic events affecting one particular company or sector invariably have *spillover effects* that wash over other companies or sectors or markets. In this regard, far too many nonprofessional traders and investors are playing checkers in a chess world. Unlike the macrowave investor, they do not look many, many moves ahead on the board. As a result, fine opportunities are missed.

One example of an opportunity that wasn't missed is offered up by our fictional chess player cum stock trader in the example that led off this chapter. In that example, Robert Fisher clearly saw the whole chessboard. He knew that the United Airlines–U.S. Air merger would immediately put pressure on United competitors like Delta and American to get bigger as well. That's why Robert immediately opened a position in acquisition target Northwest Airlines even as other checkers players in the market wound up fighting among themselves over a piece of the U.S. Air pie.

Another example of a spillover effect was offered up at the beginning of this book. When the U.S. Department of Justice sued Microsoft for antitrust violations, the savvy macrowave investor immediately opened long positions in Sun Microsystems and Oracle—the Microsoft rivals most likely to benefit from the news.

The broader point here is simply this: View the market as a giant chessboard and look as many moves ahead and across as many sectors as possible. As a practical matter, this means identifying the many spillover effects of a macroeconomic event and then quickly acting on this information. As a practical matter, this also means doing methodical research. As the old Chinese proverb says, "Chance favors the prepared mind." In a macrowave investing context, this means first and foremost familiarizing yourself with the major sectors of the economy and the strong and weak companies that make up these sectors. It is to this task we now turn.

6

IT'S THE SECTOR, STUPID!

Michelle Carrera is a position trader who follows the macroeconomic news very closely. Over time, she has learned that both macroeconomic events and economic indicator reports can have an enormous impact on broad market trends.

Today, Michelle is betting on a breakout upward move by the markets on the basis of consistently bullish economic news over the last month. Her bet: 1000 shares of Allied Capital, a financial services sector stock, and another 1000 shares of Pacific Gas & Electric in the utilities sector.

Two months later, Michelle looks like a genius—at least with respect to the broad market trend. Both the Dow and Nasdaq are up over 10 percent. However, Michelle feels like a dummy. Her financial services sector stock has traded sideways. Worse still, her utilities sector stock has actually gone down in an up market—the position trader's ultimate booby prize.

Where did Michelle do wrong? She got her market trend right but her sectors wrong. Checkmate.

Whostie the macrowave investor looks at the stock market, she does not see companies like Chevron, Dell, or Wal-Mart. Rather, she first sees *trading sectors* like energy, computers, and retailing. This is because she knows that most broad moves in the stock market are sector-driven rather than company-driven. Indeed, as we already know, over half of any individual stock's movement is typically driven by events in the company's sector rather than by the company's own earnings performance. This means that you can invest in some of the very best companies in the world but still wind up taking a bath if you happen to pick companies in the wrong sector at the wrong time. Just ask Michelle!

In this chapter, we want to look very closely at how and why the trading sectors differ and why these differences matter a very great deal when it comes to the price movements of individual stocks and the performance of your portfolio. Here's a preview of some of the most important relationships.

- *Some trading sectors like computers and leisure rely heavily on sales to consumers, other sectors like chemicals and environmental services target industrial buyers, and for other sectors like defense and aerospace, the government is a major customer. These differences matter when it comes to gauging the effects of different economic indicators like consumer confidence, durable goods orders, or the budget deficit on different sectors.*

- *Some trading sectors like retailing are labor-intensive, some like utilities are capital-intensive, and some like transportation are very fuel-intensive. These differences likewise matter when it comes to assessing how different kinds of macroeconomic shocks like wage inflation, interest rate spikes, and energy price shocks can result in individual stock price movements.*

- *Some cyclical sectors like autos and paper are closely tied to changes in the business cycle and are the first to tank during a recession. Other sectors like food and health care are noncyclical and therefore much more immune to recession. This distinction will help you find winners to ride up in a bull market and defensive sectors to flee to during a downturn.*

- *Some sectors like agriculture, electronics, industrial equipment, and pharmaceuticals are export-oriented, while other sectors such as financial services and health care derive relatively few revenues from trade. In general, the stock prices of companies in the export-dependent sectors will react much more strongly to news on the trade deficit and dollar devaluation fronts.*

• *The degree of exposure to regulatory risks such as price controls or litigation or new taxation, as well as a sector's vulnerability to exogenous shocks such as floods and drought, are likewise important sources of stock price movements in sectors like drugs, tobacco, and agriculture.*

The major, big-time, heavy point here is this: *Exploiting these kinds of trading sector differences is at the core of the macrowave investing approach and a major source of the macrowave investor's market edge. By continually viewing the stock market at the trading sector level, you will learn to pick the right stocks in the right sectors at the right time—and stay away from the wrong stocks in the wrong sectors.* You will also learn how to better diversify your portfolio against both market and sector risks.

THE IMPORTANCE OF SECTOR ROTATION

Sector rotation in the market continues on Wall Street as investors do an about-face out of blue-chip stocks into tech issues.

CNN

The concept of sector rotation is a very important one to the macrowave investor. To really get a handle on this idea, we need to first discuss how to best slice and dice the stock market into manageable trading sectors. This, by the way, is no easy task. If you define your sectors too broadly, you will not only get whipsawed, you will also miss a lot of great trading opportunities. On the other hand, if you define your sectors too narrowly, you can get lost in a blizzard of meaningless subsector minutiae and waste endless hours of time looking at distinctions without differences.

Let me first show you the problem with using an overly broad sector definition. Take a look at Table 6-1. In fact, the nine designations in this table are more like *categories* than true sectors. The reason why these categories are far too broad is that many of the true sectors within each of the categories are often moving in opposite directions from one another. For example, within the consumer cyclical category, retailing stocks may be enjoying one fine, fine day on Wall Street even as the leisure sector is taking it (literally) in the shorts. Fail to recognize this, and you have missed not one, but two, opportunities—one to go long and one to go short. Similarly, within the financial category, banking and insurance stocks will often move in opposite directions, while, under the technology umbrella, Internet stocks are notorious for moving in different directions on different days from, say, semiconductors or computers.

Okay. So we now know that we don't want an overly broad definition of our sectors. Now what about the other problem about too narrow a definition? This kind of thing can get us lost in the time drain of endless minutiae. To see why, consider that with a sector like autos, you can divide it into subsectors like manufacturing, parts, and tires. Similarly, for a sector like retailing, you can identify subsectors like discount stores, department stores, and mail order. As a practical matter, this level of detail will not be helpful in trading the vast majority of sectors. This is because as the sector goes, so too usually go the subsectors. In other words, if auto manufacturing companies are sinking, most of the time auto parts and auto tire companies will be circling the same drain.

But, and this is a very big BUT, for at least one category of sectors—namely, those grouped in the "new economy" under technology—more detail will nonetheless be useful. Why? It's the nature of the new economy beast.

Consider, for example, that the telecommunications sector is at least two sectors. One houses the traditional pole and wire companies like AT&T and Bell South. The other is home to the broadband and wireless buccaneers like Qualcomm and Motorola. Precisely because these two sectors under the telecom umbrella are engaged in what may well be a battle to the death for

---

TABLE 6-1. Broad Sector Categories in the Stock Market

- Business and industrial cyclicals
- Consumer cyclicals
- Consumer noncyclicals
- Energy and utilities
- Financial
- Health care
- Real estate
- Technology
- Transportation

the ears and mouths of the world's population, the stocks of companies in these two sectors will often move in opposite directions from one another.

So where are we heading with all of this? A drum roll please as I unveil what I think may be very workable sector maps for both the old and new economy stocks. Let's start with the old economy, which is sliced and diced in Table 6-2. It contains 34 sectors grouped under seven different categories and strikes what I believe is a pretty good balance between too much and too little sector detail.

Take a few minutes now to study this table carefully. It's our first big step to cultivating an all-important sector awareness. To best build this awareness, try to draw associations in your mind between the sectors in the left-hand column and some of the representative companies in the right-hand column.

Now that you have studied the table, you may have noticed that there are a number of sectors that have some degree of overlap. For example, the transportation sector subsumes the airline transportation sector but also includes railroad and trucking companies. Don't worry about this. Because the airline sector often responds to a different set of macroeconomic forces, it is useful in this kind of instance to also include a separate airlines sector.

Now let's turn to our sector map for the new economy technology stocks. Looking at Table 6-3, you should notice immediately that it is a little more finely grained.

For example, we don't just look at computers. We break that sector down into mainframe computer companies like Cray and IBM, PC manufacturers like Apple and Compaq, minicomputer makers like Silicon Graphics and Sun, software companies like Corel, Microsoft, and Oracle, and storage companies like Sandisk and Seagate.

Similarly, we don't just have an Internet category. We break that category down into Internet architecture companies like Cisco and Sun, business-to-business (B2B) enterprises like Ariba and Commerce One, business-to-consumer (B2C) companies like AOL and Yahoo, Internet infrastructure moguls like Akamai, Exodus, and Verisign, and Internet network companies like Juniper and Redback.

We are going for more finely grained detail here because, with the new economy stocks, there is much more volatility, not only across the various sectors but also within the numerous subsectors. In fact, if all you trade in are new economy stocks, you may want to break these sectors down even further. If that is the case, I heartily recommend a Web site visit to Changewave.com, which is one of the kings of sector mapping the new economy.

TABLE 6-2. Old Economy Sector Map

Business and Industrial Cyclicals

Basic industrial materials	Dow, 3M, Monsanto
Business services	ADP, First Data, Paychex
Chemicals	Dow, Dupont, Union Carbide
Defense and aerospace	Boeing, General Dynamics, Lockheed Martin
Environmental services	Ogden, Thermo Electron, Waste Management
Industrial equipment	Caterpillar, General Electric, Pitney Bowes
Paper and forest products	Georgia Pacific, Kimberly Clark, Weyerhauser

Consumer Cyclicals

Automotive	GM, Ford, Honda
Construction and housing	Home Depot, Fannie Mae, Whirlpool
Leisure and gaming	Disney, Seagram's, Time Warner
Multimedia	Cox, Fox, Viacom
Retailing	Costco, Gap, Target

Consumer Noncyclicals

Cosmetics	Alberto Culver, Estée Lauder, Revlon
Education and publishing	Apollo, Learning Tree, McGraw-Hill
Food and agriculture	Anheuser Busch, McDonalds, Safeway
Tobacco	Philip Morris, R.J. Reynolds, UST

Energy and Utilities

Energy	Chevron, Exxon, Schlumberger
Energy services	Halliburton, Noble, Weatherford
Oil and natural gas	Chevron, Enron, Schlumberger
Pole and wire telecom	AT&T, Bellsouth, Verizon
Utilities	American Electric Power, Duke Power, PG&E

WHAT MAKES A SECTOR A SECTOR?

Now that we have sliced and diced the markets into sectors, the next questions we want to ask are these: How are each of these sectors likely to differ, and how might these differences result in different kinds of responses

TABLE 6-2.   *(Continued)*

Financial and Real Estate

Banking	Chase Manhattan, Mellon, Wells Fargo
Brokerage and investment	Lehman Bros., Morgan Stanley, Schwab
Financial services	AMEX, Berkshire Hathaway, Citigroup
Home finance	Freddie Mac, Fannie Mae, Golden West
Insurance	Cigna, Chubb, Hartford Financial
Real estate	Burnham Pacific, Grubb & Ellis, Wilshire

Health and Medical

Health care	American Home Products, J&J, Medtronic
Medical delivery	Aetna, Cigna, Wellpoint
Medical equipment	Allergan, Biomet, Guidant
Pharmaceuticals	Bristol Myers, Glaxo, Schering-Plough

Transportation

Airlines	American, Delta, Southwest
Transportation	Burlington Northern, Eaton, Delta

to different kinds of macroeconomic news? This is, in fact, the crux of the macrowave matter. To answer these questions, we will take several additional passes at the sectors.

In our first pass, we will talk about a sector's customers. Does the sector rely more on consumers or businesses or the government? This matters because changes in key economic indicators like consumer confidence and retail sales will have a lot more impact on sectors like retailing and multimedia than on, say, biotechnology and health care.

In our second pass, we will talk about whether the sector uses relatively more workers, machinery, or fuel in its production process. That is, is the sector labor-intensive, capital-intensive, or fuel-intensive? As we will see, a sector's mix of *inputs*—labor, capital, and fuel—has an enormous impact on how the sector responds differentially to things like wage inflation, interest rate hikes, or oil price shocks.

Finally, we will look at how factors such as export dependence, regulatory risk, and vulnerability to natural disasters like droughts and floods differentially affect the different sectors.

TABLE 6-3.   The New Economy Sector Map

Biotechnology	Amgen, Genentech, Immunex, Ligand, Xoma

Computers

• Mainframe	Cray, IBM
• PCs	Apple, Compaq, Dell, Palm
• Minis	Hewlett Packard, Silicon Graphics, Sun
• Software	Adobe, Corel, Intuit, Microsoft, Oracle
• Storage	EMC, Sandisk, Seagate, Silicon Storage

Electronics

• Measuring instruments	Agilent, KLA-Tencor, Teradyne
• Semiconductors	Applied Materials, Intel, Micron, Zoran

Internet

• Architecture	Cisco, EMC, Sun
• B2B	Ariba, Commerce One, Internet Capital
• B2C	AOL, Yahoo, Amazon, eBay
• Infrastructure	Akamai, BEAS, Exodus, Real Networks, Verisign
• Networks	Juniper, Novell, Redback

New Economy Telecom and Communications Broadband

• Fiber optics	Ciena, Corning, JDS Uniphase, Sycamore
• Wireless	Ericsson, Lucent, Motorola, Nokia, Qualcomm

SO WHO'S THE CUSTOMER?

In the retail sector, stocks were given a lift after a stronger than expected July retail sales report. Sears, Roebuck rose 7/8, to 43⅛, May Department Stores rose 1⅜, to 57¾…and Woolworth rose 3/8 to 28¾.

THE NEW YORK TIMES

Declining defense budgets…have soured investors on aerospace stocks.

AVIATION WEEK & SPACE TECHNOLOGY

Our question here is simply this: Does a given sector depend more on consumers, businesses, or the government for its revenues? Table 6-4 sheds

TABLE 6-4.   Who's the Customer—Consumers, Businesses, or the Government?

Consumer Sectors	Business Sectors	Government
• Automotive (77%)	• Chemicals (91%)	• Construction and housing (22%)
• Leisure (76%)	• Energy (71%)	• Defense and aerospace (54%)
• Retailing (92%)	• Industrial materials (83%)	
• Pharmaceuticals (64%)	• Paper and forest products (86%)	

Source: United States Input-Output Tables, Bureau of Economic Analysis.

some light on that question. The numbers in parentheses show the percentage of output sold to consumers, businesses, or the government for some key sectors.

As you can see from the table, the retailing sector is very consumer-oriented. Consumers purchase 92 percent of its output. That's why when a strong retail sales report comes out, retail sector stocks like Sears and the May Company are likely to move upward. In contrast, the defense and aerospace sector relies on Uncle Sam for over half its sales, so when rising budget deficits lead to cutbacks in defense spending, the stocks of companies like Boeing and General Dynamics are going to fall.

Now here's the broader point. When tracking consumer-oriented sectors, the macrowave investor will find economic indicators such as consumer confidence, personal income, and retail sales particularly useful to watch. In contrast, indicators like the purchasing manager's report and capacity utilization are much more important when watching business-oriented sectors like chemicals and paper, while news on the budget front can have a big impact on both the defense and housing sectors.

SO HOW'S THE PRODUCT MADE?

An abrupt rise in oil prices slammed stocks by reviving inflation fears.... Traders said damage to stocks was limited only by a sharp rally in the shares of major oil and natural gas companies, which rose on expectations that last week's OPEC production accord will boost energy prices.... Airline shares were among the biggest losers. Rising oil prices would boost jet fuel costs.... Some chemical stocks [also] gave ground. Oil is a major element in the production of many chemicals.

THE LOS ANGELES TIMES

Now what about how the products or services in a sector are actually made? This question speaks to the actual mix of workers, machines, fuel, and raw materials used in the production process.

For example, some *capital-intensive* sectors like fixed wire telecommunications and electric utilities use a lot more machinery and equipment compared to workers than other more *labor-intensive* industries like retailing or computer software services. These capital-intensive industries are more *interest-rate sensitive* and more likely to react to news about any changes in interest rates. In contrast, labor-intensive sectors are likely to react more strongly to news about rising or falling unemployment and possible wage inflation.

As for fuel-intensity, the news article above clearly indicates that stocks of companies like Delta and Dow in sectors like the airlines and chemicals may react very sharply to news about rising or falling energy prices because of their dependence on the black gold of oil.

WHAT'S THIS CYCLICAL VERSUS NONCYCLICAL THING?

Usually, an upturn in the economy is spearheaded by a pick-up in consumer demand and in the housing market. Consumer and housing market-related companies are interest rate sensitive sectors that respond first to the fall in interest rates that accompanies recession.

Other interest rate sensitive areas that tend to lead off an economic expansion are retail stores, restaurants, cosmetics, tobacco and insurance as well as telephone and electric utilities.

As the recovery gathers pace, stocks of goods that have been run down during the recession need to be replaced. Manufacturing orders pick up. Finally as manufacturers start to hit capacity constraints, investment in new plant picks up. Thus stocks associated with capital spending such as steel, chemicals and mining tend to be lagging indicators.

INVESTORS CHRONICLE

This news clip speaks directly to the important distinction between cyclical and noncyclical sectors. We've already talked a lot about this distinction and how cyclical and noncyclical stocks react very differently to the business and stock market cycles. Here's a list of some key cyclical and noncyclical sectors to refresh our memory (see Table 6-5).

As we now know, cyclical sectors such as automobiles, construction and housing, paper, retailing, and transportation will react much more quickly and sharply to the onset of recession and changes in the business cycle than noncyclical sectors such as food and beverages, pharmaceuticals, and basic utilities. Why might this be so? Well, most of the noncyclical sectors produce the necessities of life—things we can't really do without, even if times are tough. The food and beverages sector and companies like Coca Cola and Quaker Oats and Procter & Gamble fit easily into this category, as do the electric utility sector and companies like Florida Power & Light and Duke Power. Many pharmaceuticals are likewise indispensable, so the stock prices of companies like Johnson & Johnson and Merck are likely to respond less to changes in the business cycle.

As for the cyclical stocks, as soon as the economy starts to go south, we, as consumers, are much less likely to travel or pop for that new car or refrigerator—so stocks like Delta Airlines, General Motors, and Whirlpool all suffer as their sales and earnings fall. Nor are we likely to be as lavish in our retail spending—so the stocks of traditional retailers like Kmart and Wal-Mart fall right along with the newer high tech retailers like Circuit City.

From a macrowave investing perspective, you should immediately see the advantage of the cyclical versus noncyclical distinction. It gives you an excellent roadmap as to which sectors to sell short when the economy is heading down and which sectors to go long in when it is back on the way up. This distinction can also help point you to which noncyclical sectors can be defensive plays when the recessionary rains start to fall. That's why

TABLE 6-5.   Cyclical versus Noncyclical Sectors

Cyclical Sectors	Noncyclical Sectors
• Automobiles	• Defense
• Construction and housing	• Food and beverages
• Paper	• Health care
• Retailing	• Pharmaceuticals
• Transportation	• Utilities

following recessionary economic indicators such as auto sales and housing starts is so important when it comes to assessing the fate of cyclicals versus noncyclicals.

TO RUSSIA, WITH A BILL OF LADING

A sharp decline in the dollar this past week cast a deep pall over the stock market, causing investors to aggressively sell large blocks of equities.... Because European interest rates have been rising at a faster clip than domestic rates, the "appeal of dollar-denominated securities versus those in other parts of the world has eroded significantly," said Hugh Johnson, market strategist at First Albany Corp.... Johnson recommended stocks of companies whose exports will in time show improvement from the weaker dollar, including IBM, Ingersoll Rand, Deere, Caterpillar, Corning and Eastman Kodak. "These do very well when continental Europe is recovering," he said.

CHARLESTON SUNDAY GAZETTE MAIL

Many sectors in the U.S. economy derive a large portion of their revenues from export sales. These *export-dependent sectors* include agriculture, computers, defense, electronics, industrial equipment, and pharmaceuticals. In contrast, sectors such as financial services, health care, pole and wire telecommunications, and transportation derive relatively few revenues from trade. In general, the export-dependent sectors will react much more strongly to macroeconomic news on the trade and currency market fronts.

To see how complex these reactions can be, consider the case of a rising trade deficit. As the deficit rises, this puts significant downward pressure on the dollar. Why? Because when Americans are buying a lot more imports than they are selling exports, more dollars are flowing out of the country into foreign hands. More dollars abroad, in turn, means that more foreigners are trying to convert their U.S. dollars into euros or Japanese yen or Korean won. This reduces the demand for dollars and by the law of supply and demand, the price of the dollar—that is, its exchange rate—falls. This happens even as the prices of euros, yen, and won are bid up.

In some sense, then, a rising trade deficit is good news for export-dependent companies like IBM and Caterpillar and Corning because a weaker dollar means that they will have more of a competitive advantage in foreign markets. But wait. Several things can happen that can make a rising trade deficit very bad news not just for the export-dependent sectors but for the broader markets as well.

For example, when the trade deficit rises and the dollar weakens, foreign investors may become much less willing to hold onto U.S. stocks because these stocks are, in effect, losing value as the dollar falls. That's why the stock market often goes down on rising trade deficit news.

SCREAMING INTO THE REGULATORY NIGHT

> Greg Valiere [chief strategist of the Schwab Washington Research Group] says the election should have an outsized effect on pharmaceutical, defense and tobacco stocks in the coming months. "If there's one pure play on the election, it's health care.... If it looks like, after Labor Day, Gore's going to win, I think it would be a clear negative for the drug stocks." The reason: Gore would more likely push for a Medicare prescription-drug benefit that would include "de facto" price controls....
>
> *BARRON'S*

While all sectors are subject to some kind of regulatory and political risks, some sectors are much more likely to bear such risk than others. For example, the elderly constitute a powerful political voting bloc in this country. Because of this, the threat of price controls or a loosening of patent restrictions on prescription drugs perennially hangs over the pharmaceutical industry. In a similar vein, the extreme volatility of oil prices coupled with the political sensitivity of prices at the gas pump makes the energy industry a frequent target of price control and windfall profit tax rhetoric.

It's not just the energy and drug sectors that fear regulation. Fearful biotech executives wake up in cold sweats from nightmares about bans on genetically engineered food. Chemical industry execs have been known to rant and rave about the unfair and costly restrictions of the Environmental Protection Agency. Ever-hopeful defense industry executives pray for hawkish presidents in the White House. Frustrated electric utility CEOs mainline Tums antacids as they maneuver a veritable Rubik's cube of constraints every time they want to build a new power plant. And frantic Internet commerce venture capitalists have been known to experience catatonic states at the very mention of the words "Internet taxation." Because of all of these different kinds of regulatory and political risks, it is important for the prudent macrowave investor to stay abreast of events in the Congress, the courts, and the White House.

And here's a good tip for you: If a stock you own suddenly tanks or soars, and it isn't earnings season, get online and go to a site like Redchip.com or CBS's marketwatch.com and check the latest news on the stock. Much of the time you will see either a new lawsuit or a new bill in Congress or some kind of government action driving the news.

WHEN IT RAINS IN BRAZIL, BUY STARBUCKS

The first big winter storms of the new century clobbered auto dealers and factories along the Eastern Seaboard early last week, curtailing sales and forcing brief production shutdowns from Georgia to Maine. By week's end, the havoc had spread inland. New storms that dumped up to 10 inches of snow on Oklahoma City and freezing rain in Dallas disrupted auto sales and production. And more severe weather was promised for the Southeast for the weekend.... Several automakers lost all or part of a day of production because workers couldn't get to work and suppliers had trouble delivering parts.

AUTOMOTIVE NEWS

Brazilian growers, who typically supply one-third of the world's [coffee] beans, have seen prices plunge in recent months because heavy rains in December, which followed a drought in the fall, caused farmers to raise yield estimates from depressed levels.... Giant coffeehouse operator Starbucks said no price cut is forthcoming, although the Seattle-based chain raised prices an average 10 cents a cup for coffee beverages last May. Starbucks has never lowered prices despite huge swings in the price of the beans they buy.

LOS ANGELES TIMES

For some sectors like food and beverages, when it *doesn't* rain, it can pour. Indeed, as the title of this book suggests, when it starts raining in Brazil to end a drought, it may well be time to buy Starbucks stock as the price of coffee is sure to fall even as Starbucks profit margins will rise. By the same token, other sectors like autos and retailing are particularly vulnerable to episodic events like blizzards, floods, and heat waves. For example, an unusually cold or snowy winter in the Midwest can show up as lower than expected earnings in the spring for auto manufacturers as well as other retailers—with the stock prices of these weather-stricken companies perhaps taking it on the chin.

Well, that completes our discussion of how the various sectors differ by factors like capital and labor intensity, types of consumers, and exposure to regulatory risks. By now, you know how important it is to view the stock market from a sector-level perspective. If that is the case, I'm sure your next two questions will be these: What is the best way to *track* each of the various sectors in the market and can I—indeed, should I—actually *trade* at the sector level? This is the topic of our next chapter.

7

ON THE TRAIL OF THE ELUSIVE SECTOR

In the trading room at Momentus Securities, the competition is intense between Danny, Zoe, and Jack. Each month, they have two standing bets: $100 on who will make the most money trading that month and another $50 on who will have the smallest draw-down or loss on their worst trade.

What is so interesting about their competition is the different styles of trading that each has adopted. Danny is strictly a market trend trader. He hates bearing either industry- or company-specific risk. So Danny only speculates in cubes and spiders, that is, the exchange-traded fund QQQ that tracks the Nasdaq market and the SPY fund that tracks the S&P 500. If Danny thinks the market is heading up, he simply goes long his cubes or spiders. If he thinks it is heading down, he shorts QQQ or SPY.

Zoe, on the other hand, is strictly a sector-level trader. Her favorite exchange-traded funds are iShares like IYD and IYF that track the chemical and financial services sectors and HOLDRS like BBH and HHH that track the biotech and Internet sectors. Zoe basically plays a sector rotation game. She simply watches the various sector indicators to see which ones are moving up or down and then rotates in and out of these sectors accordingly.

As for Jack, he's the only true macrowave investor of the bunch. For Jack, cubes and spiders and iShares and HOLDRS are all useful indicators of the market and sector trends, and he watches them closely on his computer screen—along with other even more valuable trend indicators like the TICK and the TRIN and the S&P Futures. But, when it comes to putting his money on the line, Jack is strictly a basket trader. Following his golden rule of macrowave investing, Jack only buys baskets of strong stocks in strong sectors when the trend is up—just as he only shorts weak stocks in weak sectors when the trend is down.

By the way, Danny and Zoe hate Jack. He almost always wins the most-money-made-in-the-month prize. As a rule, however, it's Danny who usually walks away with the lowest drawdown trophy. Let's find out why.

C ubes and spiders, HOLDRS and iShares, the TICK and the TRIN— this is just some of the lingo of the savvy macrowave investor. Understanding how these and other sector and market level indicators can work in conjunction with a sound basket trading approach is one of the most important steps to improving your trading performance.

In this chapter, we will look at how to use various indicators to track both the broad market and individual sector trends. We will also learn how to efficiently engage in macrowave trading using either a conservative sector level approach like Zoe or a more aggressive basket-trading approach like Jack. So hang on for the ride; this chapter should be fun.

THE TREND IS YOUR FRIEND

Dwell on the need above all other things of determining the kind of market a man is trading in.

JESSE LIVERMORE, *REMINISCENCES OF A STOCK OPERATOR*

Remember the fifth principle of macrowave investing: The trend is your friend, and you should never trade against the trend. Indeed, tracking the broad market trend is one of the most important tasks of the macrowave investor. In thinking about why this is so important, let's remember Jack's golden rule of macrowave investing:

- Buy strong stocks in strong sectors in an upward-trending market

- Short weak stocks in weak sectors in a downward-trending market

Of course to trade by these rules, you need to have a very clear sense of what the market and sector trends are and how they may be changing. In Part Three of this book, we will look at different ways you can assess these trends using various economic indicators. But for now, let's focus on how to actually track the intraday and day-to-day trends, for it is on any given day that you must consider whether to enter or exit your trades. Table 7-1 lists some of the major indicators and trading instruments that may be useful to you in tracking and trading the broad market trend.

On a day-to-day basis, one way to assess the trend might be to simply watch how the Dow Jones Industrial Average, the Nasdaq Composite Index, and the Standard & Poor's 500 Index move. Frankly, this kind of approach is strictly for Main Street and the market's "dumb money." This is

TABLE 7-1.   Key Market Trend Indicators

Main Street's "Dumb Money" Indicators

- Dow Jones Industrial Average (DJI)
- Standard & Poor's 500 Index (SPX)
- NASDAQ Composite Index (NDX)

Wall Street's Smart Money Indicators

- Standard & Poor's Futures
- The TICK ($TICK)
- The Arms Index or TRIN ($TRIN)

Trading the Market Trend

- Cubes—NASDAQ 100 Tracking Stock (QQQ)
- Diamonds—Dow Jones Industrial Average Tracking Stock (DIA)
- Spiders—Standard & Poor's 500 Tracking Stock (SPY)
- IVV—An iShare tracking the S&P 500

because none of these indicators provides any kind of forward look at the markets. In contrast, the way the Wall Street pros track the trend prospectively is to follow at least three other main indicators: the *S&P Futures,* the so-called *TICK,* and the indispensable *TRIN.*

The S&P Futures are traded in the pit of the Chicago Mercantile Exchange by some of the sharpest minds in the stock market, and most professional traders regard these futures as excellent leading indicators of the market's likely direction. For example, if the S&P futures are going up, the actual S&P 500 average usually won't be far behind. By the same token, if the S&P 500 index is rallying, and the S&P futures are not, it is highly unlikely that the rally will be sustainable. Why? Because arbitrageurs will step in and immediately exploit the gap between the futures and the actual index and bring them back toward each other.

As for the TICK and the TRIN, these are pure indicators rather than market indexes. The TICK tracks advances versus declines on the New York Stock Exchange so that if the TICK is, say, +207, that means 207 more stocks are moving or "ticking" up than down. Note that when the TICK is in positive territory, that's usually a bullish sign.

Turning to the TRIN, this is one of my own favorite indicators. The reason is that the TRIN goes beyond the simple arithmetic of comparing advances to declines measured by the TICK. The TRIN also incorporates the relative volume of stocks going up versus those going down into the formula. Specifically,

$$\text{TRIN} = \frac{(\text{advances/advances volume})}{(\text{declines/declines volume})}$$

In a nutshell, if you've got a lot more volume going into advancing issues than declining issues, the TRIN will be less than 1, and that is a bullish sign.

Now let me explain why it is important not only to watch the TICK and the TRIN separately but also to keep an eye on the all-important relationship between the two. And let me do this by showing you how Danny, our market trend trader, uses these indicators.

You see, Danny always wants both the TICK and the TRIN to be pointing in the same direction to confirm a market trend. To see why, consider a day when the TICK is happily above zero at, say, plus 200. The market must be in an upward trend, you think. But hold on. Suppose there is a lot more share volume being traded in the declining issues than in the advancing issues. This would indicate a very bearish bloodletting not visible from watching the TICK. Indeed, in this case, the TRIN would be strongly moving in the opposite direction of the TICK, and that is a very clear mixed signal. In these kinds of situations, Danny never trades because there is no clear trend.

As for how Danny goes about trading the market trend, he knows that there are a variety of so-called *exchange-traded funds* linked to the major market indices. These ETFs go under various ear-catching names like cubes and diamonds and spiders and HOLDRS and iShares, and they trade just like stocks.

For example, cubes, which trade under the symbol QQQ, track the Nasdaq 100 Index. It is a favorite of day and swing traders, and it is very widely traded, averaging over 25 million shares a day. Danny loves this stock both because of its volatility and liquidity. And if he gets the trend right with cubes, he's going to have a very good trade.

Similarly, SPY is a so-called spider fund that allows you to trade the S&P 500 Index while DIA is a diamond that tracks the Dow Jones Industrial Average. Danny particularly likes to trade in these stocks in times of Nasdaq trouble when money starts moving defensively from the Nasdaq market into the New York Stock Exchange.

THE SECTOR TREND IS VERY MUCH YOUR FRIEND, TOO

> Food, beverage and restaurant stocks replaced technology issues Thursday as the weak sector du jour.
>
> *THE ATLANTA JOURNAL AND CONSTITUTION*

Let's turn now to a discussion of how to track the sector trends. You want to do this because you don't want to be buying into weak sectors or shorting strong sectors no matter what your other stock picking information is telling you. So let's start with what should be the daily, premarket opening ritual of every macrowave investor. That would be to carefully scan two important tables.

The first table appears in the *Wall Street Journal* under the heading of the Dow Jones U.S. Industry Groups. This table lists the top five leading and lagging sectors from the previous day. The second table appears in *Investor's Business Daily*, and it is far more detailed. This table is labeled Industry Prices, and ranks almost 200 sectors and subsectors by price performance over the last six months and also highlights the previous day's best and worst performers.

Note that by watching both of these tables, you will not only get an excellent sense of the strong and weak sectors *du jour*. You will also begin to get a feel for which sectors are improving and which are deteriorating, and where the sector rotations are happening.

Now, in addition to the print media, there are also a number of excellent Web sites that track the sector trends. For example, Smartmoney.com has a *sector tracker* that tracks 120 industry groups in 10 broad market sectors using the Dow Jones industry indexes. It also sports a very sophisticated, color-coded map that gives you a bird's-eye view of which sectors are hot (the green) and which are not (the red).

In similar fashion, both Bigcharts.com and CBS.marketwatch.com not only chart sector performance, they also list the *leaders* and *laggards* in each particular sector. And don't forget the CNBC.com site, which has a *sector watch* Web page to go right along with its excellent daily sector watch feature on TV.

Okay, enough of that digression. Let's talk now about tracking your sectors during the actual trading day. To see how you might go about this, take a very careful look at Table 7-2. This is one of the most valuable tables in this book. It's one that you may want to photocopy and pin right up on the wall next to your computer.

Why is this table so valuable? Because it lists a wide variety of instruments that can be used to both track and, in some cases, trade your sectors. So take a few minutes now to study this table closely. As you do so, please note that there are two different categories of sector trackers.

In the first category, just as we have exchange-traded funds like cubes and spiders for trading the market trend, we also have *sector-level* ETFs. These include HOLDRS like BBH and SMH for the biotech and semiconductor sectors, iShares like IYD and IYH for the chemical and health care sectors, and spiders like XLE and XLU for the energy and utility sectors. Note that one of the big advantages of trading exchange-traded funds is that they are *not* subject to the uptick rule for stocks so you can short them even when the market is falling. That's one of the big reasons why Zoe loves to use them for her sector rotation plays. If the biotech sector is tanking, she sure as heck won't be able to short Amgen or Genentech. But she can short as many shares as she wants of BBH.

As for the second category of sector trackers, this consists of indexes like XAL for the airline sector, BIX for the banks, and XBD for securities brokers and dealers. These indexes are posted by a variety of sources ranging from the American Stock Exchange and the Chicago Board of Exchange to Goldman Sachs and the Philadelphia Stock Exchange.

Now here's a very good way to use these sector trackers. Before you enter a trade in a sector, you always want to check the relevant sector index for movement. That means, when you are trading online, you should create a whole window of your preferred sector trackers using the symbols in the table above, and then follow them throughout the trading day. What you want to avoid is buying a strong stock in what turns out to be a weak sector or shorting a weak stock in a strong sector. It's simply asking too much of a stock to swim against the sector tide. Remember: More than half of an individual stock's movement is related to the movement of the sector it is in.

And one other thing about this table: If you compare it to our earlier sector maps in the previous chapter, you will note that, at present, there does not exist an index or trading instrument for every sector of the stock market. While that will make your sector watching somewhat more difficult in certain cases, I also suspect that as the number of exchange-traded funds continues to proliferate, the sector coverage will become even broader.

THE VIRTUES OF BASKET TRADING

> You will consistently achieve a higher percentage of profit and lower your risk by trading a basket of stocks within a sector.
>
> MICHAEL SINCERE AND DERON WAGNER

Let's turn now to the question of whether it is better to trade at the market trend level like Danny, at the sector level like Zoe, or to use a basket trading strategy following Jack's example. Perhaps the best way to think about this question is to consider the most likely outcome of each strategy over time.

For Danny, it is true that he bears the least risk of any of the three traders. This is because he eliminates both sector-specific and individual company risk precisely because he only trades the market trend. Not surprisingly, because Danny bears the least risk, he also typically has the lowest drawdown of the three traders each month, where drawdown is defined as the biggest loss on his worst trade. Danny's problem, however, is that by limiting his risk, he is also limiting his potential reward. That's why he rarely beats Jack for the most-money-won-in-a-month prize.

TABLE 7-2. Key Indicators of Sector Trends

	Exchange-Traded Funds (ETFs)	Sector Indexes
Airline		$XAL
Automotive		$AUX
Banking		$BIX
Basic materials	IYM	
Biotech	BBH	$BTK
Chemical	IYD	$CEX
Computer		$IXCO
• Computer hardware		$GHA
• Computer services		$GSV
• Computer software		$CWX, $GSO
• Computer technology		$XCI
Energy	IYE, XLE	
• Oil		$XOI
• Oil service		$OSX
• Natural gas		$XNG
Financial	IYF, XLF	$IXF
• Financial services	IYG	
Forest and paper products		$FPP
Gaming		$GAX
Gold		$GOX, $XAU
Health care	IYH	$HCX
Industrial		$INDS
Insurance		$IUX
Internet	HHH, IYV	$INX, $GIN
• Internet architecture	IAH	
• Internet B2B	BHH	
• Internet infrastructure	IIH	
Networking		$NWX
Networking multimedia		$GIP
Pharmaceutical	PPH	$DRG
Real estate	IYR	

TABLE 7-2.   (*Continued*)

	Exchange-Traded Funds (ETFs)	Sector Indexes
Retail S&P	RMS, VGSIX	$RLX
Securities broker/dealer		$XBD
Semiconductors	SMH	$SOX, $GSM
Technology	XLK, IYW	$XCI, $TXX
Telecommunications	IYZ, TTH	$IXTC
• Telecom—broadband	BDH	
Transportation		$TRX
Utilities	XLU, IDU, UTH	$UTY

As for Jack, he used to be a purely sector trader like Zoe. But over time, Jack figured out that it was better to basket-trade for at least two reasons. The first reason is perhaps obvious. In the case of buying stocks, when you put only the strongest stocks in your trading basket, you maximize the probability of realizing the largest price movement in your favor. In contrast, when Zoe buys a whole sector using an ETF like BDH for broadband companies or IYG for financial services, she has to waste at least part of her capital carrying the weak companies along with the strong and that reduces her potential profit.

Now, the second reason why Jack prefers basket trading to sector trading is perhaps more subtle. This reason has much more to do with Jack's keeping his losses small than with boosting his profits. The fact of the matter is that when a sector goes down, the weakest stocks in the sector tend to fall the farthest and the fastest and to recover the slowest, whereas the strong stocks are much more resilient. That means, on average, if Jack is in a basket of a strong stocks in a sector and his trade starts to move against him, his downside risk will typically be much less than Zoe's with her pure sector play.

MACROWAVE INVESTING IN MOTION

Let me end this chapter by showing you how all this might work. And let me do so by describing Jack's particular approach to trading.

First, and foremost, following the advice of the legendary 1920s Wall Street speculator Jesse Livermore, Jack is always "dwell[ing] on the need above all other things of determining the kind of market a man is trading in." That is, he is constantly assessing and reassessing the market trend. At the same time, Jack is also closely watching not only for which sectors are strongest and which are weakest but for sectors that might be gaining strength or deteriorating.

As for how Jack goes about picking his strong and weak stocks, he knows that there are many ways to do that. But here is how Jack goes about it. He first uses *fundamental analysis* to create a list of the strongest and weakest stocks in every sector in which he is trading. His goal is to find the 10 or 15 strongest and weakest stocks in each sector based on factors such as earnings-per-share growth and relative price performance.

Once Jack has created that fundamentals-oriented list for buying and shorting opportunities, he uses *technical analysis* to winnow the list down and perfect his market timing. This is because technical analysis can tell him which of the stocks have the most potential for an upside or downside move at any given point in time. Now here's the punch line: Those stocks that pass both the fundamental and technical tests then comprise the basket Jack will trade.

Suppose, then, that Jack has confirmed an upward market trend and identified a strong sector like pharmaceuticals to open a long position in. That means it is time for Jack to buy shares of all of the stocks in his basket. At this given point in time, these stocks might be Avenir, CIMA Labs, Noven, and Praecis.

Now after Jack opens his positions—say $5,000 in each stock—he watches and waits. If the trade goes completely against him, he cuts his losses quickly by exiting all of his positions in the basket. However, if the trade moves in his favor, he will watch carefully for which of the stocks show the most upside move. Using this information, he will begin to eliminate some of the stocks in the basket that are the relative weaklings and perhaps build up his trades in the strongest performers. For example, Jack might sell his shares in CIMA and Noven and purchase another $5,000 worth of shares each for Avenir and Praecis. In this way, Jack maximizes his gains—and you will, too.

8

TEN RULES TO PROTECT YOUR CAPITAL

*H*ope Knot buys 1000 shares of Buy.com at $20. It immediately drops to $19½, and naturally, Hope begins to doubt the wisdom of her trade. But hey, Hope also knows Buy.com has a great future. It's been steadily moving up all year, and the Internet is as hot as a firecracker. Moreover, every single one of Buy.com's technical indicators is pointing as straight up as a Titan rocket. So the market must be wrong—not her. So Hope sits on the stock and on her loss another day and waits for the market to come to its senses.

The next day Buy.com sags down to $18. This is where it really begins to hurt. Hope knows she has skidded past the point where all of those trading gurus will tell you to exit a trade—with no more than an 8 percent loss. Still, she can't pull the sell trigger just yet.

That's because at this point, something truly insidious is happening within her. While she fears that her stock may go down further and give her an even bigger loss, she is also hoping that it will rebound. And in the battle in her gut and her ego—I'm not *wrong here, the market is wrong—Hope's hope is kicking Fear's butt. So she sits and waits a little more as Buy.com slides a few more points down to $16 and then to $12.*

Of course, at this point, Hope has lost so much money that the last thing she would ever do now is to sell the stock. Dammit! She can't do that. The loss is too big to take. The only thing to do now is to wait as long as she has to—until that stupid stock in this really dumb market gets back up to where it is supposed to be.

In the next two chapters, we are going to lay down some basic rules of the macrowave investing road. As you will soon see, many of these rules apply not just to macrowave investing but to *any* kind of trading or investing. For this reason, I'm tempted to advise professionals and experienced traders to just skim these chapters and quickly move on; nonetheless, I'm going to resist that temptation. Most of these rules are so important to successful trading that they are worth reviewing by everyone—no matter how long you have traded and no matter how deeply they are ingrained in your psyche.

As for the rules themselves, they fall in to two broad categories. In this chapter, we will look at a set of rules that will help you *manage your money* and *protect your capital*. In the next chapter, we will look a similar set of rules that will help you *manage your risk.*

Managing your money and managing your risk are two of the most important skills the macrowave investor can master. If you fail to protect your capital, you will quickly be out of the trading game. If you fail to manage your risk, you will eventually wind up a loser no matter how high your percentage of winning trades may be.

Let's begin, then, with my Top Ten money management rules. These rules, which are presented in Table 8-1, fall into three broad categories: efficient trading, efficient ordering, and minimizing your trading costs. Let's take a look at each of these rules, and let me show you why they are at the heart of managing your money and protecting your capital.

1. CUT YOUR LOSSES

The elements of good trading are: (1) cutting losses, (2) cutting losses, and (3) cutting losses. If you can follow these three rules, you may have a chance.

ED SEYKOTA

TABLE 8-1.   The Macrowave Investor's Money Management Rules

Efficient Trading

1. Cut your losses
2. Set intelligent stop losses
3. Let your profits run
4. Never, *ever,* let a big winner become a loser
5. Never average down a loser
6. Conquer the urge to overtrade—don't churn your own portfolio

Efficient Ordering

7. Never use a market order before the opening bell or with a new IPO
8. Use market orders to capture the price movement in a trending market
9. Use limit orders to capture the spread in a trading range market
10. Never chase a stock

Minimize Trading Costs

11. Think round-trip on your commissions—not one-way
12. Choose the right broker—read the fine print

Of all the advice in all the books ever written about the stock market, this rule has to be the one most frequently mentioned. The reason it figures so prominently is not only because it is a rule crucial to long-term success; it is also because this rule runs so very counter to the basic psychology of the vast majority of traders.

We are, after all, human—all too human. So instead of cutting our losses, most of us ride our small losses down until they become even bigger losses. At the root of this problem is a psychology that is to successful trading as termites are to a house. This psychology is based on two sharply conflicting emotions—hope and fear. Every time you enter a trade you, of course, *hope* it will be profitable, but you also *fear* a loss. Unfortunately, when it comes to cutting losses, hope usually overpowers fear—and that is exactly backwards.

In the story that began this chapter, I illustrated this process in gory detail. In that story, our fictional trader named Hope Knot got caught in a downward spiral in which her emotions failed to allow her to exit a losing trade. If you yourself have ever experienced this same kind of event—and most of us have at one point or another in our trading careers—then you must also know how important it is to learn the discipline to override your emotional tendencies and cut your losses. Moreover, you must learn to cut your losses with the same cold, calculating, and ruthless efficiency of the Terminator.

In Hope's case, when she failed to dump her Buy.com shares and wound up riding that dog all the way down to five bucks a share, she stopped being a *trader*. Instead, she became the living embodiment of the dreaded "I" word and the butt of the perennial Wall Street Joke: She became an *investor*.

Now there are two reasons why this is so dangerous, and while one is obvious, the other is not. The obvious problem is that, in our example, Hope has incurred a very large paper loss that she may well never recover from. The more subtle problem, which in many ways is much more powerful than the first, is that by failing to cut her loss, Hope has *tied up her capital*.

Indeed, it is not just the money you lose when you ride a loser down that hurts you. It is also the fact that the money sitting in that loser is unavailable for a new trade and a potential big winner. That's what economists call the *opportunity cost* of riding your losers down. And that's why the notion that "I've lost so much money in this stock that I might as well wait around until it comes back" is so very wrong and reckless.

In fact, at any point in time when you are holding a stock, your question should not be: Will this stock rebound and eliminate my loss? Rather, it should be: After I cut this loss and liberate my capital, is there a better stock or sector that I can buy into that will move up faster and stronger than any rebound from my loser? The answer to this question is almost always *yes*, and the thing you have to realize is that you can always free yourself from that loser at any time and only incur a small commission cost. So get out when you should get out! But what is the best way to do that? This leads us to rule 2:

2. SET INTELLIGENT STOP LOSSES

I place my stop at a point that is too far away or too difficult to reach easily.

BRUCE KOVNER

Setting protective stops is like playing financial chess. You must anticipate where the "masses" are placing their stops, and then decide whether you want to be out before they are triggered, or if you want to allow the market to take their stock without taking yours. Most of the time, it will be prudent to let the masses lose their stock while you hold onto yours.

PEJMAN HAMID

With this rule, we turn to the actual mechanics of cutting your losses and the practice of efficient trading. As a practical matter, there are three steps to setting stop losses, and each one of them requires strict discipline. These three steps are:

- Determine how much you are willing to lose

- Establish a physical or mental exit stop loss

- Take the loss if the stop is violated—no hesitation please!

Let's look at the first step—determining how much you are willing to lose on any given trade. For day traders, this can be as little as 1 percent or even one teenie—a ¹⁄₁₆. For position traders, it might be as much as that 8 or 10 percent that some investment gurus like to talk about. We'll talk more about defining the appropriate *maximum acceptable loss* in our next chapter on risk management. But the crucial point here is that you must quantify your maximum acceptable loss and do so before you make your trade. Once you do this, you must then translate this loss into a specific exit point or *stop loss*. This can either be a mental or physical stop loss, and each has its own merits.

A physical stop loss is one that you program into your trading software. For example, when you bought Buy.com at $20, you might have already decided that you would accept no more than an 8 percent loss. In that case, you could have entered a *sell stop* which basically directs your online broker to sell Buy.com at the market price if and when it falls to $18.40. On the other hand, you could have simply set a *mental stop*. This means that you have made a contract with yourself to sell Buy.com if and when you see it reach the sell stop.

As a practical matter, day traders will rely primarily on mental stop losses while swing and position traders should always use physical stop losses. By reviewing the advantages and disadvantages of each, it should quickly become apparent why this is so.

The big advantage of the physical stop loss is that it means you don't have to be chained to your computer while the market is open in order to exit the trade. With a physical stop loss, if you are at lunch or at work and Buy.com hits $18.40—bang, you're out.

The other advantage of the physical stop loss is that it helps you enforce your own discipline about cutting losses. If you have a mental stop loss and your stock hits it, you may waver before pulling the sell trigger as the battle between hope and fear rages within you. That's why physical stops are so useful.

The big *dis*advantage of setting physical stop losses, however, is that you may unwittingly get "stopped out" of what otherwise might be a very profitable trade. In fact, there are few things more unsettling to the stomach and the psyche of a trader than being stopped out of a trade and then observing your stock immediately rebound to the new highs that all your analysis predicted it would achieve. In this regard, *learning how to set your physical stop losses is one of the most important skills a macrowave investor can develop.* This is both an art and a science. Here's the big problem: Far too many traders set their stops at places where it is highly likely that they will be stopped out—even on a great trade. This can happen for three different reasons.

First, your stop loss may be set within a stock's normal range of volatility. For example, the share price of Buy.com may regularly swing 2 or 3 or even 5 points in a day. If you set your stop loss within this normal daily trading range, you could get stopped out on a dip even on an up day for the stock. We will talk more about this problem in the next chapter on risk management, but the important point here is that when you set your physical stops, you must give them plenty of room to breathe. Give your trades a chance!

A second problem arises when you put your stops too close to well-traveled technical trading *decision nodes.* In thinking about this particular problem, you have to remember that there are millions of very smart technical traders out there charting things like *support* and *resistance* levels and daily highs and lows and *double bottom breakout* levels and *pivot points.* All of these technical indicators are used as decision nodes to generate buy and sell signals.

In this regard, setting a truly intelligent stop loss means staying well out of the way of these kinds of decision nodes. For example, suppose that when you calculate your initial physical stop loss, it turns out to be just a few ticks above a key support level. In this case, if you put your stop at this point, you run a much greater risk of being stopped out in a temporary dip than if you simply adjusted your stop downwards a little more and below the support level.

Still a third problem with setting stops arises when you set your stops near round numbers like 10 or 20 or 100. For whatever reasons, round numbers draw physical stop losses like flies to buffalo chips, and if you find yourself stuck in one of those round number clusters, you are much more likely to get stopped out. This means that if your stop loss rule says "set it at $50," you might lower it slightly to $49⅞ or, better yet, to $49½.

At this point, too, I must tell you that one of the oldest games on Wall Street is for the big professional traders to tacitly collude in the normal course of a day to clear out the stops of amateur traders. If you don't believe me on this point, hear it, then, directly from a master trader, Victor Sperandeo, on *running the stops.*

> Many traders tend to set their stops at or near the previous high or low. This behavioral pattern holds true for both major and minor price moves. When there is a heavy concentration of such stops, you can be reasonably sure that the locals on the floor [of the stock exchange] are aware of this information. There will be a tendency for the locals to buy as prices approach a concentration of buy stops above the market (or sell if the market approaches heavy sell stops below the market). The locals try to profit by anticipating that the activation of a large pocket of stops will cause a minor extension of the price move. They will then use such a price extension as an opportunity to liquidate their positions for a quick profit. Thus, it's in the interest of the locals to try to trigger heavy concentrations of stop orders.

3. LET YOUR PROFITS RUN

> Milk the cows. Shoot the dogs.
>
> TOBIN SMITH

> When you have tremendous conviction on a trade, you have to go for the jugular. It takes courage to be a pig.
>
> STANLEY DRUCKENMILLER

Cows? Dogs? Pigs? Forgive me here for all the barnyard metaphors. But the above quotations, tied tightly to the animal kingdom though they may be, do aptly underscore perhaps *the* most important rule in all of trading. Ride your winners and let your profits run.

That sounds so simple, but here's the problem. Just as most traders stay too long in losing trades, most traders also want to choke off their profits by exiting trades too early. It's the same perverse human psychology at work in both cases.

When you have made a good trade and it starts to move in your favor, it should be time to hope that the stock will go higher. Instead, many traders start to fear that the stock will turn back on them and they will lose some or all of the profit they are making. So, out of fear, they sell—and usually far too soon. In such a case, what should be profit *making* turns into a premature profit *taking* as fear triumphs over hope.

This is very bad money management because you are not giving your capital the best odds-on opportunity to grow. Think of it this way: If you always cut your losses quickly but always let your winners run, you can be wrong much more than half of the time and *still* make lots of money.

To see this, suppose you make a hundred trades in a year, and only 40 percent of them are winners. You still will make good money if your average loss is 10 percent but your average gain is 20 percent. This is why the combination of cutting your losses and riding your winners is such a potent weapon for the winning trader.

4.   NEVER, EVER, LET A BIG WINNER BECOME A LOSER

> There's no victory as satisfying as coming back from the grave, and no loss as horrible as giving back what you've won.
>
> VICTOR NIEDERHOFFER

I can think of no faster way to the Trader's Funny Farm than watching a stock you have bought first go up 10 points and then go back down 12 points leaving you with a loss. It just makes you sick to your stomach because you know that it is such a waste. In almost all cases, all you would have had to do to prevent your winner from turning into a loser is to carefully turn your original stop loss into a *trailing stop.*

Suppose, then, you buy 500 shares of Dell at $50, and the next day it goes up to $52. If you at set your initial stop loss at $45⅞, now you can move it up to a trailing stop of $47⅞. Then, the next day when the stock goes to $56, you can move this trailing stop up further to, say, $53⅞. At that point, your big winner will never become a loser. At the same time, you are calming down your fear of surrendering your gains while allowing your hope of a larger gain to fully bloom.

5. NEVER AVERAGE DOWN A LOSS

> When you are in a boat that springs a leak, you don't drill another hole to
> let the water out.
>
> TONY SALIBA

Averaging down a loss simply means to buy more shares of the stock
when it goes down as a means of lowering your breakeven price on the
stock.

For example, suppose after you bought those 1000 shares of Buy.com
at $50, you might decide to buy another 1000 shares when it fell to $40.
The reason you might do this is because this would average down the price
of your total shares to $45, so Buy.com would only have to rebound to $45
instead of $50 to get you back to your breakeven point on the trade.

Don't do this! Averaging down a loss is one of the biggest sucker plays
in the stock market. Basically, when you do this, you are telling yourself
this: "Hmm. I made what I thought was a good trade, but now I see that it
is moving in the wrong direction. So rather than use my capital to find a
better trade, I think I'll pour some more of my money down the same rat
hole in the hope"—there's that dangerous hope again—"that the stock will
rebound." Not!

6. CONQUER THE URGE TO OVERTRADE—DON'T CHURN YOUR OWN PORTFOLIO

> It never was my thinking that made the big money for me. It always was
> my sitting. Got that? My sitting tight! It is no trick at all to be right on the
> market. You always find lots of early bulls in bull markets and bears in
> bear markets…. Men who can both be right and sit tight are uncommon.
> I found it one of the hardest things to learn.
>
> JESSE LIVERMORE, *REMINISCENCES OF A STOCK OPERATOR*

In the old days before online trading, unscrupulous stockbrokers used to
churn the portfolios of their clients just to generate commissions. That is,
they would make trades not to make money in capital gains for their clients
but just to make money in commissions for themselves.

The irony today is that many online investors are now doing this to themselves—they are churning their *own* portfolios! Ofttimes, they do this out of boredom or greed or an even more insidious addiction to trading. And for new traders, sometimes it's just plain inexperience. Whichever shoe might fit you in this regard, you must not do this to yourself! You *must* conquer any urge to overtrade.

In fact, a good bit of the time, market conditions warrant sitting tight— just as the above quotation from *Reminiscences of a Stock Operator* counsels. Indeed, when the market is choppy with no clear trend, when the news on the macroeconomic front is sending very mixed signals, or when the Fed is about to meet to ponder its latest move on interest rates, sitting on the sidelines can be the most brilliant and highest-return trading strategy you can adopt. That's because during such times, the odds of picking winners are considerably reduced.

7. USE MARKET ORDERS TO CAPTURE THE PRICE MOVEMENT IN A TRENDING MARKET

To limit order or to market order? That is often the question that traders face, and it is a question that can often be answered by using the power of macrowave logic to determine whether the market or a market sector is trending up or down or trading in a range. Here's an example to set the stage for our answer.

Ian McGregor had had his eye on California Amplifier all week long. Its technical indicators were all bullish. More important, the company controlled 80 percent of the budding market for transceivers—a key component of wireless broadband technology— and that's the kind of market dominance that Ian loved to exploit.

At the opening bell on Friday, CAMP was up a quarter point— along with the broader market averages. That's when Ian made his move. To try and capture the current market spread, Ian put in a limit order at the inside bid of 29. Within the next several minutes however, his order not only didn't get filled, the inside bid jumped to 29½.

So Ian canceled his first limit order and put in another one at the new inside bid. Being the cheapskate that he was, he hated to give up the spread—ever. Again, however, before his limit order was filled, the inside bid jumped up another 1/2 point.

At this point, Ian threw in the limit order towel and just went in with a market order. He grabbed his 1000 shares at the inside ask, but it was at a price a full point and a half higher than the market price when he had first placed his limit order.

The worst part of all of this is that, even as a cheapskate, Ian knew better than to use a limit order when a stock was on the move. It was a mistake that had just cost him over a thousand dollars of price movement and profit.

Now here's what's really going on with Ian: At any given point in time, you are confronted with both an *inside bid* for a stock and an *inside ask,* and the difference between the bid and the ask is the *spread.* This spread is sometimes small—1/16 or 1/8; sometimes it can be large—a quarter point or more. At any rate, if you use a market order, you likely will be filled at the inside ask. In this case, you give away all of the spread to the seller. On the other hand, if you use a limit order, you can set your limit at the current inside bid. If you get filled at the inside bid, it is you who have captured the spread from the seller.

Now, the clear danger of using a limit order is that, like Ian in our example above, you may *not* get filled. In fact, the stock that you were about to buy because you thought it was going to go up, may do just that and never return to anywhere near your limit price. In this case, your attempt to *capture the spread* will backfire because it prevents you from *capturing the price movement* that you would otherwise have enjoyed if you had placed a market order. That's what cost Ian McGregor over $1000 in forgone profits.

So which should you use? That's where the power of macrowave investing can be helpful. Here's how to think about it: Whenever your economic indicators lead you to the conclusion that the market or a sector or a stock is trending up or down, use market orders. For example, suppose you want to go long in Micron Technology, a semiconductor stock. If the market or the semiconductor sector is trending upwards, you may never get in if you simply keep offering the bid. Worst still, you may be tempted to chase the stock upwards as you keep missing the bid. In this case, you should simply use a market order.

Similarly, if the trend is down and it looks like the retail sector is tanking and you have the misfortune to be long in Wal-Mart and you want to get out, don't mess around with the ask. Just do a market order, take your loss, and be gone.

8. USE LIMIT ORDERS TO CAPTURE THE SPREAD IN A TRADING RANGE OR SIDEWAYS MARKET

> The bid-ask spread is Wall Street's form of the house edge.... [Y]ou overcome this edge by exploiting the bid-ask spread through the use of limit orders.
>
> CHRISTOPHER FARRELL

Whereas market orders typically make sense in a trending market, limit orders will generally make much more sense when the market or a sector is in a trading range and moving in a sideways fashion. In such a market, you can afford to be patient. If you want to go long, you can sit on the bid. If you want to get out or go short, just sit on the ask. Chances are you will get what you want. By so doing, you will *capture the spread.* Remember: A teenie saved is a teenie earned.

And one other point about the spread. A teenie or 1/16 of a point might not seem like a lot at any given time. However, if you are a very active trader moving tens or hundreds of thousands of shares a year, giving away hundreds of small spreads can quickly add up to thousands of needlessly lost dollars. And anything that adds up like that on the wrong side of the accounting ledger means you are not ordering efficiently and therefore not maximizing your profits.

9. NEVER USE A MARKET ORDER BEFORE THE OPENING BELL OR WITH A NEW IPO

For weeks, the buzz about the upcoming IPO for the Palm Pilot bombarded the ears of Patsy Hurt. Everywhere she turned, it was Palm this, Palm that—Palm mania. The radio, the TV, the newspapers, even her fiancé had caught the Palm IPO fever. How could Patsy resist?

So the night before Palm's IPO was to hit the Street, Patsy logged onto her online account and put in a market order for 100 shares. What Patsy figured, of course, is that she would get the order filled a little above the $38 per share price that all the articles were talking about. And so what if she paid a little more? The stock would only go higher—maybe even high enough to pay for her honeymoon in the Greek islands.

Little did Patsy know that thousands of other investors were doing the same thing—market-ordering to get in on the Palm sweepstakes. Under this intense buying pressure, when Palm's stock finally did hit the market, it immediately gapped up from $38 to $150. Then, buoyed by the flood of orders, it kept rising all the way up to $165.

Of course, Patsy got her order filled. That was the good news. The bad news was that it got filled at $160 a share. So instead of paying somewhere around $4000 for her shares, she got hit with a tab for sixteen grand. By day's end, the stock was down to $95. Two days later, it was all the way down to $60. That's when Patsy bailed out with a ten grand loss. For want of a limit order, it would be a weekend honeymoon on Coney Island rather than two weeks on Crete and Mykonos.

Perhaps the most important rule for efficient ordering is this: never, *ever* place a market order before the market's opening bell or for a new IPO. The clear danger of placing a market order in either of these situations is that a stock will, in the rather coarse language of Wall Street, "gap and crap." That is, the stock may shoot up at the opening bell under heavy pressure from accumulated market orders; then, after that pressure is released, the stock may fall back down—maybe 1 or 2 or 3 points or, as with many IPOs, as many as 30 or 40 or 50 points. Ouch!

As for why a stock other than an IPO might gap up at the market opening, this usually happens because some kind of positive news was announced after the previous day's market close. For example, Cirrus Logic might announce an unexpected increase in earnings. Or the Federal Patent Office might announce that it is expanding VISX's patents on its proprietary laser eye surgery techniques. Or MP3, the swashbuckling Internet music pirate, might announce a favorable settlement of a major suit for copyright infringement against it by Warner Brothers.

In each case, the stock is likely to gap up at the market's opening. But if you place a market order before the opening bell, you will usually pay far too much for your shares and quickly be showing a loss.

10. CHOOSE THE RIGHT BROKER—READ THE FINE PRINT

Some discount brokerages that offer cut-rate commissions, or none at all, may be quietly picking investors' pockets, by sending their orders to the market maker who will pay them the biggest fee for doing so. That may be good for the discount broker, but not so hot for the investor, who may lose out by not getting the best price on a trade.

BARRON'S

Stockbrokers are not financial consultants. They are securities salesmen.

MICHAEL B. O'HIGGINS

Well, maybe not all stockbrokers are simply salesmen. But look, O'Higgins is right about most brokers. Their job is to generate commissions first and only secondarily to make you money. That's why in most cases you will be much better off trading electronically.

But hold on right there. As the above quotation from *Barron's* warns, choosing the right electronic broker is a far more subtle task than simply getting the lowest commission. Speed of order execution and any resultant slippage between your bid price and the eventual order fill price are equally important. You must also carefully read the fine print on matters such as constraints on share size and different prices for different kinds of orders. Let me show you why all of these things matter with a little story.

Sarah Pennywise wants to become more actively involved in her portfolio, so she decides to begin trading electronically. After watching all the different advertisements on CNBC, she signs up with a deep discount broker that offers a commission of $5 per trade.

On her first trade, she places a market order for 100 shares of Conexant. While the ask was at $54 dollars, by the time she gets her order confirmation about three minutes later, she discovers she *has paid $54.75. Because of this slippage between the current ask and the eventual fill, she has paid $7.50 more for her trade, which turns out to be a true commission of $12.50. Needless to say, this irritates the heck out of her.*

Her next trade irritates her even more. On this trade, she puts in another market order at an ask of $20 for Netzero. She gets filled almost immediately, but again, her fill is 50 cents above the ask she had noted in her online order form. It's only $5 but still, that puts her true commission at $10.

Now, the third time she places an order, she decides to get smart and use a limit order at the current ask. What she finds really interesting about this is that the order gets filled almost immediately at the ask—no slippage. However, she is also very surprised to learn that using the limit order rather than the market order cost her eight bucks more because her online broker charges more for limit orders. That's a true commission of $13— the highest yet.

The last straw is when Sarah decides to buy 25,000 shares of a penny stock one of her friends had recommended. This order costs her five times the $5 commission because her online broker had a maximum of 5000 shares for any given order at the $5 discount price. Boy, did she wish that she had read the fine print.

Of all the problems Sarah is facing in this example, slippage is perhaps the most pernicious. Slippage occurs when you place a market order to buy a stock at the asking price and you get filled above the ask—or when you place a market order to sell a stock and get filled lower than the bid.

Such slippage can happen because your online broker is simply slow at executing your order. In the seconds or even minutes between the time you place your order and its actual execution, a market can move a sixteenth of a point, a half a point, or even several points. When you get filled at price higher than the asking price at the time you placed your order, that's slippage.

Besides slow execution, there is, however, a second and much more nefarious problem. It is called *payment for order flow.* Payment for order flow occurs when an online broker like Ameritrade or E-trade receives a payment from a market maker like Knight or Market Securities for routing a customer's order to the market maker. In fact, it is the market maker—not the online broker—that typically executes your trades.

The problem with this arrangement—which is essentially a blatant kickback scheme—is that the incentives are all screwed up. The online brokers have an incentive to route orders based on who gives them the biggest kickback—not the best price. Meanwhile, the market maker makes his money on his ability to capture the spread between the bid and the ask, so rather than, say, find the best match for a limit order, he will simply fill the order at the current bid. And you get the shaft—or in this case, the slippage.

Unfortunately, there is very little information about the degree of slippage across online brokers. My advice here is to watch carefully for any consistent patterns, and if you are consistently paying more than you think you should, change brokers. More broadly, you should strongly consider trading on a Level II platform such as those offered by companies like Cybercorp or Tradecast. With Level II trading, you have direct access to the market makers and the market, and thus, quite literally, avoid the broker middleman.

WHEN IN DOUBT, GET OUT: RULES TO MANAGE YOUR RISK

*O*n *his 30th birthday, Larry Lamb decided to become a day trader. So he quit his job, took out a home equity loan for $50,000 for a trading stake, and marched down to Shearem Securities to make his fortune.*

On his first day, he promptly bought 5000 shares of a highly volatile and low-volume Internet stock that had a really cool name. He bought the shares on margin for $100,000 and then licked his chops, as he got ready to scalp a point or two.

At lunchtime, the Federal Reserve announced a new interest rate hike, and his stock started to drop along with the broader market. Larry's stomach started to churn, and it wasn't from hunger.

At 1:00 p.m., a rumor hit the street that the company's quarterly earnings would be a big disappointment. Within five minutes, the stock fell another 5 points, and Larry frantically tried to bail out. Because of the stock's low trading volume and meager liquidity, there were no ready takers—just a sickening freefall.

Finally, at 1:23, Larry exited with a 12-point loss. This not only wiped out his $50,000 stake, it left him in the hole to Shearem Securities for another ten grand. That's what happens when you ignore every rule in the risk management book.

———————

M anaging your risk must go hand in glove with managing your money and, in this chapter, we will look at a dozen of the most important risk management rules. The first three focus on managing *event risk* through the careful monitoring of economic news and the regularly scheduled macroeconomic events calendars. The next six rules focus on managing *trading risk* by paying close attention to optimal share size, stock liquidity, and price volatility. Finally, rules 10 through 12 focus on how both *pretrade research* and *posttrade analysis* can significantly minimize your trading risks over time. These rules are listed in Table 9-1.

1. WATCH THE MACROECONOMIC EVENTS CALENDAR VERY CAREFULLY

———————

U p to her eyeballs in her technician's charts and too busy to read the newspaper, Jane Bollinger sees a beautiful breakout play coming on Compaq. The stock has just gotten above its resistance point at $30 on heavy volume, and it looks like it's poised to jump up big from its pivot point—about 1/8 of a point above resistance.

At the opening, Jane goes long a thousand shares and is pleased that Compaq immediately moves up a point. At noon,

TABLE 9-1.   The Macrowave Investor's Risk Management Rules

Managing Your Event Risk

  1.   Watch the macroeconomic event calendar very carefully
  2.   When in doubt, go flat
  3.   Beware the earnings announcement trap

Managing Your Trade Risk

  4.   Always trade in liquid stocks
  5.   Trade the right share and never bet the farm
  6.   Make sure your trades are not highly correlated
  7.   Match price volatility to your risk—readjust share size accordingly
  8.   Manage your entry and exit risk—scale in and out of your trades
  9.   Beware of trading on margin—adjust your risk levels accordingly

Pre- and Posttrade Analysis

  10.   Analyze your trades and especially love your losers
  11.   Do your research
  12.   Ignore hot tips and other free advice

---

however, the Federal Reserve announces a 25-basis-point increase in interest rates. The market drops sharply, pulling an otherwise strong Compaq down with it—a full 5 points. Jane doesn't even understand why. She just bails with a $5000 loss and goes back to her charts to figure out what bus just hit her.

This kind of trading is not just risky; it's reckless. This example underscores one of the most important points of this entire book: Watch the macroeconomic events calendar carefully, plan your trading accordingly, and never, *ever* get caught by new macroeconomic news like a Fed rate hike or the release of new CPI data that could otherwise have been easily anticipated.

In Jane's case, any self-respecting macrowave investor would not only have been keenly aware that the Fed was meeting that day, she would also have worked through several different scenarios as to what might happen at the meeting and traded—or not traded—accordingly. In this regard, we will learn in greater detail in the next part of this book that not all macroeconomic news is created equal. Some Fed actions and economic indicators matter more than others, just as the release of certain data at certain times will have far more impact on the markets than the release of similar data at other times. *It's all about context.*

For example, if the economy is booming and inflation is on the rise, the markets will embrace news of a rise in the unemployment rate like a long lost brother and spike up. If, however, the economy is beginning to slide into a recession and inflation is nowhere in sight, a similar rise in the unemployment rate may move the markets down.

Of course, my job in this book is to help you develop a macrowave perspective precisely so you can stay two ticks ahead of the tape. This perspective is no more and no less than a keen sense of which macroeconomic events and indicators are likely to matter most and how the markets and sectors are likely to react to each of them. In fact, the development of this perspective is the entire purpose of the next part of this book. The main reason: Watching the macroeconomics calendar helps you minimize your market risk by keeping you attuned to potential trend reversals or potential trend-extending events. Because you are a macrowave investor who knows how different sectors react to different kinds of macroeconomic news, watching the macroeconomic events calendar also helps you minimize your industry- and sector-level risks. So please, watch the macro event calendar carefully and develop a sense of the ebb and flow of the markets in response to this calendar. At least the first part of this is easy to do. This macroeconomic calendar is available in print form each week in either *Barron's* or the *Investor's Business Daily.* It's also available on line at Web sites such as Dismalscience.com.

2. WHEN IN DOUBT, GO FLAT

I don't risk significant amounts of money in front of key reports, since that is gambling, not trading.

PAUL TUDOR JONES

This is a very short rule, but because of its importance, it deserves its own billing. Here's the context: In the course of following the macroeconomic news, there will be many times in the trading year when the macroeconomic signals are mixed, and the market trades choppily. In such times, the tendency to overtrade kicks in big time.

Now, unless, you have a very clear scenario as to how the market is going to move out of this congestion, it will almost always be better to go flat and wait on the sidelines. Nobody ever lost money in a money market. The only thing you miss is opportunity, and if you do not have a clear idea as to the direction of that opportunity, you are gambling rather than speculating—a clear violation of the first principle of macrowave investing.

3.   BEWARE THE EARNINGS ANNOUNCEMENT TRAP

Jim Byelow reads an article in Money magazine over the weekend about the ten best value stocks for 2002 and decides to go long 100 shares of Whirlpool on the following Monday. That week, he is delighted to see the stock rise 4 points. In fact, he's so delighted that he buys another 100 shares on Friday.

The following Monday, Whirlpool releases its earnings for the last quarter and the next morning, the stock not only drops the 4 points that Jim was up but gives away another 3. Suddenly, Jim is sitting on a $1000 loss—$300 on the first 100 shares and another $700 on the second 100.

To add insult to injury, when Jim finally has time to read the morning paper that night after dinner, he reads that Whirlpool's earnings actually beat Wall Street's consensus estimate. Yet it tanked anyway. Boy, Jim thinks, is this stock market weird.

Or is it? What happened to Jim happens to thousands of traders and investors as regularly as clockwork. By being unaware that it was *earnings season,* Jim needlessly exposed himself to unnecessary company-specific event risk. To avoid such risk, it's important to understand how to avoid the earnings announcement trap.

The earnings season begins after the end of every quarter when companies release their earnings data. For each company, one of three things can happen. The company can fail to meet its earnings estimate, meet the estimate, or beat it. But exactly *what* estimate are we talking about? In fact, there are two: the *consensus estimate* and the so-called *whisper number.*

The consensus estimate is compiled and published by First Call. This financial data powerhouse relies exclusively on the judgment of the professional stock market analysts that follow the various stocks for the estimates it produces. And therein lies a very big problem.

In a strategy that Microsoft has now made famous, the managements of many companies try to game the consensus estimate system. The game is one of deception. It is to try to keep analyst estimates below the company's internal targets by feeding analysts misleading information. Of course, the reward for management's winning this game is that when the actual earnings number comes out and beats the consensus estimate, the company's stock price goes through the roof.

Because of this gaming behavior, so-called "whisper numbers" are now generally regarded as much better estimates of a company's likely earnings— at least in a bull market. These whisper numbers are regularly posted on the Internet at sites like Whispernumbers.com and Earningswhispers.com. They are compiled using a much broader sample of opinion; and what's important to know here is that these whisper numbers may deviate sharply from the published consensus estimates. In fact, whisper numbers often have a much better track record for accuracy than the consensus estimates.

Now let's remind ourselves as to why all of this is important. It is because stocks generally exhibit considerable movement on earnings rumors in the days leading up to an earnings announcement. Moreover, stock prices often move sharply one way or the other when the actual news finally comes out. This is classic Wall Street "buy the rumor, sell the fact" behavior, and it is as old as the New York Stock Exchange itself.

In our example above, what happened to Jim is that he wandered obliviously into a situation in which a favorable whisper number had hit the street just after he had bought his stock. On the rumor that actual earnings would beat the consensus estimate, the smart money of professional traders began to quickly accumulate the stock. After a day or so of this smart money's moving the stock up a few points, some of the public's "dumb money" of course jumped on the bandwagon. By week's end, voilà! The stock had moved up a solid 4 points. That, of course, is when Jim could have sold—as some of the smart money was already starting to do—but instead he bought another hundred shares.

Now here's the ironic end to all of this. When the newspapers and CNN reported that Whirlpool had trounced the consensus estimate on Wall Street, even more dumb money poured into the stock on the seemingly favorable news. "Cool, Whirlpool is making a bundle. Looks a like a great buy." What many of the papers did *not* report, however, was that Whirlpool's earnings fell short of the whisper number. That's when any of the remaining smart money stampeded for the exits. Selling heavily into the news-inspired dumb money rally, the smart money of course ran away with a tidy profit.

Now here is where the other shoe dropped on Jim. As the stock began to fall, some of the scared dumb money that had bought near last week's peak started to pull out, too. The result was an even sharper drop, more panic, and more selling. When the dust had cleared, a stock with seemingly great earnings wound up down 3 points from a week ago, and Jim had a $1000 loss. The broader point is this: In addition to watching the macro-economics events calendar, it is equally important to observe at least one major *microeconomic* event: Wall Street's ritual dance otherwise known as the "earnings season."

Let's turn now to a discussion of managing your trade risk and our next six rules. These rules are all closely related and they deal with factors such as optimal share size, liquidity, and volatility. In a nutshell, managing your risk means choosing the right share size given a stock's volume and liquidity for a given level of risk.

4. TRADE ONLY LIQUID STOCKS

A broker calls his client, saying: "I have a terrific penny stock. It's selling for 10 cents a share, and I think it's going to go through the roof!" The client says: "OK, buy me 10,000 shares." The next day, the broker calls back: "That 10-cent stock we bought yesterday is up to 20 cents a share, and I think it's going to go through the roof!" So the client says: "OK, buy another 5,000 shares." The third day, the broker calls again: "That 10-cent stock is now at 30 cents a share, and I think it's going to go through the roof!" The client says: "I don't care, sell my shares!" The puzzled broker replies: "To whom?"

THE BALTIMORE SUN

Remember Larry Lamb's tale of woe leading off this chapter: He learned in the hardest of ways that trading in a stock that lacked proper liquidity is one of the quickest roads to disaster. In Larry's case, when his trade went into the tank, he couldn't exit because there were no ready buyers.

So what really *is* liquidity? It's simply a level of volume traded in a stock that is high enough to allow you to get in or out of the stock rapidly. One excellent gauge of liquidity is a stock's *average daily volume*. For example, a large cap stock like Cisco Systems trades an average of more than 40 million shares a day. That's huge—a veritable sea of liquidity. In contrast, a Nasdaq niche stock like NetWolves—the Internet gateway stock—trades, on average, less than 50,000 shares a day. That's the very definition of an illiquid stock. So what's a good rule of thumb for liquidity? Never trade a stock that has an average daily volume below 500,000 shares.

Now to drive home the overriding importance of liquidity, let me give you another variation on our earlier Larry Lamb disaster. Let's make it personal.

Suppose you yourself enter a trade and then, using your money management rules, you also set a nice protective stop loss at your maximum acceptable loss. This makes you feel very comforted, does it not? You are protected by your stop loss "insurance." But wait. You just goofed big time because you are trading in a stock that trades less than 100,000 shares a day. In such a case, if your stock's price starts to fall, it just might plunge right through your stop loss without attracting any buyers. Indeed, when your stop loss market order finally kicked in at 2 or 5 or even 10 points lower than you intended, you'd wind up with a loss far larger than you ever imagined.

Interestingly, this kind of worst-case scenario was actually more the norm during the penny stock crash of 2000. In fact, the lack of high liquidity is why *penny stocks*—those which sell for less than a few bucks—are often so dangerous. Such stocks are like the Hotel California of Eagles fame—you can check in, but you can never leave. In the case of the penny stock crash in the year 2000, volume in these *pink sheet* or *over the counter* stocks fell from a flood of shares to a trickle. The results were devastating as many investors found it almost impossible to exit the suddenly illiquid market at anywhere near their breakeven levels.

The bottom line: Trade in high-liquidity stocks to minimize your downside risk.

5. TRADE THE RIGHT SHARE SIZE—NEVER BET THE FARM

"Mr. Stupid, why risk everything on one trade? Why not make your life a pursuit of happiness rather than pain?"

PAUL TUDOR JONES

Remember how Larry Lamb bet the farm on a single stock. That's bad money management. As we learned in the last chapter, no loss should ever be able to take you completely out of the game. Having said that, the more subtle problem here and one that speaks more directly to the issue of managing risk is this: How do you determine the right share size for each of your trades?

That is hard to say. But most successful traders never use more than 10 to 20 percent of their capital on any one trade. The primary reason is to diversify their risk.

As for how much you might be willing to lose on any one trade, for most successful traders, the number ranges from 1 percent to 8 percent. Whoa, you say here. There's a very *big* difference between 1 percent and 8 percent. On a $20,000 trade, that's $200 versus $1600. So which is best?

I can't really tell you that. It will depend first and foremost on your style of trading. If you are a day trader, you want to be a lot closer to the 1 percent guideline than the 8 percent guideline. But if you position-trade over a few days, a few weeks, or a few months, you will want to be much closer to the 8 percent guideline to let your trades breathe.

More broadly, there really are no right or wrong or hard and fast rules here. Ultimately, *you* must make the decision based on how much risk *you* want to bear. But a good rule to follow, handed down from an old cotton trader, goes something like this: Bear only as much risk as will allow you to sleep at night.

6. MAKE SURE YOUR TRADES ARE NOT HIGHLY CORRELATED

> Through bitter experience, I have learned that a mistake in position correlation is the root of some of the most serious problems in trading. If you have eight highly correlated positions, then you are really trading one position that is eight times as large.
>
> BRUCE KOVNER

This rule is both short and sweet. It is as an important corollary to the previous rule 5 and is best explained by an example: Suppose you place a maximum bet on Yahoo and then the next day, you put a new maximum bet on Amazon. You have not diversified your risk across trades. Instead, you have effectively violated your maximum bet rule. This is because these Internet stocks are highly correlated and tend to move up and down together, depending upon the rising and falling fortunes of their sector. The best way to implement this rule, then, is to spread your maximum bets across several sectors that exhibit both strength and a lower degree of correlation.

7. CHOOSE A LEVEL OF VOLATILITY THAT MATCHES YOUR RISK LEVEL—ADJUST YOUR SHARE SIZE ACCORDINGLY

Volatility represents opportunity rather than risk, at least to the extent that volatile securities tend to provide higher returns than more placid securities.

PETER BERNSTEIN

Volatility measures how much prices move—*not* whether they move up or down. Put another way, volatility measures the size of price changes but *not* the price direction. When you enter a trade, you have to take volatility into account to properly manage your risk.

To see why, first understand that on an average day, low-volatility blue chip stocks like General Motors or Dupont typically trade in a very narrow range—no more than 50 cents to a dollar up or down. On the other hand, highly volatile biotech or Internet stocks like Celera Genome or Yahoo can rise or fall by $10 to $20 on any given day. Why does this matter?

The more volatile a stock, the more risky the trade—and the greater potential for reward. It's that simple. What is more complex is factoring in a stock's volatility when it comes time not only to set your stop losses (as we discussed in the last chapter) but also to adjust your maximum trade share size. To see this, suppose you have $100,000 in trading capital and you follow a *20 and 5* rule. That is, you will risk no more than 20 percent of your trading capital, or $20,000, on any one trade and you will risk losing no more than 5 percent of that $20,000, or $1000, on any one trade. Now further suppose that your trading system—whatever it may be—sends you a buy signal for PLX Technologies. With PLXT trading at $50 a share and following your 20 and 5 rule, you go ahead and buy 400 shares. And of course, as soon as you open your position, you also immediately set up a protective sell stop loss at $47½.

Unfortunately, you have just made a very big mistake. The reason is that PLXT is a highly volatile stock. Because it is so volatile, in the normal course of most trading days, the stock is likely to dip as low as $47 and trigger your stop loss. Of course as soon as it does this, it is just as likely to zoom up to $53 where, if you were still in the stock, you would have a nice little profit.

By the way, when this kind of thing happens, you are likely to lose some of your hair—either from the stress of getting stopped out on what would have been a great trade or from pulling the damn stuff out of your head yourself in frustration. How to avoid going bald? It's simple. You adjust your share size to the volatility. In this case, you might start by buying just 200 shares of PLXT and setting a stop of $45—well outside the range of the volatility cycle but still within your $1000 trade risk limit. Then, once the trade moves far enough in your direction, you can add the other 200 shares. This is called *scaling in* to a trade, and it is the subject of our next rule for managing your risk.

8. MANAGE YOUR ENTRY AND EXIT RISK—SCALE IN AND OUT OF YOUR TRADES

> Let us suppose, for example, that I am buying some stock. I'll buy two thousand shares at 110. If the stock goes up to 111 after I buy it I am, at least temporarily, right in my operation, because it is a point higher; it shows me a profit. Well, because I am right, I go in and buy another two thousand shares. If the market is still rising, I buy a third lot of two thousand shares. Say the price goes to 114. I think it is enough for the time being. I now have a trading basis to work from. I am long six thousand shares at an average of 111 3/4, and the stock is selling at 114. I won't buy any more just then. I wait and see.
>
> JESSE LIVERMORE, *REMINISCENCES OF A STOCK OPERATOR*

Scaling in to a trade allows you to test the market waters. At the same time, it also allows you to move systematically to your maximum bet size when it is constrained by volatility.

In the case of our PLXT example above, you might start by buying 200 shares at $50. Then, when the stock gets to $55, you buy another 200 shares to complete your full position. At this point, you are in with an average price of $52.50 a share and a profit of $500. At this point, you can set your protective sell stop as low as $50. This should put you out of harm's way from the stop's being triggered by a normal volatility swing.

Note, however, that this isn't the only benefit of scaling in. You have also accomplished something else that is very important. By entering the trade with a small bet, you have been able to confirm the direction of the trade with less risk exposure. Now, as you scale further in, you are poised for a bigger payoff. But note also that if the trade had gone the other way, your loss would have been much smaller than if you had not scaled in.

As for scaling out of a trade, this has its benefits, too. In our PLXT example, you might sell 200 of your 400 shares once the stock hits $58 or

$60 or $65. This scaling out allows you to book at least some profits. By doing this, you should feel more comfortable holding on longer to the rest of the shares so that you can let your profits run—which we now know is one of the most important keys to successful trading.

So manage your entry and exit risk: Scale in and out of your trades, particularly when trading in highly volatile stocks.

9. BEWARE OF TRADING ON MARGIN

On April Fool's day in the year 2000, Julia Edgewater moved her $25,000 trading capital over to Plunge Online, a discount broker with the most lenient margin rules in the business. Over the next several days, Julia proceeded to open up $75,000 worth of new positions on "can't miss" swing trades.

Of course, on April 14, Julia got caught in the Nasdaq massacre. With the value of her portfolio cut almost in half, she quickly got a margin call from Plunge. But Julia couldn't meet the call. She had already poured every last penny into her account and had no assets to borrow on.

The worst part of this for Julia wasn't watching Plunge Online liquidate her account. No, what really ripped at her stomach lining was seeing the stocks she had once owned quickly bounce back to their full value within a matter of weeks. If only she hadn't been on margin.

Unfortunately, our fictional Julia Edgewater was joined by thousands of very real people with very real mortgages and very distraught families during that dark spring of 2000. Unfortunately, this kind of *margin squeeze* happens all the time, particularly during sharp market corrections.

So does this mean you shouldn't trade on margin? Not at all. It simply means that you have to make some important adjustments—particularly if you, like Julia, do not have any backup funds in the case of a margin call.

The first adjustment is to be absolutely religious about setting protective stop losses. However, the much more important other step to take is to follow your capital allocation and maximum loss rules as if you were *not* trading on margin. To see how this works, let's look more closely at Julia's situation.

She's got $25,000 and wants to follow a 20 and 5 rule. In the absence of any margin buying power, Julia's maximum trade size is therefore $5000 and her maximum acceptable loss is $250 per trade. Now, when Julia uses her margin buying power, she can get her stake up to $75,000. At this level, Julia might be tempted to increase her maximum trade size to $15,000 and her maximum acceptable loss to $750. But this is far too risky. The better strategy to minimize her trading risk is for Julia to simply keep her bet size and loss size down at the original level. In other words, maintain her maximum trade size at $5000 and her maximum loss at $250 and just make more trades. While this will mean she won't be able to make as much money on any one trade with her expanded margin stake, it also means she can't lose as much money either.

Bottom line: When you are trading on margin, it's a good idea to set your optimal share size based on your actual cash, not your margin buying power. Let's turn now to our next set of rules about pre- and posttrade analysis.

10.   ANALYZE YOUR TRADES—LOVE YOUR LOSSES

> The market is not a casino. It is a thinking person's game that requires hard work and a solid understanding of the psychology of the market.
>
> DAVID NASSAR

The goal of this rule is minimize the "tuition" that all new traders and investors must invariably pay to the market in the form of losses. You can do so by keeping a log of every trade and carefully analyzing each trade— both winners and losers.

Of the two, analyzing your losses is far more important than analyzing your winners. This is because many of your losses, particularly your early losses, will happen precisely because of rookie mistakes you will not want to repeat. For example, you might have used a market order before the opening bell and got caught in a gap opening. Or you might have set a stop loss too tight—or not at all. Or you might have bought two stocks that turned out to be in the same sectors, and they tanked in tandem. Or you might have unwittingly bought into a stock on an earnings announcement rally and gotten burned when all the smart money sold on the news. Any time you make one of these kinds of mistakes, you are paying tuition to the market. The gift that keeps on giving is a trading log that helps you articulate your mistakes and then learn from them.

In this regard, the worst thing that can happen when you don't do this is not that you make the same mistake twice but rather that you keep making it over and over and over. Unfortunately, this is where typical trading psychology can be such a dangerous enemy.

The rub here is that most nonprofessional traders and investors not only remember better their winners, they also want to completely forget their losses. It's basic human nature: We embrace what feels good and shun what hurts. To overcome this problem, you must embrace your losses—you must learn to love them. You must treat them as you would one of your very best friends who, in the future, will protect you from making similar mistakes.

11. DO YOUR RESEARCH

Always respect the marketplace. Never take anything for granted. Do your homework. Recap the day. Figure out what you did right and what you did wrong. That is one part of the homework; the other part is projective. What do I want to happen tomorrow? What happens if the opposite occurs? What happens if nothing happens? Think through all the "what-ifs." Anticipate and plan, rather than react.

TONY SALIBA

The more research you do, the less risk you face. But there's an important catch. You must do the right kind of research. Here are some of the things every macrowave investor should know:

- Know your sectors. Know the leaders and laggards in your sectors.

- Know how and why your stocks move in relation to different macroeconomic events and how they move in relationship to one another.

- Know the technical characteristics of your stocks—the spreads, the volumes, the trading ranges, the moving averages, and the patterns of accumulation and distribution.

- Know the fundamental characteristics of your stocks—the earnings growth, price performance, management structure, institutional ownership, and so on.

- Watch the macroeconomic events and earnings calendars—don't trade a stock around earnings time unless you are specifically trading on earnings news.

In short, do your homework before you trade—it is the ultimate risk insurance policy.

12. DON'T FOLLOW OTHER PEOPLE'S ADVICE—IGNORE HOT TIPS

Systems that work are not for sale.

FERNANDO GONZALEZ AND WILLIAM RHEE

If your trading system consists of following the advice or hot tips of others, you do not have a trading system—you have massive exposure to risk. And, as with traders who don't have the time or inclination to do their research, you would be far better off just plopping your funds into a low-risk, indexed mutual fund. Let's look at the dangers inherent in the Wall Street advice game.

Suppose you slavishly follow the advice of analysts in picking your stocks. You need to know that analysts rarely downgrade stocks or issue sell orders. One reason is that many of the analysts work for stock brokerage houses, brokers need stocks to sell to their customers to generate commissions, and it is the job of these *sell side* analysts to provide a steady stream of buying opportunities.

A second reason why analyst recommendations are usually worthless has to do with the fact that brokerage houses not only sell stocks, they also underwrite new stock offerings. While there is supposed to be an ethical wall that separates the brokerages' research divisions from their underwriting arms, analysts are often under pressure not to rankle clients with negative reports.

As for hot new Web site and message board stock tips, they get old a nanosecond after they hit the Web. Worse yet, they may even have been started as part of a *pump and dump* campaign by some unscrupulous traders who want to run a stock's price up on rumors, dump that stock, and then watch with a smirk as everyone else takes a bath.

In earlier days, this kind of thing went on all the time through telemarketers pumping stocks out of "boiler room" shops. Today, however, the new boiler rooms often can be chat rooms on Web sites. The tragedy here is that there is a lot of very good information that passes through the Yahoo Finance and Raging Bull and Motley Fool and Silicon Investor message boards; nonetheless, it is often very difficult to tell the difference between the pearls of wisdom and the pump and dump bunk. Accordingly, the macrowave investor will sort and filter and carefully weigh all of these sources of information; but in the end, he will make up his own mind based on a set of objective criteria he has set forth in his system.

As for those "hot tips" that may often come across your radar screen from a friend who has a friend who has a friend at Tips R Us, they should generally be ignored. By the time this allegedly fresh information has gotten to you, a thousand other people have probably already acted on it.

NO MATTER WHAT YOUR STYLE

A lice is a day trader in Los Angeles, Benjamin is a swing trader in Boston, and Carla is a buy-and-hold investor in Atlanta. Then, there is Dietrich, the technical trader in Chicago, Evan, the fundamental investor in Dallas, Fran, the value investor in San Francisco, and Giorgio, the change wave investor in Washington, D.C. Over the next few weeks, all of these Wall Street players are about to share two things in common. They are all going to buy 1000 shares of a stock—each for radically different reasons. And they are all going to lose money because they failed to bring a macrowave perspective to the trading table.

O ne of the most important themes of this book is that a macrowave perspective on the markets can help you add to your bottom line—no matter what your style or strategy of investing is. This is true for at least three reasons.

First, a macrowave perspective can help you better predict and anticipate broad trends in the markets. As we have already discovered, the trend is your friend, and you will rarely, if ever, want to trade or invest against the trend. Second, as we have also seen, a macrowave perspective can help you sort out the differential impacts that different kinds of macroeconomic news can have on the various sectors of the market. Indeed, as we now know, while all market sectors may go up in a bull market, some are much more likely to travel much higher and faster than others. By the same token, some sectors tend to crash much harder when macrowaves like inflation or recession trigger a bear market correction. Of course, this kind of information is very powerful when it comes to crafting profitable trades—as well as avoiding large losses.

Third, and in some ways most important, a macrowave perspective helps you to see the market chessboard more clearly. From such a strategic vantage point, you begin to think many more trading moves ahead. As you do so, you also begin to see much more complicated relationships between macroeconomic events and eventual stock price changes. Thus, when it rains in Brazil, you realize it's time to buy Starbucks stock. Or when the trustbusters from the U.S. Department of Justice crack down on Microsoft, you know it's time to make a play on Oracle. Or when United Airlines merges with U.S. Air, you immediately go long Northwest Airlines.

In this chapter, I want to take this theme—that a macrowave perspective can help every kind of trader and investor—several steps further. I'm going to do that by analyzing some of the most common styles and strategies of trading and investing from a macrowave perspective. To begin then, let's ask this question: What really distinguishes the various styles and strategies of investing from one another? The answer lies in these two key dimensions:

- How do you pick your stocks?

- How long do you hold your stocks?

For example, the distinction between a technical versus fundamental trader or between a value investor versus a growth investor or between a small cap versus a large cap approach has to do with the first dimension—how you pick your stocks. In contrast, the distinction between day trading, swing trading, and buy-and-hold investing focuses on the issue of time and how long you hold your trades. In both dimensions, a macrowave perspective can help you improve your trading odds. Let me show you how by talking first about the dimension of time.

A DAY IN THE LIFE OF A DAY TRADER

*A lice is a day trader in Los Angeles with the fastest computer in
the West. It's a custom box she's put together with a 133-
megahertz front side bus, a 1.13-gigahertz Pentium processor, a
100-gigabyte hard drive, 1000 megs of RD-RAM, and four jumbo,
flat-paneled, 19-inch monitors. She is strapped into that trading
rocket right now carefully watching the market makers do their
speculation dance on her Nasdaq Level II screen.*

*Alice's scalping target today is good ole reliable Cisco, and
she likes what she sees so far. The three-minute intraday chart is
starting to show an uptick with increasing volume and the S&P
futures chart, which usually leads Cisco's moves, shows a strong
upward-accelerating trend. Best of all, in her market maker
screen window, it looks like the market maker Ax—the ever-wily
Goldman Sachs—is ready to make a long move. With two
lightning keystrokes, Alice goes for a Small Order Execution
System market order—and boom, she's got an immediate 1000 -
share fill.*

*In the blink of an eye, Cisco ticks up a teenie—1/16. Oooooh,
Alice likes that. Now, in another blink of an eye, it's up two more
teenies. Even Alice's cat named Teenie likes that.*

*But wait—something's wrong. The Ax is exiting the buy side,
and suddenly there is intense selling pressure. Cisco's Big Mo—the
momentum that had been driving it upward—grinds immediately
to a halt, and it levitates right there in cyberspace before Alice's
disbelieving eyes.*

*Then Cisco starts to fall. There go both teenies. Now the third.
"Eject, eject!" shouts Alice to her cat as she bails out with a
market order. But with a sickening thud, Cisco's price falls a full
point more before the order is executed as a wave of selling
overwhelms the Small Order Execution System.*

*Argh! Alice has just lost over a thousand bucks. No steak
tonight for Alice. And no tuna for her cat Teenie.*

And so it goes in the life of a scalping day trader. It is a risky, high-stress business that makes a job like air traffic controller look like a walk in the park. In this case, what Alice has tried to do is scalp a few teenies. It's a pure momentum play based on the bidding patterns of the various market makers she can observe on her Nasdaq Level II screen. Sometimes she's in and out within as little as 30 seconds with her teenies. Other times, it can go as long as five minutes, and she can capture as much as a full point or *stick*. And if, by chance, she happens to hit a really good stock on a rocket up, she might stay with that right up until the close of the day and take home several sticks. But Alice *never* holds her trades overnight.

Now, it is a simple fact of life that many good day traders never pay any attention to anything more than their Nasdaq Level II screens. Like Alice, they simply watch the bid and ask patterns of the market makers; and from those patterns, they gauge the direction of a stock's momentum and make their plays accordingly. These kinds of day traders couldn't care less about macroeconomic events.

Having said that, it is perhaps equally true that the very best day traders are supremely aware of the importance of following the macroeconomic news. This is because it is the macroeconomic context that often sets up the day's trading environment, and a great day trader never allows herself to be ambushed by the release of macroeconomic data. Consider this quote from one of the best books available on day trading:

> It is a common misconception that the professional day trader ignores the big picture. While this may hold true for some profitable day traders, the majority of the best, most profitable, and most consistent traders pay attention to and correctly understand the big picture. Total awareness of the market is akin to having a mental compass. While not often perfect, it serves as a guide to traders toward the best-odds direction of the market— be it an individual stock, a specific sector, or the entire stock market—and [it] helps them to avoid dead ends and traps.

FERNANDO GONZALEZ AND WILLIAM RHEE

In Alice's case, she has just lost money because she happened to hit her buy button on her computer seconds before the release of the latest data for the Index of Leading Economic Indicators. The news was bad—an unexpected sharp drop in the index—and it sparked a brief wave of panic selling that washed over the market, taking Cisco down with it.

Alice's $1000 lesson: Watch the news, gauge the trend, and minimize your risk by trading in sectors with little exposure to the day's news.

GETTING INTO THE SWING OF SWING TRADING

---

*B*enjamin is a swing trader in Boston. He buys stocks and holds them from a few days to a few weeks, hoping to pick up 2 to 5 points or maybe, if he is really lucky, 10 points. To find his swing trading targets, Ben subscribes to several stock picking services. Each of these services has an excellent track record, but for some reason, Ben is never able to do quite as well as the services.

In fact, today he is about to take a bath in 1000 shares of Pacificare Health Systems. He figures it will be good for at least 2 to 3 points within a few days—but he figures wrong. Not two hours after he opens the position, it's gone against him by a point and a half. Since it hits his mental stop loss, he has the discipline to quickly exit the position for a small loss. And it's a good thing he does because, over the next week, the stock falls 3½ more points. What went wrong?

Ironically, it was a deadly case of *good* macroeconomic news. In the early morning, the CPI indicated that inflation was moderating, while just before noon, the Chairman of the Federal Reserve testified before Congress and all but promised that he would end any more interest rate increases for the foreseeable future. On this bullish news, many investors, including some large mutual funds, rotated their money out of the health care sector, which they had been in for defensive purposes, and moved back into more speculative technology sectors like biotech, the Internet, and semiconductors. Because of this sector rotation, Ben's stock went on its 5-point slide.

Of course, Ben blamed his stock picking service for steering him in the wrong direction. But Ben could just as easily have blamed himself. After all, he had opened up a new position just a few hours before two regularly scheduled major macroeconomic events, each of which had the potential to significantly impact the sector he had targeted.

The broader point here: Before entering any trade, carefully review the upcoming flow of macroeconomic news and *scenario-build* accordingly. Which economic indicator reports will be coming out over the interval of the trade? What are the estimates for those numbers? How might the numbers affect not just the broad market but the particular sector to be *swung* if the

numbers come out in an unexpected way? If the Chairman of the Federal
Reserve is scheduled to testify on Capitol Hill, what is he likely to say, and
how might that influence the markets? Is there any other kind of news that
might likely affect the market and the sector you are trading in? And so on.

THE BUY-AND-HOLD INVESTOR

----

*A*t 55, Carla is a buy-and-hold investor and a relatively young
widow living in one of the many minimansions that dot
Atlanta's suburban landscape. Fortunately, Carla's dear departed
husband, a retired pharmacist, has left her with a million dollar
portfolio—half in stocks and half in bonds—and she is able to both
pay her bills and live fairly comfortably on the dividend and
interest income. Unfortunately, the only stocks Carla owns—J & J,
Merck, and Pfizer—are concentrated in the sector in which Carla's
husband had toiled all his adult life.*

*Today, a $50,000 long-term bond has come due, and Carla's
financial advisor, Joe Butterworth, has just called to suggest that she
move that money into the stock market. According to Joe, the market
is looking up, and Joe tells Carla that since J & J is now at a bargain
price, that's the stock her husband would have wanted her to buy.*

*Naturally, Carla goes along with Joe's suggestion. Her
husband had always trusted Joe—stock-churning charlatan though
he may be. So Joe buys Carla 500 more shares of J & J.*

*The next day, J & J, along with both Merck and Pfizer, all fall
hard on the news that Congress will consider new legislation to
impose price controls on prescription drugs eligible for Medicare
reimbursement. Carla's total loss is over $50,000. It was as if the
proceeds from the bond sale had just been vaporized—along with
5 percent of the value of her retirement nest egg.*

Macrowave investors *never* make this kind of mistake. This is because
macrowave investors always view the market from a sector perspective and

use that perspective to properly diversify their portfolio. For buy-and-hold investors, this may be the most powerful insight of the macrowave approach.

In addition to guiding buy-and-hold investors to diversify, a macrowave perspective may also help such investors be at least somewhat more flexible in the hold part of their strategy. For example, you may recall the story of Ed Burke that opened this book. Ed was a retired petroleum engineer heavily invested in oil stocks like Exxon and Chevron and Halliburton. Not only was Ed's portfolio highly undiversified, like Carla's, Ed also missed out on a great chance to realize a large capital gain when he failed to sell some of his stock on a large run-up in the price of oil and a collateral spike in oil stock prices.

Okay, now that we have covered the dimension of time with regard to investing styles and strategies, let's turn to the issue of how investors actually pick their stocks. In many ways, stock picking techniques are like fingerprints; they are unique to each individual. Nonetheless, it is possible to identify broad categories of stock picking methods. These methods range from a technical versus fundamental approach and value versus growth investing to a small cap versus large cap focus and more modern and innovative techniques such as change wave investing and IPO lockup plays.

THE TECHNICAL TRADER

*D*ietrich is a technical trader in Chicago. Right now, he is poring over his charts looking for his next breakout stock. Maybe Nanometrics will be it. The 10-day, 20-day, 50-day, and 200-day moving averages are all stacked up nicely one above the other, and on-balance volume shows strong smart money accumulation. Moreover, the stochastic oscillators indicate an oversold condition and therefore an excellent entry point. Best of all, the three-month chart shows clear seven-week basing and a distinct cup with handle pattern, and the stock has just moved a full half point above its pivot point.

As Dietrich goes over the data one last time, his hands actually start to tremble. It doesn't get much better than this. So here he goes: 1000 shares of Nanometrics. He's in the hunt!

Unfortunately, Dietrich is about to become the hunted rather than the hunter. Yes, he has chosen a stock that is technically very strong, and yes, it will even hang above its pivot point all day long as it strains to move up and finally break free of its resistance-level chains. But the volume will just not be there.

Worse still, tomorrow, that technically sound stock is going to crash and burn all the way back to its support level, and Dietrich is going to lose a bundle on what will turn out to be a false breakout. Why will this happen? Because Dietrich has ignored the broader market trend.

Indeed, while Dietrich was engrossed in his technical charts, he failed to realize that for the past month, every single major macroeconomic indicator has been negative. Retail sales, durable goods, consumer confidence, business inventories, housing starts, the jobs report—you name it. They have all pointed to recessionary trouble on the horizon.

What is perhaps most interesting about all of this is that the price of Nanometrics was able to weather the choppiness in the overall markets during this bad macroeconomic time precisely because its technical characteristics were so strong. It truly is a stock ready for a big breakout. But even a stock with such strong technical characteristics will be unable to move up when the overall market trend turns sharply down. A falling tide does indeed take every ship down with it—and that's exactly what happened to Dietrich's stock pick when the Nasdaq dropped several hundred points during the week.

Take a look at Table 10-1 now because I really want to drive this point home. This table lists 31 stocks that were definite buy candidates based purely on technical signals generated during a two-week period when the market trend was decidedly down. Note that column one lists the various companies, column two their trading symbols, column three the date that the technical buy signal was generated, and column four the price the stock was at when the buy signal was generated. As for column five, it measures the percent gain or loss of the stock pick to date, and, as you can see, it's a veritable sea of negative numbers. Indeed, 24 of the 31 recommendations were losers at that point in time, and any technician who slavishly followed these buy recommendations would have lost a ton of money.

Now the purpose of this example is not to dump on technical analysis. In fact, I regularly use technical analysis myself as part of my stock screening process, and I heartily recommend it as part of a broader macrowave strategy. No, the point I'm trying to make with this table is that during this particular two-week period, the broader market trend was as down in the dumps as any day trader facing a big margin call. This made it very difficult

TABLE 10-1.   Technical Analysis Stock Picks Buried by the Market Trend

	Symbol	Buy Signal Date	Buy Target Price	% Gain or Loss as of 7/31/00
Gart Sports Co	GRTS	7/10/00	6.88	27.18
Nextlink Comm	NXLK	7/10/00	39.69	−16.86
Leap Wireless International Inc	LWIN	7/11/00	54.62	13.05
Unitedglobalcom	UCOMA	7/11/00	52.25	−5.49
Whole Foods Market Inc	WFMI	7/11/00	46.19	−0.95
Broadwing Inc	BRW	7/12/00	27.50	−2.51
Canadian National Railway Co	CNI	7/12/00	30.56	5.73
Wal-Mart Stores Inc	WMT	7/12/00	62.00	−5.34
The Cit Group Inc	CIT	7/13/00	20.25	−11.11
Jabil Circuit Inc	JBL	7/13/00	58.69	−19.59
Applied Micro Circuits Corporation	AMCC	7/14/00	153.50	−12.99
American Tower Corp	AMT	7/14/00	46.50	−10.09
Gatx Corp	GMT	7/14/00	37.88	1.80
Home Depot Inc	HD	7/14/00	56.19	−6.23
Kenneth Cole Productions Inc	KCP	7/14/00	45.00	−3.60
Ralcorp Holdings Inc	RAH	7/17/00	13.56	−3.24
MBNA Corp	KRB	7/18/00	30.16	10.68
MGIC Investment Corp	MTG	7/18/00	54.06	6.14
Tyco International Ltd	TYC	7/18/00	53.62	−1.87
Cerprobe Corp	CRPB	7/19/00	19.88	−17.30
Gap Inc	GPS	7/19/00	37.25	0.83
Motorola Inc	MOT	7/19/00	37.62	−10.29
Pegasus Communication Corp	PGTV	7/19/00	44.88	−5.99
Southtrust Cp	SOTR	7/19/00	25.44	−2.95
Time Warner	TWX	7/19/00	87.50	−13.85
Best Buy Co Inc	BBY	7/20/00	75.44	−4.56
Burlington Northern Santa Fe Corp	BNI	7/20/00	25.00	−2.48
Children's Place Retail Stores Inc	PLCE	7/20/00	26.12	−7.39
Razorfish Inc	RAZF	7/20/00	20.62	−13.77
Yahoo Inc	YHOO	7/20/00	134.00	−5.41
J P Morgan Chase and Co	JPM	7/21/00	134.50	−3.02

for even the best technician's stocks to move up. In other words, technical trading does not happen in a trend vacuum.

SHOULD YOU BUY ON THE DIPS OR BUY ON THE PEAKS?

Because this point is such an important one, I want to digress briefly now and talk more about one of the great strategic debates that perennially rages in the stock picking world. This debate revolves around the issue of whether you should *buy high and sell higher* as Dietrich was trying to do on his breakout play or, alternatively, whether you should *buy on the dips and sell on the peaks* as so many bargain hunting investors attempt to do.

In fact, either strategy can make you a lot of money—or lose you a lot of money. The trick is to choose your strategy based on the appropriate market context. And that's where a macrowave perspective can be so very helpful.

Let's look at the buy-on-the-dips, sell-on-the-peaks strategy first. This can be a moneymaking strategy—but *only if* the stock market is in a so-called *trading range*. In a trading range market, stocks themselves as well as the broad market indexes tend to move up and down within a clearly identifiable range. During such a time, the buy-on-the-dip, sell-on-the-peak trader can often eke out a nice little profit exploiting cyclical movements within this range. In contrast, in a *trending* market, both stocks and the broader market indexes will continue to exhibit cyclical price movements. However, in addition to those daily movements, there is a weekly or monthly upward or downward movement in the overall market. In this kind of trending market, the buy-low, sell-high investor can get absolutely killed for two reasons.

First, the only stocks that will keep finding their support levels or lows are the ones that are most likely to go against the trend and dip further. In other words, *buying on the dips in an upward-trending market is a perfect recipe for picking losers.* Second, and even worse, selling at the peaks in an upward-trending market is to miss the real meat of a profit move when a stock breaks through its existing resistance level, trends upward with the broad market trend, and finds a new peak. In this scenario, the buy-low, sell-high investor winds up violating one of the most important principles of macrowave investing, which is to let your profits run.

Now what about Dietrich's buy-high-and-sell-higher approach? This strategy is predicated on a so-called stock *breakout*. Such a breakout can occur when a stock finally bumps through an area of resistance and reaches a new high, while a *breakdown* occurs when a stock finally falls through a level of support and reaches a new low. Technical traders like Dietrich love to go long on such breakouts and sell short on the breakdowns because once a stock finally does break free of its support or resistance chains, it is likely to enjoy a strong move. Indeed, this buy-high, sell-higher philosophy is one of the important linchpins of the *Investor's Business Daily* approach to investing which is followed by millions of investors.

Nonetheless, this strategy can get you into as much trouble as the buy-the-dips, sell-the-peaks strategy *if* it is attempted in a trading-range market. And it can get you into even more trouble if you attempt this strategy against the market trend. In the first case, it is difficult for most stocks to complete a breakout move in a market trading sideways in a trading range. In the second case, it's virtually impossible for even the strongest of stocks to move sharply upward when the broader market is heading downward. Look what happened to Dietrich with Nanometrics.

Having said this, the buy-high-and-sell-higher strategy can be an absolutely brilliant one in a trending market. In such a market, you can indeed let your profits run and enjoy the biggest gains. The broader point, of course, is that a macrowave perspective will help you better distinguish between trading and trending markets. Carefully watching the macroeconomic indicators will also help you better spot trend reversals. In either case, what you are looking for is the right market context for your particular strategy of investing.

THE FUNDAMENTAL INVESTOR

---

*E*van *loves his Dallas Cowboys almost as much as he loves his stock picking. As a fundamental investor, his bottom-up approach always begins with a mastery of a stock's financial vital signs— market capitalization, earnings per share, sales-to-profit ratio, leverage, institutional ownership, float. You name it, Evan knows it.*

And once Evan has got these fundamentals down, he also carefully reviews the firm's management structure and style—is it innovative and creative or traditional and reactive? And Evan is so thorough that he even assesses the labor market situation. Is the work force unionized? If so, when is the next collective bargaining session? And have labor costs been rising or falling?

Unfortunately, despite the depth of Evan's preparation, he is about to make a very big mistake. He's going to buy 1000 shares of a great company with bulletproof fundamentals. But over the next year, Evan is going to take a very different kind of loss than Dietrich did. It will not be from money actually lost but rather from a lot of money Evan otherwise could have made. You see, over the next year, the sector in which Evan's latest stock is in is going to simply tread water while other fundamentally great companies in other much more robust sectors are going to go on to reach new highs.

The fundamental investor who fails to adopt a macrowave perspective will invariably fall into two kinds of traps. The first trap is to invest in a great company in a bad overall *market*. The second and more subtle trap that Evan fell into is to invest in a great company in a bad market *sector.* In either case, the fundamentalist often winds up scratching his head and wondering just what went wrong.

Having said that, I confess here that I may have short-changed the fundamental approach just a bit. In fact, the *true* fundamental investor may start by studying all aspects of the firm—from financial performance and the pattern of share ownership to management and marketing performance. But he will also look very carefully at the broader economic and political context that a company operates in. Unfortunately, far too many self-described fundamental investors stop at the company-specific level, and they invariably find themselves in Evan's trap—buying great companies in bad sectors.

THE VALUE INVESTOR VERSUS THE GROWTH INVESTOR

Fran is a dog lover in Minneapolis. She's a value investor who spends her evenings Web-surfing Yahoo Finance and the Motley Fool and Wallstreetcity.com and Smartmoney.com in the hopes of finding an undervalued stock that she can scoop up at a Kmart price.

Last night Fran found a Nasdaq dog with a perfect pedigree: a market capitalization of over $100 million, a price-to-earnings ratio *of less than 10, and a price-to-book ratio of way below 1. Before she goes to bed that night, Fran puts in a limit order on her online account to buy this Schnauzer at tomorrow's market opening.*

Value investors like Fran represent a particular breed of the fundamental investor. They look for stocks with things like low price-to-earnings ratios and current market values that they believe are below the true value of the company. The idea is that when the market eventually realizes its mistake in valuation, the stock price will rise to reward the value investor.

Of course, those on Wall Street who believe the stock market is a so-called *efficient market* love to ridicule *dog hunters* and *cigar butt* investors like Fran. They argue that a stock's price always reflects the true value of the company at any given time, given investor expectations. Thus, no stock can ever be truly undervalued, so there can be no real mistakes. But tell that to the millions of value investors who have used this strategy to periodically outperform both the S&P 500 index and the value investor's archrival—the growth investor.

Growth investors buy stocks that have both higher-than-average growth in sales and earnings and expectations for continued growth. To these kinds of investors, a price-to-earnings ratio for a stock like Adobe or Cisco that is over 50 or 100 need not indicate an overvalued stock that should be dumped. It just means the stock is highly successful and will continue to be even more so.

As for whether the growth or the value approach is better for the macrowave investor, there is no real answer to that. Basically, the debate boils down to the time frame in which the strategy is evaluated and the same kinds of considerations any style of investing must address: What is the broad market trend? And what are the more focused sector trends?

In Fran's case, she chose to buy a Dow dog that happened to be in a highly *cyclical* sector. If Fran had bought into this sector during a recession when the stock market was down, this might have been a very intelligent move. This is because cyclical stocks like Alcoa, Caterpillar, and Dupont realize their greatest gains during the initial phases of an economic recovery. But Fran hasn't done that in this case. Instead, she has chosen a cyclical stock in the later stages of an economic recovery and towards the most recent top in a very strong bull market. In this case, any cyclical stock that remains "undervalued" is not undervalued at all. It is a true dog that will *never* hunt profits for Fran, even if the market keeps going up. And even worse, if the market trend reverses, this kind of Dow dog will fall farther and faster than most of the other stocks on the list.

As for the kinds of perils a growth investor can fall into, it likewise is all about market trend. Indeed, for the growth investor, there is no phrase more true than "the trend is your friend." That's because the whole thrust of growth investing is price appreciation of the stock, and it is a very rare stock indeed whose price can climb quickly when the overall market is trending downward or when the sector which you have invested in has fallen out of favor.

From this discussion, it may now be apparent why in some periods growth stocks outperform value stocks, while in other periods the reverse is true. The trick, of course, is to figure out which kind of period we are in and where we are in the business cycle, and that is where a macrowave perspective can be so very helpful.

THE CHANGE WAVE INVESTOR

Giorgio is a change wave investor living in Washington, D.C. He lobbies Congress by day and speculates on new economy stocks by night.

Using the change wave approach, Giorgio looks for emerging-game-over-dominators with killer value propositions that reside in super spaces of the stock market. Using this approach, Giorgio has already made a bundle on stocks like BEA Systems, Bluestone Software, JDS Uniphase, Verities, and Wind River—all of which netted him more than a 200 percent profit.

Today, Giorgio thinks he has found his latest change wave gem—a company called Phone.com. The company sells proprietary software that turns ordinary cell phones into Internet Web browsers. It is being billed as the "next Netscape of the wireless Web," and a wide range of cell phone companies from Ericsson and Nokia to Nextel and Sprint are all standardizing to its technology. That's a recipe for a change wave killing if Giorgio ever heard of one. So Giorgio goes long 1000 shares on margin.

Within a week, Giorgio will be facing a margin call that he can't meet with additional cash, and he will wind up losing every

*penny he invested in the stock. Giorgio's problem: He fell into an
earnings trap lined with punji sticks.*

Change wave investing is one of the hottest and most exciting new styles of
investing that has appeared on the Wall Street scene in the last several
decades. You may want to study it carefully for three reasons. First, it is a
great example of how a sector approach to investing can be quite lucrative.
Second, it is an equally good example of how to divide broad sectors up
into various subsectors for investment purposes. Third, its results to date
have been absolutely astonishing.

Still and all, even change wave investors like Giorgio can get into trouble by failing to maintain a macrowave perspective. Indeed, the same rules
apply to change wavers that apply to everyone else. In this case, Nokia, the
cell phone giant, announced solid earnings for the quarter. But in the fol-
low-up conference call with reporters, Nokia's chief executive officer also
warned that the next quarter's earnings would be much lower than
expected. This news promptly sent Nokia's stock tumbling as it lost more
than 25 percent of its value. Unfortunately, the bad news quickly engulfed
not only Ericsson and Nextel and other cell phone providers, it also put a
very heavy hammer down on Phone.com—guilt by association, or so the
stock market often goes.

By the way, six months after Giorgio's earnings ensnarement, Phone.com
was up by more than 150 percent. Too bad Giorgio no longer owned it.

Of course, there are other examples I could offer you of the different
styles and strategies of trading and investing. There's the small cap versus
large cap approach; there are the spinoff specialists and the IPO speculators;
and then there are those investors who are constantly searching for turnaround
or takeover candidates. But by now, I think you have gotten the big picture.

A macrowave perspective can enhance your portfolio performance no
matter what your style or strategy of trading is *if* you use this perspective to
do at least these three things: Follow the market trend; follow the sector
trends; and watch for the connections between sectors within the stock market, as well as for connections across the stock, bond, and currency markets.

As for how to systematically accomplish these three goals, that's the
topic of the next chapter. It examines the checklist that every macrowave
investor should review before making any trades.

C H A P T E R

THE MACROWAVE INVESTOR'S CHECKLIST

Well, you know, Copper Mountain. The folks over there could not be too happy today. I'm sure these people work awfully hard, and they produced some great numbers today, earning 24 cents. The Street was looking for 23...yet the stock is getting crushed.... It is down about $24 or $25 to about $100.... The problem is the "whisper number." The whisper number is 28 cents. That's what I'm hearing.

ANDY SERWER, EDITOR-AT-LARGE, *FORTUNE MAGAZINE*
Appearing on CNN's In The Money

Before every takeoff, a good pilot methodically goes through an extensive checklist. He does so to minimize the risk of an accident and thereby protect his aircraft and the passengers and cargo he is ferrying.
The prudent macrowave investor likewise works his way through an extensive checklist before opening a new position. He does so to minimize his trading risk and thereby protect his trading capital. The macrowave investor's checklist includes these three categories:

• Assessing the broad market trend

- Assessing individual sector trends
- Choosing potential trade targets

Ultimately, the macrowave investor is seeking to trade according to these two Golden Rules:

- Buy strong stocks in strong sectors in a stable or upward market trend
- Short weak stocks in weak sectors in a stable or downward market trend

Following these two rules will never guarantee a profit on any individual trade. But over time, the macrowave investor also knows that a strict adherence to these rules will put the odds of winning in his or her favor and thereby offer the path of least resistance to long-term success. Let's work our way, then, through the macrowave pilot's checklist with the help of two fictional traders, Charles Yeager and Angela Earhardt.

Charles is a macrowave investor living in Long Beach, California. For his day job, he's an aerospace engineer at Hughes Space and Communications. Because Charles doesn't have to be in his office until 8:30 a.m., he can trade every morning for at least an hour once the stock market opens at 6:30, West Coast time. And usually, Charles can trade the market close as well during his noon to 1:00 p.m. lunch hour. That's plenty of time to make plenty of money, and Charles is as meticulous in his own stock research as he is with his operations research at the Hughes plant.

Angela, on the other hand, is an airline pilot based in Atlanta. When she's not flying Boeing 767 jets to London, Madrid, or Tokyo, she actively trades. Like Charles, she is meticulous about her trading preparation. However, as you will see from observing these two distinctly different individuals, there are many different ways to assess market and sector trends and to choose your trading targets.

Indeed, it is ultimately *you* who will be the one to develop your own unique macrowave investing style. Nonetheless, watching how Charles and Angela go through their checklists can only help you in that process. So let's start with how Charles and Angela each, on their own, go about assessing the broad market trend.

FOOL ME ONCE, SHAME ON *BARRON'S*

While Wall Street sweltered in unseasonably hot weather, technology shares buckled amid concerns over high valuations. An article in *Barron's* questioning Cisco's high price/earnings multiple, and its acquisition and accounting practices, triggered a sharp sell-off in tech stocks.

CNN

Charles Yeager's trading motto is "Fool me once, shame on you. Fool me twice, shame on me." After Charles got caught in the Nasdaq Crash of 2000, he decided he wouldn't be fooled again by any phony euphoria. Indeed, if that crash taught Charles anything, it is how important macroeconomic events are in shaping the broad market trend. That's why every Saturday morning, Charles starts his trading week by pulling his issue of *Barron's* out of the mailbox and turning right to the Preview This Week section.

This section provides a detailed calendar of upcoming macroeconomic indicator announcements. These announcements begin each month with indicators like car sales, construction spending, and personal income and end each month with indicators like consumer confidence and the Federal budget.

As he scans the list of indicators, Charles likes to make mental notes of which reports are coming out on which days. He also notes which of the reports are more important, like retail sales, the Consumer Price Index, and the jobs report, and which are of lesser importance, like chain store sales and consumer credit. He then begins to scenario-build accordingly. For example, if the CPI number comes out unexpectedly hot, the Federal Reserve may well raise interest rates at its next meeting. This will drive the broad market trend down. Alternatively, if the jobs report shows an increase in the unemployment rate, this actually might be good for the trend if the market is sensing inflationary pressure. But Charles also knows that the market might react very negatively if it interprets the data as an early signal of recession.

After Charles finishes reviewing the macroeconomic calendar, he turns to the *Barron's* columnists and articles. Basically, he is looking for two things. The first is the various views on where the market has been the past week and, more important, where it might be going. The second has more to do with his stock picking than with assessing the trend. Specifically, Charles wants to determine whether any particular stock or sector is receiving really favorable or unfavorable coverage. In fact, Charles once took a pretty big loss after a *Barron's* story slammed his beloved Cisco. He doesn't want that kind of thing to happen to him again—fool me twice, shame on me.

Once Charles finishes the columns and articles, his hard work really begins in earnest. That's when he tosses on his reading glasses and starts combing the fine print. For example, one of his favorite sections is the report on Short Interest which shows whether the number of short sales are increasing or decreasing. Charles believes that a big drop in short sales will often point to an up trend.

In addition, Charles looks very carefully at several other *sentiment indicators.* His favorite is the Investment Advisors Bullish versus Bearish Readings. This contrarian indicator is compiled by Investors Intelligence, which polls a sample of investment advisors on the likely market trend. Charles knows that when the percentage of bulls gets too high, there won't be enough additional buyers in the market to sustain a rally and a move to the downside is likely. By the same token, when the bearish reading really gets high, there is so much cash sitting on the sidelines that there is ready fuel for the market's next strong advance.

As for Angela Earhardt, she's no early *Barron's* bird like Charles. Instead, when she's not flying, she always sleeps in on Saturday. Partly, it's from the perennial jet lag of a pilot. But mostly, its because most nights she's up surfing the Internet until 2 or 3 in the morning looking for new stock targets and market trends.

As for how Angela follows the macroeconomic calendar, she much prefers the Internet. That's why on Saturday afternoon she scans Web sites like Dismalscience.com. These sites not only list all of the upcoming events, they also provide in-depth analysis of each macroeconomic report. Angela uses this kind of information to develop her own market-trend scenarios.

WATCH CNBC—PROFIT FROM IT

> Throughout the day, CNBC features in-depth news stories and interviews CEOs about market rumors and events that influence stock prices. This coverage will always affect the supply and demand in the stocks that are featured.
>
> CHRISTOPHER FARRELL

While Charles and Angela live in different time zones and have very different sleep patterns, come Monday morning, when the trading week begins in earnest, they each will have two important things in common. Both will have their television sets tuned to the business news; both will be particularly attentive between 8:30 and 9:30 a.m. Eastern time.

This early morning window before the stock market opens is the macroeconomic data witching hour. It's the time when many data reports are released by the government; and even though the stock market isn't open, the bond market is. Both Charles and Angela know that the reaction of the bond market to the first day's news is often a good indication of how the stock market is going to open.

For example, an unexpected spike in the CPI or GDP numbers might signal inflation. If bond prices fall sharply in response to that news, you know the bond market is signaling that the Federal Reserve is more likely to raise interest rates. That, in turn, will likely mean that the stock market will open down.

It's not just the macroeconomic data that make the 8:30 to 9:30 time frame so important. During this time, the options market has also opened in Chicago. That means people are actively trading both Standard & Poor's futures and Nasdaq futures; both Charles and Angela watch these futures closely in the little sidebar windows on their TV screens. If these futures are up significantly relative to the actual indexes and their so-called *fair value,* it means it could be a very good day for the market. And, of course, if the futures are way down, it may well be time to batten down the hatches or go short.

As for which TV shows they watch, Angela is partial to Bloomberg TV. At least part of the reason is that Bloomberg has excellent coverage of both European and Asian news—places where she flies all the time. This news helps Angela follow the more global components of her portfolio—stocks like Bookham Technology, Deutsche Telekom, and Ericsson. Even more important, Angela believes that a down market in Europe often presages a down market in the U.S.; so it's a great market trend indicator.

Charles, on the other hand, believes that the European market is usually just reacting to yesterday's U.S. news and therefore is a lousy predictor of the current day's market opening. So he usually just tunes in to CNBC. It focuses more on the U.S. market. It also features a great cast of characters and some really great features, like Michelle Caruso-Cabrera's sector watch, Maria Bartiromo's machine gun analysis of the market opening, Tom Costello's sprint down the Nasdaq lane, Joe Kernan's sardonic movers and losers, and Charles's all-time favorite, the fastest mouth in the bond market, Rick Santelli.

THE MACROWAVE INVESTOR'S JOURNAL

A stream of economic data since the end of May—ranging from housing, manufacturing to employment trends—had raised hopes that the need for much higher interest rates to stem the red-hot economic pace...was diminishing. But government securities slid after Friday's stronger-than-expected June retail sales.... Market prices now point to a growing sense among market players that central bankers may tighten credit further at their meeting on Aug. 22.

INVESTOR'S BUSINESS DAILY

Interestingly, both Charles and Angela share one other thing in common besides a penchant for stock market TV. Both keep a running tab of the key economic indicators in a journal that they keep right next to their computers. Table 11-1 illustrates Angela's approach. Here, she has listed in column one the major economic indicators in the order that the reports typically appear each month or quarter, with the quarterly reports in italics.

As for column two, it rates the impact the report is likely to have on the markets, with a four-star report like the CPI far more likely to get a strong reaction than, say, a two-star personal income report. Note that the remaining columns use the letters U for up, D for down, and N for neutral to indicate in which direction Angela believes the latest indicator news will push the market trend.

For example, if the construction spending report for May shows a modest increase in spending and inflation is not a threat, that's good news and Angela will pencil in a "U" under the assumption that this news will help move the markets up. In contrast, if the Purchasing Managers' Index shows a decline into the recessionary range, Angela will pencil in a "D" for bad news and a downward market trend.

Now looking at Angela's notations in the table, you can see that in some cases, like in column three, the news for a month—in this case May—will be quite mixed. Some reports are flashing positive signs for the market, some are flashing negative signs, and sometimes, the report is just plain neutral. This last is useful information in and of itself because it will often point to a sideways or congested market with no clear trend. Angela loves to scalp trade in this kind of market—it points to a trading-range market and what comes up to resistance levels in such a market invariably must fall back down to support levels. That's a great environment in which to buy low and sell high.

But now look at column four. You can see that during this month, almost every indicator was bearish. That points to a clear downward trend. However, if you weren't keeping a journal like Angela's, you would likely miss this clear pattern and might get caught in the downdraft. Angela didn't—she had a field day shorting all that month.

TABLE 11-1.   Angela's Macroeconomic Indicator Market Trend Checklist

Indicator	Rating	May	June	July	August
Construction spending	*	U	D		
Purchasing Managers' Index	***	D	D		
Auto and truck sales	**	N	D		
Personal income and consumption	**	U	D		
New home sales	**	U	D		
Chain store sales	*	N	U		
Factory orders	*	D	D		
The jobs report	****	U	D		
Index of Leading Indicators	*	N	U		
Consumer credit	*	D	D		
Productivity and costs	****	*U*	*D*		
Retail sales	****	N	D		
Industrial production and capacity utilization	***	U	D		
Business inventories	*	D	D		
Producer Price Index	***	N	U		
Consumer Price Index	****	U	D		
Housing starts	***	U	D		
International trade	***	D	D		
Consumer confidence	***	N	D		
The Federal budget	**	D	D		
Durable goods orders	**	U	D		
Employment Cost Index	***	*D*	*U*		
Existing home sales	**	U	D		
Gross domestic product	***	*D*	*D*		

As for how Angela goes about filling in her table, she relies heavily on the *Investor's Business Daily* and *Wall Street Journal* analyses of each report, as well as that of Dismalscience.com. She also carefully reads *IBD's* Big Picture feature. This feature relates the movements of the market both to the latest macroeconomic news and to other market catalysts like earnings surprises, mergers, and new government legislation.

SOME USEFUL MARKET INDICATORS

While watching the calendar of macroeconomic indicators to determine
how the broad market trend fits into the category of fundamental analysis,
both Charles and Angela also make very good use of several technical trend
indicators. Charles's favorite is the so-called "TICK," which he includes in
his online portfolio using the symbol $TICK. You might remember from an
earlier discussion that the TICK is a summary statistic that subtracts the
number of stocks that are advancing on the New York Stock Exchange from
the number that are declining. Charles knows that a positive TICK during
the trading day reinforces a bullish market trend. On the other hand, a negative TICK indicates that declines are leading advances and that the bears
are in control.

Angela likes using the TICK, too, but never without also watching
the TRIN and the S&P Futures. When the TICK stays steadily above
zero, the TRIN ranges between 0.5 and 0.9, and the S&P Futures is
trending upward, Angela can ring her scalp-trading cash register all day
long. However, when the TICK and TRIN are running opposite to each
other, Angela knows there is great danger. The bulls and bears are fighting it out, and if she gets in the middle of that fight, she can get badly
mauled. That's why she usually sits on the sidelines when the TICK and
TRIN are at war with one another.

SECTOR WATCH

Let's turn now to how Charles and Angela, each in their own way, go about
assessing sector trends. The important questions are: Which sectors are
strong and which are weak? Which are improving and which are deteriorating? And what is the pattern of sector rotation? For example, is money
moving out of the telecom and computer sectors into defensive sectors like
food and health care? Or is the flow of funds in the other direction?

As a print media kind of guy, Charles looks at several features in the
Wall Street Journal to try to answer these questions. One is the Dow Jones
U.S. Industry Groups table that lists the leading and lagging sectors from
the previous day, as well as the strongest and weakest stocks in the groups.
The other feature is the DJ Global Groups Biggest Movers. This table likewise lists the leading and lagging sectors and representative stocks, but
does so both with more detail and from a global perspective. For a more

detailed look at the subsectors, Charles will also review the *Investor's Business Daily* Industry Prices feature. It ranks almost 200 sectors and subsectors based on their price performance over the past six months. It also highlights the previous day's best and worst performers.

Angela, on the other hand, takes a totally Internet-based approach to her sector watching. For her technical analysis of the sectors, she uses Market Edge's Industry Group Analysis. This tool can rank the sectors from strongest to weakest over various time periods using various technical criteria. It also indicates which sectors are improving and which are deteriorating. Significantly, this tool also allows Angela to easily identify both the strongest and weakest stocks in a sector. This helps when it comes time to implement the only-buy-strong-stocks and only-short-weak-stocks parts of her Golden Rules of trading. In addition, Angela always carefully monitors Smartmoney.com's Sector Tracker, as well as its color-coded Map of the Market. The latter is a particularly useful tool to detect sector rotations throughout the trading day.

TARGETS OF OPPORTUNITY

Besides assessing the market and sector trends, the other big task that Charles and Angela face each week is to find their trading targets of opportunity. Because they are both macrowave investors, they each understand that the best way to go about this is to rely on both fundamental and technical analysis. What is interesting about the two of them, however, is the order in which they do their stock screening.

Charles is a reformed value investor whose early heroes were Benjamin Graham and Warren Buffett. Because of his value-investing roots, Charles takes a bottom-up approach to his macrowave-investing stock research. With this approach, he begins with a stock's fundamentals. Only after he has found fundamentally sound stocks will he then check that the technical aspects of the target are also favorable.

As for the stocks he actually researches, Charles is rather eclectic in his approach. Of course, he is an avid reader of such blue-chip magazines as *Bloomberg Personal Finance, Business Week,* the *Economist, Family Money, Forbes, Fortune, Kiplinger's, Money, Smart Money,* and *Worth.* But Charles also subscribes to a variety of magazines like *Active Trader, Individual Investor, Red Herring,* and *Stocks and Commodities.* From his avid reading, he is constantly finding new stocks to investigate. Once Charles finds a stock, he only grudgingly logs on to the Internet. This is because even Charles must now admit that the Internet is far faster and more efficient than any print form of fundamental analysis. In fact, for this reason, Charles finally and unceremoniously dumped his subscription to *Value Line* after 15 loyal years.

Today, Charles uses Web sites like CNBC.com, Financialweb.com, Hoovers.com, Fool.com, and Wallstreetcity.com. Many of these sites have very sophisticated stock-screening tools that sort stocks based on everything from cash flow, dividend yield, and market capitalization to earnings per share, P-E ratios, and institutional holdings. These sites also offer historical price data, which Charles uses to calculate his stop losses. Being the meticulous engineer that he is, Charles will also check both Yahoo Finance and Earningswhisper.com for the earnings calendar for each of his potential trading targets. He not only wants to know the date of the next earnings announcements, he also wants to carefully compare the consensus number that represents the judgment of industry analysts to the typically much more accurate whisper number which is developed from a much broader sample of opinion. The last thing Charles wants to do is fall unwittingly into an earnings trap.

Once Charles completes his fundamental analysis, he moves on to the technical side of the stock picking equation. However, in this realm, even Charles would admit that his technical approach is rather primitive. In fact, the only thing he will ever do is to pull up a chart on Bigcharts.com and review a stock's 50-day and 200-day moving averages. Charles's rule of thumb is to never buy a stock that has fallen below either of these averages. He knows that when these moving averages are broken, mutual funds tend to start dumping large share blocks. This can send a stock down faster than a skydiver without a parachute.

In sharp contrast to Charles's bottom-up stock screening, Angela prefers to go the top-down route. That's why she always starts at the top with technical analysis. Sometimes, she does her own using the Cyberquant feature of her Cybercorp trading software. On a daily basis, she also checks in with Market Edge's Money Runner for Today's Buys, as well as with several stock picking subscription services like the Pristine Swing Trader, eGoose.com, and Changewave.com. As for Money Runner, this technical tool identifies both buy and sell targets based on a wide range of technical characteristics. These include not only moving averages but also much more complicated statistics like stochastic oscillators, relative strength indicators, Bollinger bands, and moving average convergence-divergence crossovers. In addition, Market Edge's Second Opinion tool is an excellent source of support and resistance levels for stocks, and Angela uses these levels to help set her buy and sell stops.

Angela is, however, very cautious about basing her stock picks solely on technical analysis—or *any* subscription service for that matter. She not only knows from painful experience that the best buy or short recommendation is only as good as the sector and market trends that the position will be opened in, she also knows that the black box of technical analysis will often recommend buying a stock whose fundamentals are absolutely in the gutter or shorting a stock with stellar fundamentals. In such cases, she knows it is far too risky to take that technical advice.

That's why Angela always checks a stock's fundamentals after it has survived her technical screen. What she does to save time is to use a very simple but highly effective tool. This is the five-category rating system that *Investor's Business Daily* uses to rank stocks daily. This system includes ratings for earnings per share, relative price strength, industry group relative strength, sales and profit margins, and the degree of accumulation or distribution of the stock. In using this *IBD* data, Angela's decision rule is very simple. She won't buy any stock in a position trade unless it has an earnings-per-share rating over 85 and a sales-plus-profit-margin rating of B or higher. And she won't short a stock unless it has an EPS under 50 and sales-plus-profit margin of C or less.

As for falling into any earnings trap, Angela will never again let that happen. In the space of just two weeks several summers ago, she lost more than $25,000 on just three stocks—Nokia, VISX, and Worldcom. Each of them plummeted sharply on negative earnings news. In fact, the experience was so traumatic that Angela now schedules both her flying trips and vacations around earnings season so she won't have the temptation to trade.

Moreover, because Angela got caught very early in her trading career holding a basket of drug stocks when the Clinton Administration proposed a health care reform bill that was a disaster for both Clinton and the pharmaceutical sector, Angela also knows to follow the political and legislative news very carefully. In fact, she is the only trader she knows who regularly reads the online edition of the *Washington Post.*

SOME STOCK PICKING SCREENS

More broadly, both Angela and Charles always check the latest news on their potential targets. They are particularly interested in any regulatory or legislative developments affecting the stock, the stock's sector, or, most subtly, the stock of a leader in the sector.

Charles usually does his News Screen at Redchip.com. This Web site even has a nifty portfolio tracker that e-mails Charles all the latest news stories about the stocks in his portfolio. Angela, on the other hand, prefers to use CBS' marketwatch.com for her news check. And unlike Charles, who is offended by the coarse language often bouncing off the walls of the stock-picking chat rooms, Angela will always check the major Internet message boards. She knows there are many pearls of wisdom that can be gleaned from these boards despite the coarse language and the more than occasional swine who will spread false rumors about a stock in the hopes of causing a rise or drop in price.

As for checking the message boards, Angela always takes a short cut to CNET.com. At this site, she can type in the symbol for any stock and the search engine will pull in all of the messages from her four favorite boards: the Motley Fool, the Raging Bull, the Silicon Investor, and Yahoo Finance. As their final stock-picking screen, both Charles and Angela must determine whether a stock is a leader or laggard in its particular sector. Here again, the *Investor's Business Daily* ratings are helpful to both of them. In addition, both Charles and Angela especially like to use the industry analysis feature of Bigcharts.com. It provides a list of the best- and worst-performing stocks over different time periods ranging from a week or a month to one or five years.

Both Charles and Angela know how much work it is to assess the market and sector trends and find excellent stock trading opportunities. But from personal experience, both of them also know how important it is to go through their macrowave investing checklist in preparation for the trading week. That's why each, in their own way, is an excellent macrowave pilot.

Where the Macrowave Rubber Meets the Stock Market Road

LEAD, LAG, OR GET OUT OF THE WAY

To begin this chapter, allow me to repeat an important passage from the introduction to this book:

> The Federal Reserve hikes interest rates, consumer confidence falls, war breaks out in the Balkans, drought shrinks the coffee crop in Brazil, oil prices spike sharply in Rotterdam, and the U.S. trade deficit reaches a new record high. Each of these macroeconomic waves—some of them thousands of miles away—will move the U.S. stock market in very different but nonetheless systematic and predictable ways. If you come to fully understand these macrowaves, you will become a better investor or trader—no matter what your style of investing or trading is. That's the power of macrowave investing, and that's what this book is about.

Well, the purpose of this part of this book is to illustrate in more detail those systematic and predictable ways the stock market and its sectors do indeed move in response to macroeconomic events. The overarching goal is to help you as a trader or an investor to use the flow of macroeconomic information to better time your trades and to better identify the sectors that you want to trade within.

To achieve this goal, we must undertake the at times difficult task of learning about each of the various macroeconomic indicators that are released on a weekly, monthly, or quarterly basis. To help you do this, I have organized the various indicators by the type of macroeconomic problem that each indicator is most closely associated with.

For example, in Chapter 13's discussion of taming the recessionary bear, you will be introduced to two of the most important leading indicators of recession—declining housing starts and auto sales. Similarly, when we stalk the inflationary tiger in Chapter 15, you will come face to face with the Consumer Price Index and the Producer Price Index. But please note this about the way I've organized things. The segregation of the various indicators into specific chapters and specific problems will be, in many ways, a very artificial one. The fact is, at any given time, any one of the major economic indicators can provide important evidence on any given macroeconomic problem—be it inflation or recession or growth or productivity. So when we seek to read the indicator tea leaves as a means of improving our trading performance, we must always do so within the broader context of current economic conditions.

WHEN GOOD NEWS IS BAD NEWS

A huge spike in new jobs shattered expectations that the Federal Reserve Board will cut interest rates. The resulting stock sell-off sucked $182 billion out of market capitalization on the Nasdaq and the S&P 500.... The good news that began all of this bad news—the Labor Department this morning reported that unemployment in February fell to 5.5 percent, as the economy added 705,000 new jobs.

MONEYLINE

Does this quotation help you see why I am emphasizing the importance of context? In the Alice in Wonderland world of Wall Street, bad news can be good news and good news can be bad news, and only the economic context for this news can help us resolve these paradoxes.

For example, an increase in the unemployment rate or a decrease in industrial production or a fall in consumer confidence can all be very *bad* news for Wall Street and send stock prices plummeting *if* the economy has begun to soften. In that particular context, the Street's primary fear is recession, and such bad news strongly reinforces this fear.

But here's the perversity of it all: That same seemingly bad news—rising unemployment, falling production, and sinking consumer confidence—may also be embraced as very *good* news by the Street and send stock prices soaring *if* the economy is in the later stages of an expansion and inflationary pressures are high. In such a case, what the Street is most worried about is not economic stagnation but rather whether the Fed will raise interest rates. In that context, any signs of an economic slowdown can help assuage those fears and reassure the markets. So, as we move through these next several chapters examining the various economic indicators, please keep this crucial point about King Context always uppermost in your mind.

With that said, let's complete two more tasks before diving into the thicket of economic indicators. One is to review the very important distinction between so-called *leading indicators, lagging indicators,* and *coincident indicators.* The other is to revisit the role of expectations in driving stock market prices.

NOT ALL INDICATORS ARE CREATED EQUAL

A *leading indicator* provides us with a signal of what is about to come. For example, housing permits usually start to fall months before the economy actually enters a recession. Hence, housing permits are a leading indicator of recession, and macrowave investors love leading indicators because they are the best tools for prediction and anticipation of changing market and sector trends.

In contrast, a *lagging indicator* only changes direction *after* business conditions have changed. For example, the *average duration of unemployment* is considered to be a typical lagging indicator. This is because decreases in the average duration of unemployment invariably occur *after* an expansion gains strength, while the sharpest increases tend to occur *after* a recession has begun. In this sense, lagging indicators can only provide us with a confirmation of what has already begun to happen. Accordingly, lagging indicators are much less useful in a macrowave context—although they can be important in confirming changes in the trend.

As for so-called *coincident indicators,* these rise and fall, or *coincide,* with the trend and are designed to indicate the current state of the economy. Some examples include nonfarm payrolls, personal income, and industrial production. As with lagging indicators, macrowave investors find coincident indicators useful more for confirming than predicting trend changes. Now take a look at Table 12-1. It lists the major ingredients of the so-called Index of Leading Indicators. The nonprofit Conference Board releases this index during the first week of every month for the preceding two months. Note in the table that the left-hand column lists the specific indicators that make up the index, while the right-hand column provides a brief comment on why each item is considered a leading indicator.

TABLE 12-1.   The Index of Leading Economic Indicators

Leading Indicators	Rationale
The average workweek	• More overtime precedes an expansion and less a recession.
Initial jobless claims for unemployment benefits	• Claims rise as the economy begins to enter a recession and fall with an expansion.
Percent of companies receiving slower deliveries	• Slower deliveries mean business is booming; faster deliveries signal an economic weakening.
New factory orders for consumer goods	• This is the first step in the production process. As orders increase, production soon follows. As they fall, there's trouble ahead.
New building permits	• As the Fed raises or lowers interest rates to slow or stimulate the economy, this sector is the first to feel it.
Consumer confidence	• When consumer spirits start to soar, the economy will start to roar; when confidence falls, the GDP goes with it.
New orders by manufacturers for non-defense capital goods	• A bullish sign when rising investment foreshadows expansion; a bearish sign when falling investment signals contraction.
S&P 500 Stock Market Index	• Historically, the market peaks months *before* a recession hits and troughs months *before* the recovery begins.
The money supply (M2)	• More money means lower interest rates and more investment; less means just the opposite.
The interest rate spread (10-year bond less Fed funds rate)	• When short-term interest rates rise above long-term interest rates, this inverted yield curve signals recession.

Now chances are, if you have heard about any one macroeconomic indicator, the Index of Leading Indicators is the one. It certainly gets a lot of attention in the press. The irony, of course, is that the Index of Leading Indicators has a relatively poor track record accurately forecasting turns in the business cycle. In fact, one of my favorite jokes on Wall Street is that this index has predicted ten of the last five recessions. More important, this index has much less impact on the stock market than many of the other individual indicators we will soon discuss. The primary reason is that it is constructed from previously announced data, so that, in many ways, by the time the Index of Leading Economic Indicators is released, it is simply old news that the markets have assimilated. You will see what I mean in the next several chapters. But before we go there, let's finish this chapter with a discussion of the critical role that *expectations* play when it comes to gauging the stock market's reaction to economic data.

IF SOMETHING DOESN'T HAPPEN, IT PROBABLY ALREADY HAS

To better understand the critical role of expectations in moving stock prices, I want to introduce you to the technique of using so-called *event studies* to gauge the market's reaction to new macroeconomic news. The essence of an event study is to compare stock market prices just prior to and just after a major *unexpected* macroeconomic event. Note that the most important word in that last sentence is the word "unexpected." Here's the issue.

Virtually all the best Wall Street professionals carefully watch the macroeconomics event calendar. As this "smart money" watches this calendar, it also forms expectations about the actual event. Indeed, this is a very highly developed ritual in which Wall Street's analysts and economists regularly estimate and come up with consensus predictions about what the latest numbers to be released will be.

Now the bigger point here is that this smart money not only makes predictions, it also trades on that information *prior to the actual event.* Thus, if the consensus on Wall Street is that the Consumer Price Index is going to show a big increase, Wall Street's smart money is likely to move out of the inflation-sensitive sectors and into more defensive sectors in the days—and perhaps even weeks—*before* the actual news hits. In fact, *when* the news hits and *if* the news meets expectations, *the market is unlikely to react much at all.* The reason: *it already has.*

That Wall Street trades heavily on expectations creates problems for the naïve statistician trying to gauge market reactions to macroeconomic events. In this particular example, suppose that Professor Simpleton were to look at prices just before the CPI was released and just after. Because nothing moved, he would conclude with a high degree of statistical significance that "inflationary signals appear to have no impact on stock prices." Of course, this is nonsense. What Professor Simpleton has failed to notice is that the stock price movements have already taken place over some much more difficult-to-define time period—it might three days, four days, a week, or maybe even two weeks or a month.

TAMING THE RECESSIONARY BEAR

After six Fed rate hikes in less than 16 months, Roy Siegfried figured that it was just about time for Alan Greenspan's ever-tightening noose to finally choke off the economic expansion. That's why Roy was hardly surprised when auto sales slumped for the second straight month, housing starts came out with their third straight monthly drop, and the average work week began to shrivel.

Time to move, thought Roy. And his move was as swift as it was sure. He cashed out his entire stock portfolio—including 2000 shares of his beloved Oracle—and moved right into bonds.

Four months later, the recession that Roy had foreseen was officially underway. And over the next year, as the Fed lowered interest rates by over 200 basis points, both the bond market and the value of Roy's portfolio soared—even as the Dow and Nasdaq hit five-year lows.

Roy slept very well at night during this whole, dark time. He was also one of the relatively few consumers in America who splurged on a new luxury car. It was a sleek brown Porsche that Roy affectionately nicknamed The Bear.

———————

A s Roy Siegfried clearly understood, the onset of a recession spells disaster for the stock market. The reason lies in understanding this vicious little downward spiral.

Higher interest rates raise the costs of doing business for a large segment of American industry. These higher costs lead to higher prices which in turn lead to reduced demand—even as consumer credit is being squeezed by rising interest rates. As consumer demand falls, business inventories build, and businesses cut back on the hours their employees work. With less money in their pockets, workers spend less, sales fall, more inventories pile up, and soon, businesses start laying people off. But this means even less money spent by consumers, even lower sales, less production, and more layoffs. This circling around the recessionary drain hits the bottom line of almost every business hard, and because stock prices are ultimately driven by earnings, stock prices must inevitably fall during a recession.

Of course, during these hard times, those morticians in pinstripes—also known as bond traders—are having a field day picking at the economy's carcass. They know that when recession hits, the Federal Reserve must invariably begin to lower interest rates. In reaction, bond *yields* must fall, and since bond prices are inversely linked to yields, this means bond *prices* must rise. That's why buying bonds just as interest rates are peaking and just before a recession hits is one very excellent route to the Rich House—or to Roy Siegfried's house, as the case may be.

The question, of course, is, How can you tell when a recession is looming on the horizon? At least part of the answer lies in Table 13-1, which provides a summary of the key recessionary indicators as they are rated on a five-star scale.

As you can see from the table, the savvy macrowave investor will do well to first look at two particular sets of economic reports: one for auto and truck sales and the other for the housing sector. These two sectors typically are the first to lead the economy into—and out of—recessions.

In addition, two more key signals of an approaching recession may be found in several reports released by the U.S. Department of Labor. The *initial jobless claims* report counts how many people have filed the preceding

TABLE 13-1. Key Recession Indicators

Recession Indicators	Market Rating Reaction	Data Source	Release Date
Auto and truck sales	***	Department of Commerce	Monthly; third business day of the month.
Housing starts and building permits	****	Department of Commerce	Monthly; between the 16th and 20th of the month.
Existing home sales	**	National Association of Realtors	Monthly; around the 25th of the month.
New home sales	**	Department of Commerce	Monthly; around the last business day of the month.
Construction spending	*	Department of Commerce	Monthly; first business day of the month.
Initial claims	***	Department of Labor	Weekly; every Thursday.
The jobs report	*****	Department of Labor	Monthly; first Friday of the month.

week for unemployment benefits. More important, the five-star, 800-pound gorilla of a *jobs report* not only tracks the nation's unemployment rate by different sectors, regions, and demographic groups, it also provides valuable information on factors like the average workweek and hourly earnings. Let's look now at each of these indicators in more detail.

AUTO AND TRUCK SALES—WHAT'S GOOD FOR GENERAL MOTORS...

The industry's health is important because highly variable auto sales tend to be a leading indicator of recessions. Auto manufacturing accounts for about 4 percent of economic output in the United States, for instance. The General Motors Corporation and the Ford Motor Company are the world's two largest companies in terms of sales and share of global economic output....

NEW YORK TIMES

Years ago, this indicator used to be referred to simply as "car sales." However, with the advent of family-toting minivans and gas-guzzling sports utility vehicles—both of which are classified as light trucks—it is now better to include the truck portion of the moniker when talking about this report. As for the auto and truck sales data, each of the Big Three automakers—DaimlerChrysler, Ford, and GM—reports sales individually along with foreign producers. The Department of Commerce then uses these individual reports to calculate a total annual seasonally adjusted *sales pace*. It is this sales pace that the market focuses on, and these data are released during the first week of the month.

The report on car and truck sales is a solid three-star report that you should pay considerable interest to—particularly around key market turning points (when it then merits five stars) and particularly if you are trading in any of the sectors in the *auto cluster*. These are the sectors that make the tires, glass, aluminum, and steel for the industry.

The importance of this report lies in the fact that it tracks the very first economic indicator—along with housing starts—to turn down when the economy begins to slide into a recession. This is because when consumers begin to worry about the economic outlook, one of the first things they do is postpone or cancel decisions to buy big-ticket items like autos or homes. Accordingly, auto and truck sales represent one of the macrowave investor's most important leading indicators.

THE HOUSING REPORTS—CANARIES IN A COAL MINE

The housing industry is a leading indicator for the rest of the economy. When housing sales slow, people don't purchase as much furniture, appliances and accessories. The result is that retail activity decelerates and employment in that sector slows.

THE RICHMOND TIMES DISPATCH

The housing industry is a huge part of our economy, accounting for over a fourth of all investment spending. When tracking this industry, the four main reports to follow include: housing starts and building permits, new home sales, existing home sales, and construction spending. Of the four reports, the most important by far is housing starts and permits. This is because, like the auto and truck sales report, it is a big-time leading indicator of recession.

HOUSING STARTS AND BUILDING PERMITS—I LOVE THE SOUND OF HAMMERS IN THE MORNING

> The stock market surged to a new post-crash high in active trading Tuesday, after new economic data signaled moderation in the economy and helped ease fears about inflation.... Share prices leaped at the opening following a sharp rally in the bond market on news that housing starts were down dramatically.... Although the housing numbers raised recession concerns, stock analysts said the market interpreted the report as good news because it signaled a slowing economy that could lead to lower inflation.
>
> ASSOCIATED PRESS

The Department of Commerce reports housing starts and building permits between the 16th and 20th of the month. This four-star report is broken down by region and covers the Midwest, Northeast, South, and West. Note, however, that the regional data are highly volatile due to weather changes and natural disasters.

Housing starts and building permits are very important leading indicators and, as we have already noted, building permits are included in the Conference Board's Index of Leading Indicators. Together with auto and truck sales, the housing sector is the first to turn down as the economy enters a recession and the first to rise when it rebounds. Indeed, almost all of the economic turnarounds over the past 50 years have been precipitated by changes in these sectors.

As with all of our reports, the stock market reaction to a change in housing permits is a matter of where we are in the business cycle. As the above news excerpt from the Associated Press illustrates, if inflation is a concern in the middle or later stages of an expansion, the stock market views a strong housing start report as bearish, while earlier in the cycle or in a recessionary trough, good news on the housing front is decidedly bullish.

NEW AND EXISTING HOME SALES—MORTGAGING THE AMERICAN DREAM

> For the second day in a row, stocks tumbled more than 200 points amid growing concern that the global economic turmoil will spread to the United States by next year.... This week's drop in stock prices was triggered by a series of negative reports from around the world, which economists said add

up to a pervasive sense of gloom.... U.S. manufacturing activity declined for the fourth month in a row, due largely to slowing exports. And sales of new and existing homes were down for the second month in a row.... "It's like you're putting a mosaic together, with all these pieces," said Robert MacIntosh, vice president and portfolio manager for Eaton Vance Management in Boston. "And the picture that's emerging...is not pretty."

AUSTIN AMERICAN-STATESMAN

The National Association of Realtors releases the *existing* home sales report around the 25th of the month for the preceding month. Such sales are highly sensitive to changes in mortgage interest rates and will react very quickly, with only a few months' lag.

Besides sales, this report also provides data both on inventory and median price. The inventory data are important because a low level of inventory can be a signal that new housing starts may increase. At the same time, the median price is a good indicator of inflation in the housing market.

The Department of Commerce publishes the *new* home sales data around the last business day of the month. This indicator is a moderately useful measure of the *demand side* of the housing market, while housing starts measure the *supply side*. Indeed, new home sales tend to surge as the economy comes out of recession. This is because of pent-up demand as cautious consumers wait on their big-ticket purchases when times are tough.

Note that both of these two-star reports are subject to large revisions. Note also that the sales reports of both new and existing homes are typically old news to the stock and bond markets by the time they hit. This is because these reports follow housing starts in the reporting queue, and the sales data are highly correlated with the housing start data.

But note finally that, as the above news excerpt from the *Austin American-Statesman* illustrates, even relatively unimportant reports can, at critical times, become part of an important mosaic that allows analysts to see the bigger macroeconomic picture.

CONSTRUCTION SPENDING—THE BIG SLEEP

Construction spending fell 1.1 percent in June after four consecutive monthly gains, pulled down by declines in housing and commercial building.... Wall Street showed little reaction to the report.

THE COLUMBUS DISPATCH

The U.S. Department of Commerce releases this report on the first business day of the month for the two preceding months, and it is usually greeted on the Street with a big yawn. The problem is that the data are both super-volatile and subject to major revisions. Because of this, this monthly report barely rates a single star.

Nonetheless, at least some analysts watch this report for emerging trends over a longer time period. In addition, it can be useful to watch the residential component of the data. This is because residential construction begins to recover a little sooner than the overall economy.

INITIAL CLAIMS—OR HOW I FOUND MY WAY TO THE UNEMPLOYMENT LINE

The market was pounded early in the session by news that initial claims for unemployment benefits climbed by 47,000 to 498,000 in the week ended April 13, indicating no signs of relief from the recession.

THE WASHINGTON POST

Every Thursday at 8:30 a.m., the Department of Labor releases the latest data on new claims for unemployment benefits. This three-star report is a very timely one, but it is also very volatile. That's why most analysts prefer to look at it more as a four-week *moving average*. The advantage of viewing the data in this fashion is that it smooths out the volatility and allows you to better spot trends.

As previously noted, initial jobless claims are one of the components of the Index of Leading Indicators. The reason should be obvious: New people going on the unemployment line represent a very early warning that all is not well in production land. By the same token, prior to an economic recovery, the initial claims start to decline.

THE JOBS REPORT—THE BIG KAHUNA

"[The Jobs Report] has become such a big deal that nobody on Wall Street wants to touch it," says Jim Bianco, research chief at Arbor Trading. Most traders clear their positions ahead of the report because both stocks and bonds can open sharply lower the day it's released. "Going in with a position is a career trade," Bianco says. "You can blow up in five minutes."

USA TODAY

The jobs report provides key data on the nation's unemployment rate, non-farm payrolls, average hours worked, and, as we already discussed in the last chapter, average hourly earnings. This jobs report is released by the Department of Labor on the first Friday of every month for the previous month. Like many data reports, it comes out at 8:30 a.m. before the stock market opens. But unlike most other reports, this one truly is the Big Kahuna. This is so for at least two reasons.

First, the jobs report helps set the macroeconomic tone on Wall Street for the month—and therefore the market trend. This is not only because the unemployment rate and average hours worked are two crucial pieces of data. It is also because from the jobs report, it is possible to estimate many of the other macroeconomic indicators that will follow in its wake.

For example, if we know how many people have been working, if we know how many hours they have worked, and if we know how much over-time they have accumulated, then we can predict how much these workers have produced. This information will show up two weeks later in the report on industrial production. Similarly, if we know how much workers have been paid, we can likewise make a reasonable guess about the data for personal income, while looking at a specific sector like, say, the construction industry can help us predict housing starts.

The second reason why the jobs report has superstar status on the Street is equally important. Along with the inflation rate, the unemployment rate generated by this report can be absolute political dynamite. Indeed, a sharp rise in this rate is likely to lead to a very swift fiscal or monetary policy response—particularly in an election year.

THE UNEMPLOYMENT RATE—THE THIRD RAIL OF POLITICS

The nation's unemployment rate, the most politically sensitive economic indicator in an election year, rose sharply in June. Minutes after the report was released today, the Federal Reserve responded by cutting its key interest rate in an attempt to stimulate the sagging economy.... Analysts said the unemployment statistics were so grim that the central bank had little choice but to act, despite its concerns that it would appear to be bowing to political considerations.... Concerned about the weak economy, stocks slid today on the New York Stock Exchange.... Bonds rose, however, as long-term interest rates dipped in reaction to the Federal Reserve's rate cut.

THE NEW YORK TIMES

On Wall Street, the unemployment rate is not generally regarded as a leading indicator. Nonetheless, changes in the unemployment rate can be very important to the markets because of their political implications and the likelihood of a swift fiscal or monetary policy response—as the above news excerpt from the *New York Times* indicates.

The other point of interest about the unemployment rate is that while both Main Street and the nation's politicians always love a lower unemployment rate, Wall Street gets very nervous when this rate approaches the so-called *natural rate* of unemployment. We talked about this natural rate earlier in Chap. 2 where we learned that if the unemployment rate falls below the natural rate, inflationary pressures start to build. This is because labor markets get tight and wages get bid up as labor shortages force businesses to begin to poach on other companies for workers. Accordingly, when the unemployment rate gets near this natural rate, Wall Street begins to watch movements in the unemployment rate more for signs of inflation than recession.

As a final comment on this indicator, you should be aware that major aberrations in the data can occur during the summer when teenagers end school and start job hunting. For example, when fewer than expected teens enter the market, the total labor force will shrink on a seasonally adjusted basis, and this will push the unemployment rate down. In contrast, when student workers go back to school in the fall, the unemployment rate may rise again. More broadly, the data can be highly volatile.

NONFARM PAYROLLS—PUTTING AMERICA TO WORK

The US economy, which had been thought to be on the mend, unexpectedly shed more than 100,000 jobs in June, helping drive up the nation's unemployment rate to an eight-year high.... A startled Federal Reserve quickly cut key interest rates in hopes of averting a new round of stagnation or actual economic contraction. Commercial banks followed by lowering the prime rate they charge their best customers.... On Wall Street, the Dow Jones average of 30 industrial stocks finished down....

THE BOSTON GLOBE

As a second key measure of the level of unemployment, the jobs report also contains statistics on *nonfarm payrolls*. A big problem with these data can be *double counting*.

To see this problem, suppose you are working full time at your job. However, suppose you also take a part-time job to earn a little extra money for your trading account. Then, once your trading starts to generate income, you quit your part-time job. In the jobs report, that looks like a drop in employment, but this kind of "unemployment" would hardly be cause for concern. A second problem with the nonfarm payroll numbers can be labor strikes. When workers go out on strike, nonfarm payrolls can fall dramatically. The irony here, of course, is that such strikes often occur during economic booms when labor markets are tight and union negotiating power is at its peak. And the point is simply this: Don't mistake a drop in jobs from a big strike for a faltering economy.

Still a third problem has to do with how surges in government employment can skew the data. This is particularly true with the census workers the Federal government hires periodically. This large surge in workers can create the impression of a rapidly growing economy even when the number of private sector jobs is actually falling. Again, the message here is this: Look behind the numbers and don't be fooled.

Finally, there is a fourth and more subtle issue that is very important to our macrowave sector perspective. When reviewing the data, look carefully to see if the job gains or losses are distributed evenly across the sectors or, alternatively, if they are concentrated in specific sectors. Why is this important? Well, if, say, service sector jobs are surging while manufacturing jobs are stagnant or falling, this is not as good a signal of healthy economic growth as if all sectors of the economy are humming.

THE AVERAGE WORKWEEK—OVERTIME OR UNDERWORKED?

A surprisingly weak employment report and a decline in the government's leading forecasting gauge have some economists wondering if the economy's soft landing is turning into a recession.... Average hourly earnings fell and so did the length of the average workweek—clear signs that businesses are cutting back on production, but also signs that there is little inflation producing wage pressure.

The Nightly Business Report

In addition to our two measures of unemployment, the jobs report also generates numbers on the *average workweek*. This statistic measures the number of hours that people have worked, and it is a very important one because it is considered a leading indicator of economic activity. This is because businesses tend to increase the number of hours their workers put in as a first step *before* hiring additional workers. They also tend to start cutting hours of their work force in a downturn *before* they begin laying people off.

More broadly, when the average workweek rises in the early stages of a business cycle, this may be the first signal that employers may begin to boost their payrolls—a very bullish sign. In contrast, when the workweek is falling late in the business cycle, a rising workweek may indicate a tight labor market and potential wage inflation—and that's nasty bear stuff.

Besides its signaling value, the average workweek data can also help us predict the direction and magnitude of other monthly indicators such as industrial production and personal income. Indeed, as we noted earlier, if we know how many people have been working, if we know how many hours they have worked, and if we know how much overtime they have accumulated, then we can predict how much these workers have produced.

WHY BONDS LOVE THE RECESSIONARY BEAR AND OTHER MARKET PERVERSITIES

Yes, indeed. Bond prices will rise on the expectation of lower interest rates when the data start sending off recessionary signals—provided, however, there are no inflationary pressures. In contrast, the dollar will fall on that same expectation of lower interest rates. This is because, as interest rates fall, foreign investors will pull out of U.S. financial markets. This reduces the demand for dollars and pushes its value down.

As for the reaction of the stock market to the recessionary bear, both the Dow and the Nasdaq will tend to fall on the expectation of lower earnings. As for how each of the sectors in the market is likely to fare relative to the others during this fall, let's defer that discussion to our next chapter where we will look at the crucial macrowave concept of sector rotation. By coming to understand this concept, we will come to see just how the smart money on Wall Street systematically moves in and out of different market sectors, not just in and around a recession, but also throughout the entire business cycle. Indeed, because of this sector rotation, there is a very well-defined stock market cycle that closely tracks the business cycle—and need I say here that there are great riches to be had by mastering the subtleties of these twin cycles?

STOCKS TO PEDAL DURING THE BUSINESS CYCLE

*E*very September, Lancer Armstrong takes several weeks off *from his duties as a finance professor at the University of California to compete in Europe for the title of senior world champion amateur cyclist. And while Professor Armstrong has won that title three out of the past five years, that's not why his friends call him a "master cyclist." Rather, he has earned that sobriquet through his highly lucrative sector rotation strategy of investing.*

Right now, with the economy on its way to hitting a recessionary rock bottom and the stock market in its late bear phase, Professor Armstrong has already begun to move cash out of defensive sectors like food and drugs and pharmaceuticals into several key cyclical sectors, including automotive and housing. While Professor Armstrong knows that most of the time, these cyclical sectors are dogs, he also knows that as the stock market cycle moves from late bear to early bull, they will definitely get some run. And after they do and the market moves on to its middle bull period, it will then be time to rotate first into stocks in the technology sectors, and later into the sectors that sell capital equipment and basic materials.

Finally, as the business cycle approaches its peak and the stock market enters its late bull phase, Professor Armstrong will do a pure play on energy stocks. Like the cyclicals, these can be dogs much of the time. But hey. When the major economies around the globe are hitting on all cylinders, that's when these energy dogs definitely will have their day.

Of course, at the first sign of trouble, Professor Armstrong will once again become an early bear. At that point, he will move back into his defensive sectors. The bad news is that the stocks in these sectors will only earn him, at best, a single-digit return. The good news is that while these stocks are yielding that 4 or 6 or 8 percent return, the rest of the market and its sectors will likely be net losers. And Professor Armstrong hates to lose—as he demonstrates just about every year in that championship bicycling race.

L et me warn you here. This is not only one of the most important chapters in this book, at times, it can also be one of the most demanding. But let me exhort you now to slog through it all because at the end of this rainbow of business cycle theory and dry economic reports is a solid analytical foundation with which to understand the complex game of *sector rotation*.

To set the stage for our discussion, let's remember two of the most important rules in the macrowave investing firmament:

- Buy strong stocks in strong sectors in market uptrends
- Short weak stocks in weak sectors in market downdrafts

With these rules in mind, let's take a look at Fig. 14-1, which I first introduced to you way back in Chapter 1. It should of great help in finding those strong and weak sectors that we always want to be on the watch for.

FIGURE 14-1   The twin cycles and sector rotation.

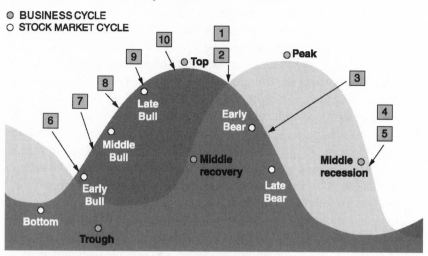

1. Consumer Noncyclicals (e.g., food, drugs, cosmetics)
2. Health Care
3. Utilities
4. Consumer Cyclicals (e.g., autos, housing)
5. Financials
6. Transportation
7. Technology
8. Capital Goods
9. Basic Industry (e.g., aluminum, chemicals, paper, steel)
10. Energy

Now, to carefully study this figure is to observe at least three important things. First, there is both a stock market cycle *and* a business cycle, each of which consists of very distinct phases. For example, in the business cycle, we can see a peak at the top of the economic expansion and a trough at its bottom. We also see a middle recession phase between peak and trough and a middle recovery phase between trough and peak. By the same token, in the stock market cycle, there are both early bear and late bear phases on the downswing, just as there are early bull, middle bull, and late bull phases on the upswing. As for why there is no middle bear phase, it is simply because bear markets happen much more quickly than bull markets and are, as a rule, of much shorter duration.

As for the second observation from the figure, it is a far more important one, and it is simply this. Not only do the stock market cycle and business cycle move in tandem, the stock market cycle is actually a leading
indicator of movements in the business cycle. To see this, look at the bottom of the stock market cycle at the late bear stage. Its trough typically well
precedes the recessionary trough of the business cycle. Similarly, you can
see quite clearly that even before the economy reaches its expansionary top,
the stock market cycle has already entered its early bear phase. Now the
trick in all of this is to clearly understand which sectors are strongest and
which are weakest at different points in the stock market cycle. Indeed, to
understand this market dynamic is to cut to the very heart of the matter of
sector rotation and effective macrowave investing. That is where our third
observation from the figure comes in.

In the figure, you can see a clear progression through nine different categories of sectors beginning with the transportation and technology categories in the early bull phase of the market and ending with the financial
and consumer cyclical categories in the late bear phase. Our task now is to
use of the power of macrowave logic to come to understand why the stock
market typically follows this progression during the business cycle.

ROUND AND ROUND WE GO, WHERE TO TRADE THE SMART
MONEY KNOWS

Let's start, then, at the top of stock market cycle with the transition from
late bull to early bear. At this point, the business cycle is in the late stages
of an expansion and heading towards a red-hot, and perhaps even white-
hot, peak. By this time, the Federal Reserve has probably already raised
interest rates three, four, or even five times or more in an effort to bring the
high-flying economy in for a soft landing.

Nonetheless, despite these Fed rate hikes, the unemployment rate
remains very low, retail sales continue at a Christmas-like sizzle, the cup of
consumer confidence runneth over even as consumer credit becomes per-
ilously overextended, both factory production and capacity utilization rates
are banging loudly up against inflationary thresholds, energy prices are
spiking, and every new economic report that comes out suggesting any further inflationary pressure is just one more reason for Wall Street to get
more nervous. It is at precisely at this point in this early bear phase that the
Street's smart money starts to defensively rotate funds into the health care
sector and consumer noncyclical sectors like cosmetics and food and phar-

maceuticals. This happens because the smart money knows just how hard it is to fine tune the economy using monetary policy. Indeed, at this point, the pros are betting that the Federal Reserve will raise interest rates just one too many times and thereby knock the economy right on to its recessionary keister—with no pillow handy for a soft landing.

Of course, once the economy crests and begins its ugly slide into a recession, falling production, sinking consumer confidence, a rising unemployment rate, a shrinking workweek, and increasingly idle factory capacity will all lead the Federal Reserve to conclude the now painfully obvious. Oops. It hit the interest rate brakes too hard. Crash!

With this realization—but no doubt after some months of gnashing its teeth—the Fed will finally reverse course and begin to lower interest rates as a means of resuscitating the patient it has just finished killing. But here's the Fed's dilemma in this middle recession phase: With sales slowing and inventories building, business executives will be in no mood to take advantage of the Fed's new easy money. Hence, these executives will refrain from any new investment in new plant and equipment that would otherwise stimulate the flagging economy. Nor are wary consumers—now fearful of winding up on the unemployment line like one of their neighbors—likely to go on any new spending sprees even if interest rates are falling. As a result of the reluctance of both businesses and consumers, the first of what will likely be many Fed interest rate reductions will have little or no impact on the economy. Instead, the recessionary spiral will continue on its way down to find some inevitable, and hopefully not too deep, bottom.

It is at this point, somewhere near this bottom, that the stock market moves towards its late bear phase. In this phase, the smart money begins to rotate first into utilities and then into both consumer cyclical and financial stocks. Utilities become attractive because they are very capital-intensive and therefore their earnings are very sensitive to the level of interest rates. At the same time, in this late bear phase, energy costs tend to be declining during the recession because of reduced worldwide demand for oil, gas, and coal, so this helps the bottom line of utilities as well.

As for consumer cyclical sectors like autos and housing, they have typically reached the nadir of their valuations under ever-weakening demand. However, as interest rates head toward a bottom, both of these sectors are now likely to perk up as consumers rush in with their pent-up demand for these big-ticket items. This, in turn, will help key sectors in the financial category like banking and home finance, just as ever-lowering interest rates are helping other sectors within the financial category like brokerage and financial services.

By now, the collective effect of the lower interest rates on a variety of sectors has been to prime the economic pump; with this priming, the broader economy soon begins to move back up. Of course, the first signs of a pulse become evident in surface transportation sectors like the railroads and trucking, and that's why the smart money begins to rotate funds into the transportation category in this now early bull phase of the market. Indeed, at this point, things are beginning to percolate nicely as businesses now steadily begin to increase production and output, even as sales continue to rise.

Interestingly, however, at this point there is still no need for businesses to invest in new plant and equipment. Nonetheless, the smart money knows full well that as the economy moves inexorably towards the middle recovery phase, equipment will begin to wear out even as increased demand speaks to the need for expanding capacity. For this reason, as the stock market enters the middle bull phase and factory orders begin to increase, the Street's smart money will begin to rotate first into the technology category and then into all those sectors that will benefit from the boom in capital goods—from agricultural equipment and industrial machinery to machine tools and basic electronics.

Now the economy is hitting on all cylinders. In this phase, retail sales are humming, the jobs report is showing the economy at full employment with lots of overtime and a longer workweek, the National Association of Purchasing Managers' Index is well up into the 60s and showing very slow delivery performance, and both factory orders and capacity utilization are reaching new peaks in the current cycle. This is a clear signal for the smart money to rotate into sectors in the basic industry and basic materials categories as the demand for aluminum, chemicals, paper, and steel heads toward a zenith.

But guess who's coming to take the punch bowl away at this party? Yep. It is at this point that the Federal Reserve once again is likely to insert itself into the process and begin raising interest rates over concerns about a budding inflation. It is also at this point that the demand for energy begins heading toward a razor-sharp peak. Indeed, with supplies tight, the OPEC oil cartel will begin trying to manipulate the price of oil ever upward and both fuel-oil and gasoline shortages may begin to emerge. By then, the smart money has already rotated into energy stocks that, with their notorious volatility, will soon be spiking upward right along with the price of a barrel of OPEC crude.

Finally, as the Fed continues to raise interest rates and energy price shocks continue to batter both businesses and consumers, the business cycle will reach its inevitable peak. At this oscillation point, the economic data will become very confusing. While some economic reports like the CPI and PPI will continue to throw off inflationary signals, others like retail sales and the initial jobless claims may suggest contraction. Meanwhile, one company after another will start showing the negative effects of the Fed's interest rate hikes by missing its earnings estimates At this point, individual stocks start getting picked off one by one by disgruntled investors until whole sectors like technology and telecommunications start to fall with them. Of course, by this time, the smart money has already recognized this early bear phase and either shorted the now falling stocks or moved back into food, drugs, and health care stocks as a defensive measure. And as the recession deepens, we move back to where we began and the twin cycles repeat.

Whew. That was some ride, wasn't it? But it should be obvious from riding this twin-cycle roller coaster just how many trading opportunities can pop up along the way. Our task now is to figure out how to better get in tune with both the business and stock market cycles. That means it's time to introduce our next set of economic indicators. These are summarized in Table 14-1.

THE GDP REPORT—HOW LOW CAN YOU GROW?

> Stock prices plunged in reaction to the GDP report, with the Dow Jones industrial average dropping 230.51 points....
>
> *THE WASHINGTON POST*

The Department of Commerce releases the quarterly report on the gross domestic product in the third or fourth week of the month for the prior quarter. As we have already learned, the gross domestic product equals consumption plus investment plus government spending plus net exports. Adjusted for inflation, real GDP gives us the most precise measure of the rate of economic growth over the longer term, as well as shorter-run output and spending.

Now, you might think that the GDP report is one of the most important in helping us to follow the rate of economic growth and where we are in the business cycle. But you'd be dead wrong. Sure, this report is important—and certainly among all the reports issued quarterly, it is one of the most essential. But, in truth, this report merits no more than three stars, for at least three reasons.

TABLE 14-1.   Key Business Cycle Indicators

Business Cycle Indicators	Market Reaction	Data Source	Release Date
• Gross domestic product	***	Department of Commerce	Quarterly; third or fourth week of the month.

Consumption Indicators

• Retail sales	****	Department of Commerce	Monthly; between the 11th and 14th of the month.
• Personal income and expenditures	**	Department of Commerce	Monthly; first business day of the month for two months prior.
• Consumer confidence	***	Conference Board	Monthly; last Tuesday of the month
		University of Michigan	Preliminary, Friday following the second weekend of the month;
		Survey Research Center	final, Friday following last weekend of the month.
• Consumer credit	*	Federal Reserve	Monthly; fifth business day of the month.

Investment Indicators

• NAPM report	*****	National Association of Purchasing Managers	Monthly; first business day of the month.
• Durable goods orders	*	Department of Commerce	Monthly; third or fourth week of the month.
• Factory orders	**	Department of Commerce	Monthly; about a week after the durable goods report.
• Business inventories and sales	*	Department of Commerce	Monthly; around the 15th of the month.
• Industrial production and capacity utilization	***	Federal Reserve	Monthly; around the 15th of the month.

First, the report only comes out quarterly. Second, the data are highly volatile and subject to frequent revisions. Third, and most important, by the time the GDP data roll around, there is so much other information available that we already have a pretty good idea of what the GDP numbers will be. This is because virtually all of the other indicators that we look at have something to say about some portion of the GDP.

Accordingly, when it comes to charting the rate of economic growth and stages of the business cycle, it is far better to focus on the monthly data generated for the two most important components of the GDP—consumption and investment.

CONSUMPTION—THE KING KONG OF GDP

There is a distinct difference beween a "consumer recession" and a "producer recession." The slowdown of 2000 was indeed a producer recession, not a consumer recession. Housing remained strong while manufacturing practically collapsed. If it had been a consumer recession, housing would have collapsed. Recognizing the distinction between these two types of recessions allows the proper trading or investment theme to be developed.

PEJMAN HAMIDI

Consumer spending accounts for about two-thirds of the gross domestic product. For this reason, when something does go wrong in Consumerville, a slowdown in economic growth cannot be far behind.

In following consumption patterns, the savvy macrowave investor will want to look at at least four reports: consumer confidence, consumer credit, personal income and consumption, and retail sales. Of the four, the retail sales report is the most important, followed by consumer confidence.

RETAIL SALES—WHICH WAY TO THE MAUL?

Blue chip stocks took their biggest fall in two weeks and bonds slumped as a strong retail sales report and a sagging dollar stirred up investors' inflation fears. The Dow Jones industrial average fell 120 points to 10,910.

MONEYLINE

The retail sales report merits at least four full stars—and maybe another half of a star thrown in for good measure. This report is very important because it provides us with the first major evidence of consumption patterns for the month, as well as the most timely indicator of broad consumer spending patterns. Because of this, it is generally regarded as being one of the most important stock market movers, and any unexpectedly negative retail sales report can lead to a severe market mauling.

The Department of Commerce collects the retail sales data using a monthly survey of almost 15,000 retail establishments of all sizes and types across the country. It releases these data, which measure the total receipts of retail stores, between the 11th and 14th of the month. About 35 percent of the sales are of durable goods like autos, building materials, furniture, and home appliances; the remaining receipts come from the sale of nondurable goods like clothing and apparel, drugs, gasoline, food, liquor, mail order, and other general merchandise.

When analyzing retail sales, it is best to evaluate the data excluding auto and truck sales, which account for almost 25 percent of sales. This is because auto and truck sales can move swiftly from month-to-month and these wild fluctuations can obscure the broader underlying trend. In addition, it is equally important to gauge the impact of both the gasoline and food components on retail sales. This is because changes in both of these components often can be traced more to changes in the prices of these goods than to actual changes in consumer demand. Accordingly, a failure to take this into account might lead one to falsely conclude that consumption is on the rise when just the opposite may be true.

Besides sorting out the different effects of autos, gas, and food, the savvy macrowave investor will also want to review the data from a sector perspective. In particular, you should always look carefully to see whether any changes in consumption patterns are broad-based or, alternatively, are linked to a specific sector or set of sectors.

Now, a few final caveats when perusing the retail sales data. First, even though these data are highly prized on the Street, they are also highly volatile and subject to big revisions. So be careful. Second, retail sales do *not* include any expenditures on services—even though services make up over half of total consumption. Thus, the retail sales report tells us nothing about what the consumer may be spending on things like air travel, dry cleaning, education, hair cuts, insurance, legal expenses, and other kinds of services. In fact, the data on services aren't available until two weeks after retail sales data, as part of the next report we will discuss—personal income and consumption.

PERSONAL INCOME AND CONSUMPTION—AN INSIGHT INTO SERVICES

> Real personal consumption dropped by a steep 3 percent in the first quarter, following a 3.4 percent drop last fall. According to Wall Street economist H. Erich Heinemann, "the outlook is grim."
>
> *SAN DIEGO UNION-TRIBUNE*

The Department of Commerce releases the personal income and consumption data on the first business day of the month for the two months prior. The largest component of personal income is wages and salaries. This component accounts for the lion's share of the total. Other categories of income include rental income, government transfer payments like social security payments to retirees, and subsidies like welfare, as well as dividend and interest income.

This report is moderately useful if for no other reason than that the data on personal consumption help fill in the *services blank,* which is not included in retail sales. However, because service purchases tend to grow at a fairly steady rate, the personal income and consumption report is fairly predictable and far less important than retail sales. This is all the more true since at least some of the data for this report come from the retail sales report. Indeed, this report should garner no more than two stars when it comes to the Street's reaction, precisely because much of it is already old news.

CONSUMER CONFIDENCE—NOTHING TO FEAR BUT FEAR ITSELF

> Consumer confidence, a driving force in the economy's long expansion, has soared to its highest level in the 33 years the statistic has been kept, driven by the booming stock market and plentiful jobs.
>
> *CHATTANOOGA TIMES*

There are two major measures of consumer confidence released monthly by private institutions—one by the Conference Board and the other by the University of Michigan Survey Research Center. Perhaps the most important thing to note about these solid, three-star reports is that the *future expectations* portion of consumer confidence is considered a leading economic indicator. That should be very intuitive: If consumers look into their crystal ball and see a storm coming, they will, of course, begin to reduce their spending; this will soon ripple through the economy like a recessionary wave. And that's why consumer confidence is included as an important component in the Index of Leading Indicators.

As for how the Conference Board and the University of Michigan actually measure consumer confidence, their approaches are remarkably similar. For example, the Conference Board conducts a monthly survey of 5000 households in which consumers are asked about both their current appraisal of economic conditions and their expectations for the future. They are also asked more specific questions, such as whether they are going to buy any big-ticket items like housing, cars, or appliances. The resultant report includes an index of consumer confidence and is released on the last Tuesday of every month. Expectations make up 60 percent of the index, while current conditions account for the other 40 percent.

While the University of Michigan Index is very similar to the Conference Board Index, one big difference between the two reports is that the Michigan data are released twice during the month. The first, preliminary data are released on the Friday following the second weekend of the month, while the final data are released on the Friday following the fourth weekend of the month.

A final comment on these measures: They both took on heightened importance to the markets beginning in the 1990s after they were favorably mentioned by Fed Chairman Alan Greenspan. In this regard, note that these measures can be very helpful at times in predicting sudden and large shifts in consumption patterns. However, most of the time, small changes in the index merely represent noise to be ignored.

CONSUMER CREDIT—JUST CHARGE IT

> Consumer credit growth roared back in August, beating expectations. The monthly gain was $13.4 billion, about $3 billion above consensus. Revolving gains were particularly strong, rising at a double-digit annualized pace.... Consumer credit has yet to slow in line with the underlying consumer spending it finances. More disturbing, consumer credit growth is once again outstripping income gains pushing debt service burdens upward.
>
> DISMALSCIENCE.COM

The Federal Reserve reports the net change in consumer installment credit on the fifth business day of the month for the previous two months.

Consumer credit is broken down into three major categories: autos, credit cards and other revolving credit, and the catchall "other." The data are based on a survey of banks, consumer finance companies, credit unions, and savings and loan associations.

The consumer credit numbers barely merit a single star. One reason is that they are highly volatile and subject to large and frequent revisions. A second reason is that this report in some sense represents the consumer data caboose in that it follows other consumer spending indicators like auto and truck sales, consumer confidence, retail sales, and personal consumption. Still a third reason is that periods of strong consumer spending can be accompanied by relatively weak growth in consumer credit, just as periods of weak spending can be accompanied by sharp increases in consumer credit. Accordingly, this measure fails as either a coincident or even a lagging indicator.

Now that we have consumption covered, let's turn to a second key part of the GDP equation: investment and, implicitly, production.

INVESTMENT AND PRODUCTION—SMALL WITH A BIG WALLOP

Investment spending accounts for less than 20 percent of the gross domestic product as compared to almost 70 percent for consumption spending. Nonetheless, tracking investment can be every bit as important to the macrowave investor because of the extreme volatility of investment expenditures and their sometimes dramatic effects on the business cycle. Indeed, the growth in investment usually runs much faster than GDP growth during an expansion, while it also declines more sharply during recessions.

As for the various investment indicators, these include: business inventories and sales, durable goods, factory orders, and the purchasing managers' report from the National Association of Purchasing Managers. Of the four, the most important is the purchasing managers' report, which is the one we will start with. Indeed, the other three reports are worth discussing more for alerting you to their very limited effect on the financial markets than for their usefulness in guiding your trading.

THE PURCHASING MANAGERS' REPORT—A FIVE-STAR GENERAL

At Oryx Energy Co. in Dallas, Ralph Kauffman knew the economy was developing some slack in February, when steel-tube suppliers began cutting prices and giving him more attentive service.... A traffic jam in the delivery pipeline is, ironically, a sign of economic vitality because it means suppliers have more business than they can handle. That's why the National Association of Purchasing Managers keeps an index on supplier performance, published monthly by the Commerce Department.

U.S. NEWS & WORLD REPORT

The National Association of Purchasing Managers report uses a survey of purchasing managers in more than 300 companies, representing over 20 industries in all 50 states, to construct one of the most comprehensive and timely indexes available to the macrowave investor. Indeed, this is a very clear five-star report, and it is very closely watched for at least two reasons. It comes out at on the first business day of the month, so it has very comprehensive data very early in the month. It's also one of a handful of indicators that the Federal Reserve Chairman has identified as important.

As for the Purchasing Managers' Index itself, it is actually a composite of five series dealing with new orders, production, slow delivery performance, inventories, and inflation. New orders are a leading indicator of economic growth because they lead to increases in production. Both production and employment are coincident indicators reflecting the current status of the manufacturing sector. Inventories represent a lagging indicator because the buildup of inventories usually occurs after a cyclical downturn has begun, while inventories become depleted as an expansion accelerates. Finally, slow delivery performance, which is also known as supplier delivery or vendor performance, is a key component of the Index of Leading Economic Indicators. It is useful to watch because, as our excerpt from *U.S News & World Report* indicates, when producers can't fill their orders quickly, it means they are busy, while faster deliveries mean a slowing economy.

From these five series, the purchasing managers create what is called a *diffusion index*. The total index is based on these weights: 30 percent for new orders, 25 percent for production, 20 percent for employment, 15 percent for deliveries, and 10 percent for inventories. This diffusion index is a very different animal from the usual numbers posted on Wall Street. It is calculated by adding the percentage of positive responses to one half of those who report conditions unchanged. Thus, for example, if 60 percent of the purchasing managers say that things are unchanged, while 21 report a positive response, the Purchasing Managers' Index will be at 51. Any number over 50 and the manufacturing sector is considered to be in an expansion phase, and the higher the number, the bigger the expansion. When the index is between 44.5 and 50, this suggests that the manufacturing sector has stopped growing, but the economy may continue to expand. However, when the index falls below 44.5, this is a strong signal of recession.

In addition to looking at the overall index, the savvy macrowave investor will also want to look carefully at some of its individual components. As we have indicated, only two of the five components are leading indicators—new orders and slow delivery performance. These are the ones to watch most closely for changes in the business cycle and market trend.

Before leaving the subject of the purchasing managers' report, it is also useful to make several other points. First, the report also includes both a price index and a new export orders index. The price index is useful to monitor for early signs of inflation. This is because prices may start rising in the manufacturing sectors before these inflationary pressures show up downstream in the CPI. By the same token, watching the new export order index can be helpful not only if you are following companies heavily dependent on exports, but also for predicting the broader economic trends. This is because exports have become an increasingly important part of overall GDP growth. As a second point, the purchasing managers' report fits in nicely with the durable goods orders, the index of industrial production, and the jobs report. When all of these reports are pointing in the same direction, it is hard to argue with whatever trend they suggest.

Finally, in following the Purchasing Managers' Index, the size of the changes in this index will be less important than the actual index trend. So look carefully to see whether this is showing up or down momentum.

DURABLE GOODS—JUMPING JACK FLASH IN THE PAN

> The orders for durable goods are a leading but erratic indicator of the nation's investment spending and industrial production. Economists cautiously greeted today's unexpectedly strong increase as an indication that the economy may be in less danger of slipping back into a recession only a few months after it began growing again.
>
> *THE NEW YORK TIMES*

The Department of Commerce releases its durable goods report three to four weeks after the end of the current month. It encompasses manufactured products with a service life of over three years.

With the production of durable goods accounting for about 15 percent of the total GDP, it would seem that this report would be very important.

However, as a practical matter, the data on durable goods are so volatile and so prone to massive revisions as to render this Jumping Jack Flash report almost worthless much of the time. The underlying problem has to do with the "lumpy" nature of durable goods orders. The key culprits are civilian aircraft and military orders. For example, when Boeing completes a deal with China for 10 new jumbo jets, the durable goods data jump up by billions of dollars—all in one month! Then, the next month, the numbers plummet.

Still and all, while the financial markets rarely react to this barely one-star report, as a macrowave investor, you can sometimes use the data to your advantage. The best way to do so is to look at durable goods orders excluding both defense and transportation orders, and then look at the data using a moving average to smooth out the volatility in the data.

FACTORY ORDERS—CORNED BEEF REHASH

> The Dow Jones industrial average took its third big spill in four sessions yesterday, wiping out almost all that remained to this year's robust gains.... The only significant economic news yesterday was that factory orders rose 0.8 percent in February.
>
> *THE CLEVELAND PLAIN DEALER*

Roughly a week after the release of the durable goods report, the Department of Commerce releases the factory orders data series as part of its manufacturers' shipments, inventories, and orders report. While much of the factory orders report is merely a rehash of the durable goods data, this report also features new information on orders and shipments for non-durable goods, as well as some useful data on manufacturing inventories.

Regarding the nondurable goods portion of the report, one might think that it would be of at least some interest to Wall Street. After all, non-durables like food and tobacco account for about half of the factory orders total. But the problem here, and the reason why this report merits no more than two stars, is that the nondurables tend to grow at a very consistent rate. That means they are very easy to predict even without the new data.

As for the inventories section of the report, these data are of slightly more interest because they provide a first look at the inventory picture for the month. As a more important point, the inventory data can also take on heightened interest at possible key turning points in the business cycle. At such times, if the economy is growing and demand is increasing, then an inventory buildup points to more growth. However, if the economy is contracting and demand is falling while inventories are building, that is a very clear bearish signal.

THE BUSINESS INVENTORIES AND SALES REPORT—WHAT'S ON THE SHELF?

In the United States, the Government reported further signs of slowing economic growth. Business inventories rose four-tenths of a percent in November, to a seasonally adjusted $1.04 trillion, the 17th month without a decline, while business sales slipped two-tenths of a percent, to $758.1 billion....

THE NEW YORK TIMES

The Department of Commerce releases the business inventories and sales report around the 15th of each month as part of its manufacturing and trade inventories and sales report. The data are compiled from a monthly survey of manufacturers and from the merchant wholesalers and retail trade surveys. The report includes both inventory and sales statistics for all three stages of the manufacturing process, including manufacturing, wholesale, and retail.

In theory, Wall Street should be very interested in any buildup in business inventories or reductions in sales as signals about the business cycle. This is because of this recessionary chain reaction: In Step One, when sales start to slump and inventories begin to build, businesses start to cut back on production to trim inventories and begin laying people off. In Step Two, the unemployed workers have less to spend so inventories build some more as sales fall further. This leads to more production cutbacks and layoffs in Step Three, and the downward recessionary spiral continues.

In practice, however, the business inventories and sales report is on a par with both the durable goods and factory orders reports in that all rate only one or two stars, and each is greeted on the Street with considerable lack of interest. Why is this so? Simple. This report contains no new information other than on retail inventories. In fact, by the time this report hits the Street, all three of its sales components and two of its inventory components have already been reported as part of the durable goods, factory orders, or retail sales reports.

Now, one last tip regarding this report for the more discerning macrowave investor. When looking at the numbers, it can be at least somewhat useful to look at the split between total retail inventories and retail inventories minus cars and trucks. If you see a large buildup in car and truck inventories on dealer lots, this could signal a fall in auto and truck production, and, of course, we now know this is a leading indicator of recession.

INDUSTRIAL PRODUCTION AND CAPACITY UTILIZATION—TAKE IT TO THE LIMIT

Production of the nation's factories rose 1.1 percent in June, the seventh gain in a row, the Government reported today. Economists said the increase in this broad measure of business activity showed that the economy was now following the lively pace of the early stages of most recoveries, and, like most, would begin to slow later this year.

THE NEW YORK TIMES

Around the 15th of each month, the Federal Reserve simultaneously publishes reports on both industrial production and capacity utilization. Both measures move in tandem, but industrial production is viewed as a better signal of economic growth, while capacity utilization provides a better signal of inflation. Let's get to know them because, from a sector trading perspective, they can be of considerable use when trading cyclical sector stocks. In addition, as three-star reports, these data are also quite capable of moving the broader markets, at least at key turning points in the business cycle.

Let's start, then, with the Fed's Index of Industrial Production. This index encompasses three main categories in the economy—manufacturing, mining, and utilities—and it has been designed to measure *physical volume* of output. The index number itself is constructed from about 250 individual series of data that account for roughly a quarter of the GDP. This may seem like a relatively small portion of the GDP but note this: The index covers a very *large* portion of our cyclical sectors, including paper, chemicals, machinery, and equipment. That cyclical coverage makes the index well worth watching, particularly for traders who use movements in the business cycle to rotate in and out of sectors.

More broadly, the ebb and flow of the Industrial Production Index provide a very good coincident indicator of changes in the business cycle. In fact, this measure is one of the four coincident indicators used by the Conference Board to help define key turning points in the business cycle. In this regard, a falling index can confirm the onset of recession, while a rising index can indicate expansion and, in the later stages of an expansion, possible inflationary pressures. Hence, the index is said to be "procyclical."

Now, what about the Fed's measure of *capacity utilization?* This is simply the ratio of the Index of Industrial Production to a related index of capacity. It is designed to measure the extent to which our nation's manufacturing plants are being used to produce manufacturing goods. For example, if our plants are all running at full capacity, capacity utilization will be at 100 percent. If, however, we are in a recession, capacity utilization may fall to an anemic 50 percent. You can immediately see, then, how tracking capacity utilization gives us a signal as to where we are in the business cycle. But there is an even more important reason why this report can be important as the economy moves into the later stages of expansion. This reason lies in its *threshold effect* on inflation.

Specifically, economists believe that when the rate of capacity utilization rises above 85 percent or so, inflationary pressures will begin to build rapidly. This happens because, at this point, further increases in demand will outstrip the ability to produce. At higher levels of capacity, bottlenecks may also emerge in the production process. This, then, would be a clear bearish sign, since it raises the probability that the Federal Reserve will raise interest rates.

THE SECTOR ROTATION PAYOFF

> Successful market timing depends on understanding the impact of the business cycle on different types of assets at different stages of the cycle.... Sector rotation—the process of rotating a stock portfolio through time in order to concentrate on specific market sector and take advantage of changes in relative performance—is one of the most important decisions an investor makes. Timely sector rotation has the potential to add significantly more to returns than stock selection.
>
> JON GREGORY TAYLOR

To complete this chapter, let's return briefly now to our discussion about the relationship between the stock market cycle and the business cycle that began this chapter. Table 14-2 summarizes the progression of sector rotations that we outlined in this discussion. Please review it carefully now because such a table should be very helpful to you in planning your trades and investments during this progression.

TABLE 14-2.   Sector Rotation and the Stock Market Cycle

Stock Market Phase	Rotation Category	Best Category Sectors
Early bull	Transportation	• Railroads • Shipping
Early to middle bull	Technology	• Computers • Electronics • Semiconductors
Middle to late bull	Capital goods	• Electrical equipment • Heavy-duty trucks • Machinery and machine tools • Manufacturing • Pollution control
Late bull	Basic industries and materials	• Aluminum • Chemicals • Containers • Metals • Paper and forest products • Steel
Late bull to market top	Energy	• Oil • Natural gas • Coal
Early bear	Consumer staples and health care	• Beverages • Cosmetics • Food • Health care • Pharmaceuticals • Tobacco
Approaching late bear	Utilities	• Electric • Gas • Pole and wire telecommunications
Late bear	Financials, consumer cyclicals	• Autos • Banking • Home finance • Housing • Real estate • Retailing

STALKING THE INFLATIONARY TIGER

*A*rmed with a steaming mug of double mocha latte, Ernest Hunter flicks his TV on to CNBC. It's 8:32 in the morning, and as Ernie logs on to his direct access trading platform, he hears that the Producer Price Index is showing a sharp spike in inflation. Rising oil prices are to blame, according to CNBC's macro data goddess Kathleen Hayes.

Boy, that ought to drive the market down, thinks Ernie. So he fires off an order to short a thousand shares of cubes, the tracking stock for the Nasdaq. Minutes later, his shorted cubes not only don't go down, they go up—way up—and Ernie winds up losing almost $10,000.

Two days later, Kathleen Hayes reports on the latest Consumer Price Index numbers. Like the PPI, the CPI has come out very hot. But the culprit this time isn't a spike in oil prices, says Kathleen, but rather a jump in the CPI's core rate of inflation.

So what? thinks Ernie. He won't be fooled again. So this time he goes long a thousand shares of cubes. Only problem is, this time the Nasdaq goes down on the inflation news...and down...and then down some more. At this point, Ernie is beginning to hate Kathleen Hayes.

Hey, Ernie, don't shoot the messenger. Just understand Kathleen Hayes' message. Here it is: When stalking the inflationary tiger, the macrowave investor must first be aware that there are at least three species of this very dangerous beast.

First, there is the *demand-pull* variety that comes with economic booms and too much money chasing too few goods. This tiger is perhaps the easiest to tame—although with inflation, nothing is ever truly easy. Second, there is the *cost-push* variety that results from so-called *supply shocks* like oil price hikes or drought-induced food price spikes. This inflation moves with deadly swiftness, inflicts great pain, and often gives the Federal Reserve fits. Finally, there is *wage inflation*. It can be the most dangerous of all, slow and plodding though it may be; it can be triggered by either demand-pull or cost-push pressures.

Now here's the broader point: If, like Ernie in our little story above, you are unable to quickly and clearly distinguish between these three species of inflationary tigers, you will be prone to misinterpreting the real message of inflation indicators like the Consumer Price Index and the Producer Price Index. The likely result will be that one of these inflationary tigers will eat your trading capital for lunch, belch loudly, and then move on to its next victim with nary a thank you. This will be true for one very simple reason: In the face of inflationary news, both the Federal Reserve and Wall Street are likely to react quite differently depending on which species of the inflationary tiger they actually fear. If you get caught on the wrong side of such a reaction, you will be doomed! That's why, right now, we need to roll up our sleeves and dig into some inflation theory.

THE LOWDOWN ON HIGH THEORY

Big Government, Big Labor and Big Business all accept the notion that no one should lose ground to inflation. So does the average worker, whether an executive or a janitor. The result is a series of practices and customs that make the basic inflation rate the floor for most wage increases....

THE NATIONAL JOURNAL

In modern industrial nations like the United States, most economists believe that there is a *core* or *inertial rate* of inflation that tends to persist at the same rate until some kind of shock comes along to change things. At the heart of this idea of *core* inflation is the concept of *inflationary expectations*. Inflationary expectations are important because the *expectation* of inflation can significantly contribute to *actual* inflation. The reason is that inflationary expectations strongly influence the behavior of businesses, investors, workers, and consumers.

For example, during the 1990s, prices in the U.S. rose steadily at around 3 percent annually, and most people came to expect that inflation rate. This expected rate of inflation was, in turn, built into a core rate of inflation for the economy through institutional arrangements such as negotiated labor contracts. To see how this happens, suppose that an economics forecaster like Standard & Poor's DRI predicts that the rate of inflation for the coming year will be 3 percent—the same rate as the previous year. Further suppose that labor negotiators at the United Auto Workers union believe that workers will achieve a 1 percent increase in productivity. Because increases in real wages are tied to labor productivity, this means that autoworkers arguably deserve a 1 percent increase in their real, inflation-adjusted wages. There-fore, under these conditions, the union negotiators will demand a minimum 4 percent increase in the nominal wage—1 percent to get the real increase based on productivity gains and 3 percent to adjust for the expected or fore-cast inflation.

Now, when Ford, General Motors, and DaimlerChrysler all agree to this 4 percent wage demand, the increase in wages caused by the union's inflationary expectations will lead to an *actual* increase in the auto indus-try's labor costs. This, in turn, will put upward pressure on auto prices so that the expectation of inflation becomes a self-fulfilling prophecy, and the inertial or core rate of inflation is maintained.

From this little story, you can see that once inflationary expectations are built into an economy, they are very hard to eliminate. The reason is that people tend to assume that inflation will continue to be what it already is, and they will behave accordingly—a phenomenon known as *adaptive expectations*. From this little story, you can also see the intimate relation-ship between inflation at the retail level where, for example, cars are sold, and wage inflation at the wholesale level, where cars are manufactured.

Now the broader point of this story is that at any given time, the econ-omy's inertial or core rate of inflation tends to persist until a shock causes it to move up or down. The next question is: What kinds of shocks might cause the inertial rate to move? The answer is either demand-pull or cost-push inflation.

OF BOOMS AND PUNCH BOWLS

> If Alan Greenspan has someone to thank for his rock-star status, …it is surely William McChesney Martin. He ran the Fed under five presidents (Truman, Eisenhower, Kennedy, Johnson and Nixon) and seems to have had a generally low opinion of presidential economic acumen…. When in 1965 he decided to raise interest rates to try to stave off inflation brought on by the Vietnam War, Lyndon Johnson called Mr. Martin to his ranch in Texas to berate him about the political consequences of a rate rise. Mr. Martin stood firm. The Fed had to "lean against the wind" of inflation, he said. His job, as he famously quipped, was to "take away the punch bowl just when the party gets going."
>
> *THE ECONOMIST*

Right up until the Vietnam War in the 1960s, inflation was largely viewed as a demand-pull phenomenon. That is, when there was a general rise in the price level, it was typically attributed to excess aggregate demand—too much money chasing too few goods in a booming economy. In this sense, *demand-pull inflation is a very bullish phenomenon,* and all the more so because it is more readily curable using either contractionary fiscal or monetary policies—or so the Keynesian theory goes.

Indeed, from a Keynesian perspective, all the party-pooping Federal Reserve has to do to fight demand-pull pressures is to take away the proverbial punch bowl. How does it do so? Simply by raising interest rates. And if all goes well, the economy will come in for a very nice soft landing as demand-pull pressures ease.

Alternatively, to fight demand-pull inflation, Congress and the President can apply contractionary fiscal policy by either cutting spending or raising taxes. However, with fiscal policy, the effects take a much longer time to take hold and the outcome is much more uncertain. That's why fighting demand-pull inflation usually falls in the Federal Reserve's lap.

OVER THE OPEC BARREL AND UNDER EL NIÑO'S THUMB

> The Fed has raised [interest] rates six times…to the highest level in nearly a decade. The economy's continued strong performance has policy-makers fearing inflation…. [But] higher energy costs may have the same impact as a tax [increase] or [interest] rate hike. That would argue against further

Fed tightening. Higher prices for airfares and natural gas simply limit the purchasing power in some other sector of the economy.

INVESTOR'S BUSINESS DAILY

Now let's contrast the demand-pull situation with *supply shock* or *cost-push inflation,* and let's use the now infamous supply-side shocks of the early 1970s to help illustrate this concept. During those years, the economy was hit by dramatically higher oil prices due to the Arab oil embargo and higher food prices due to an El Niño weather condition. At the same time, the Nixon Administration moved to a flexible exchange rate, the dollar's value fell precipitously, and this likewise raised business costs. Taken together, these supply-side or cost-push shocks put a severe crimp in the American economy's ability to produce.

Let me show you what I mean with a picture of how cost-push inflation winds up hitting the economy with the double whammy of *stagflation.* Figure 15-1 illustrates the economy before and after a supply-side shock. In the left-hand side graph, the horizontal axis measures the economy's output or gross domestic product, while the price level or level of inflation is measured on the vertical axis. In addition, aggregate demand in the economy is measured by the downward-sloping AD curve while the economy's ability to produce is measured by the upward-sloping aggregate supply curve AS. Note the intuition behind these supply and demand curves. Higher prices for their products mean businesses will produce more, so the aggregate supply curve slopes up; but higher prices also mean consumers will demand less, so the aggregate demand curve slopes down.

Now, the graph on the left side illustrates the economy before the supply-side shock. It is in equilibrium at point Q1 where the supply and demand curves cross. At this point, the price level in the economy is at a modest level of P1, and everyone is fully employed. But now take a look at the right-hand graph. This shows what happens after a supply-side shock like higher oil prices hits the economy. This shock shifts the aggregate supply curve, AS1, inward to AS2 because business costs are now higher. And note that this shift causes two things to happen—both of them bad.

First, the economy's output falls to Q2 as the economy falls into a recession. Second, and simultaneously, the price level rises to P2. In other words, we get both recession and inflation at the same time. This is a classic case of cost-push inflation, and you can see how, if it persists, it can lead to the deadly economic disease of stagflation—recession and inflation.

FIGURE 15-1 Cost-push inflation.

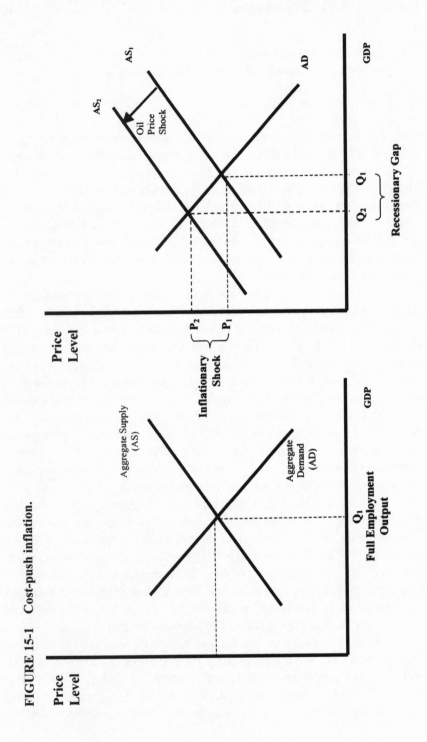

In this sense, cost-push inflation is much more of a *bearish* kind of inflation than demand-pull. The problem is that there is no simple Keynesian policy solution to cost-push inflation. Using either expansionary fiscal or monetary policy to reduce unemployment and end the recession will only create even more inflation, while using contractionary policy to curb inflation will just plunge the economy deeper into the recession. This is precisely why cost-push inflation can give the Federal Reserve such fits. Indeed, in the presence of cost-push inflation, the Federal Reserve is often as helpless as a baby caught in a riptide. More important, the Fed also knows that this kind of inflation has a much different impact on the economy than demand-pull inflation.

A case in point is offered up by the events of the year 2000. In that year, the Fed suddenly found itself fighting both cost-push and demand-pull inflation. The demand-pull inflation was, of course, the result of years of an economic boom. The cost-push inflation began to surface, however, primarily in the form of rising energy prices. At the root of this problem was the OPEC cartel. It began to ratchet oil prices up sharply, and as the cost of a barrel of oil zoomed towards $40, gasoline prices sprinted for the $2-a-gallon mark.

Now what is most interesting about these two conflicting forces of demand-pull and cost-push pressures was that Fed Chairman Alan Greenspan was smart enough to understand that at least in some perverse sense, OPEC was actually helping the Fed do its job of bringing the economy under control. The reason is that OPEC's oil price shocks acted in much the same way that contractionary fiscal policy in the form of higher taxes works on an economy. In this case, as oil prices rose, consumers had to spend more of their money on energy. But that meant that they had less money with which to buy goods being produced in other sectors of the economy. That, in turn, meant lower consumption and less stimulus for the booming economy. So the Fed could be less aggressive about raising interest rates to fight demand-pull inflation.

The broader point here, and one that brings us back to our earlier story about Ernest Hunter, is this: *While the Fed is likely to very swiftly raise interest rates when demand-pull inflation is pushing up the core rate of inflation, the Fed is much less likely to raise interest rates when supply-side shocks like rising energy prices are creating cost-push inflationary pressures.* That's why the Fed always tries to determine what kind of inflation is pushing up our economic indicators before it decides on a course of action to take. And that's why the savvy macrowave investor always goes through the same thought process as a means of anticipating the Fed's actions.

ENTER THE DRAGON

These points lead us to a discussion of the third species of inflation. *Wage inflation* tends to occur in the later stages of an economic recovery, usually as a result of demand-pull pressures. At this stage in a recovery, labor unions, in particular, will likely see their bargaining power rise to a maximum. The resultant labor negotiations may yield large wage increases that, in turn, may ripple through other industries. In addition, as labor markets in the nonunion sector get tighter and tighter, firms will begin to bid against one another for workers, likewise driving wages up.

Note, however, that wage inflation can also be driven by cost-push pressures. In fact, way back in the 1970s when stagflation reigned supreme and inflation soared into the double digits, a number of key labor unions were able to successfully negotiate the inclusion of cost of living adjustment clauses into their contracts. The result of these so-called COLAs was that as cost-push inflation soared, wages were automatically driven up. The irony, of course, is that these higher wages led to higher consumer prices, fewer sales, faster layoffs, a deepening recession, and much higher unemployment.

Now the point here is simply this: Whether it is from demand-pull or cost-push pressures, *any* sign of wage inflation is likely to be met with the strongest of Fed responses and the harshest of market reactions. This is because both the Fed and the Street know that wage inflation usually occurs in the more advanced stages of the inflationary cycle. Because of this, the Fed and the Street also know that wage inflation will typically require the strongest medicine to cure and take a much longer time to cure than simple demand-pull inflation.

It follows from this discussion that when inflation starts to rear its ugly head, discretionary fiscal and monetary policies cannot be too far behind. And for the stock market, that always means trouble. The particular kind of trouble, however, will be a function of the particular kind of inflation the Fed and the Congress and the White House are forced to fight. That's why the major inflationary indicators, which are listed in Table 15-1, are so important to watch. These indicators include the Consumer Price Index, the Producer Price Index, the GDP deflators, average hourly earnings, and the Employment Cost Index. Note that in the table each indicator is ranked with from one to five stars. Five stars indicate the strongest reaction from the stock and bond markets, while one star indicates the least reaction.

TABLE 15-1.   The Major Inflation Indicators

Inflation Indicators	Market Reaction	Data Source	Release Date
Consumer Price Index	*****	Department of Labor	Monthly; between the 15th and 21st of every month.
Producer Price Index	****	Department of Labor	Monthly; around the 11th of each month for the prior month.
GDP deflator	***	Department of Commerce	Quarterly; third or fourth week of the month for prior quarter.
Average hourly earnings	***	Department of Labor	Monthly; first Friday of month.
Employment Cost Index	****	Department of Labor	Quarterly; near end of month of the quarter for prior quarter.

EVERYTHING YOU EVER WANTED TO KNOW ABOUT THE CPI

Consumer prices surged in March, reflecting higher costs for everything from gasoline to housing. The unexpected news on inflation triggered the worst one-day point drop in Wall Street history.... Most troubling to investors and economists: the core rate of inflation, which ignores volatile food and energy prices, jumped by the largest amount in five years.

SOUTH BEND TRIBUNE

The Consumer Price Index or CPI is the ultimate inflation tea leaf. It is arguably the most closely watched and important of the major inflation indicators, with a clear five-star rating, and any unexpected change in the CPI is likely to have a major impact on the stock and bond markets.

The latest CPI data are released by the Department of Labor between the 15th and 21st of every month. As with many economic indicators, the data are always released at 8:30 a.m. Eastern Standard Time before the stock market opens. The CPI measures inflation at the *retail* level. It is a fixed-weight index that tracks the average price change over time of a *fixed* basket of goods and services. The pie chart in Fig. 15-2 illustrates the major categories of goods and services and shows the relative importance of each category. Note that the largest CPI category by a very large margin is housing, accounting for roughly 40 percent of the index. It is

FIGURE 15-2   Slices of the CPI pie.

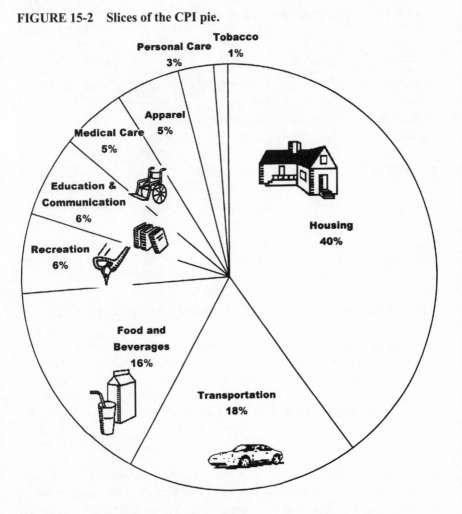

followed in importance by transportation, food and beverages, recreation, education, and medical care.

When analyzing the CPI data, Wall Street analysts are very careful to concentrate on the CPI excluding food and energy. This care speaks to the importance of distinguishing between demand-pull inflation, which is likely to spur the Federal Reserve to raise interest rates, and cost-push inflation, which may make the Fed much less likely to raise rates. In this regard, Wall Street views the CPI excluding food and energy as the best measure of the economy's core rate of inflation. If this is rising, it usually means demand-pull pressures are building, and the Fed is more likely to take away the punch bowl. That's why in our example leading off this chapter Ernest Hunter made such a serious mistake. He should have interpreted a rise in the core rate as very bad news likely to move the market down—a clear sign to go short. Instead, he went long, and it wound up being his trading capital that got a lot shorter.

As for the impact of higher food and energy prices on the CPI, the thing you need to know here is that these prices are not only highly volatile, they are often symptomatic of cost-push inflation. As we now know, this kind of inflation cannot be cured by raising interest rates to cool off the economy. In fact, cost-push inflation is recessionary in and of itself. If the Fed tries to cure it with an interest rate hike, the only result will be a greater recessionary shock.

Now, here's a more subtle but equally important point about the CPI. Unlike the Producer Price Index that you are about to meet, the CPI includes imported goods in its calculations. This is particularly useful to know during times when the value of the dollar is fluctuating rapidly, because during such times the CPI can generate misleading inflationary signals. The problem is simply this: If the dollar is depreciating rapidly, this will drive the cost of imports up and move the CPI up. However, this kind of inflation will likely be viewed as far less troublesome by the Federal Reserve than, say, a similar rise in the cost of domestic goods.

MORE THAN YOU EVER WANTED TO KNOW ABOUT THE PPI

The producer price index, which measures inflation at the wholesale level, rose 0.6% in June—a bit more than expected and 4.3% year over year. The culprit was higher energy prices, which jumped 5.1% for the month. But core PPI, which strips out the volatile food and energy sectors, actually fell 0.1% for the month. That was better than expected. The drop is likely to soothe the nerves of the inflation wary Federal Reserve.

INVESTOR'S BUSINESS DAILY

While the CPI measures inflation at the retail level, the Producer Price Index or PPI measures inflation at the wholesale level. It is based on over 30,000 commodities and more than 10,000 price quotes. The PPI data likewise are released by the Department of Labor, usually around the 11th of each month for the prior month.

In terms of Wall Street reaction, the PPI ranks at least one star below the CPI. However, for the macrowave investor, the PPI is, in many ways, much more interesting. This is because changes in the PPI often foreshadow changes in the CPI—at least over the longer term.

To see this, we need to understand that the PPI is actually three indexes rather than one. The first PPI reflects prices of *crude materials* such as grains, livestock, oil, and raw cotton. A second PPI reflects prices of partially processed *intermediate* goods like flour, leather, auto parts, and cotton yarns. The third PPI looks at *finished goods* such as bread, shoes, autos, and clothes that are available for sale at the wholesale level.

Technically, each PPI beginning with crude materials can be seen as a leading indicator of changes in the next PPI. For example, an increase in the cost of a crude material like grain will soon show up as an increase in the cost of an intermediate material like flour, and soon thereafter this higher intermediate good cost will be reflected in the cost of a finished good like bread. It is perhaps for this reason that when you read about the PPI in the news or see it discussed on CNBC, the reporters and analysts are usually referring to the *finished goods PPI*. It is also this finished goods PPI that gets the most attention and reaction on Wall Street.

The pie chart in Fig. 15-3 shows the relative importance of each of the major categories of finished goods in the PPI fixed-weight index. The capital goods slice of the pie includes equipment and machinery, as well as civilian aircraft. In the nondurable consumer goods category, we have necessities like clothes, electricity, and gasoline, while in the durable goods category, we have big-ticket items like cars and trucks.

Perhaps the most interesting thing to note about this pie chart is that the finished goods PPI is heavily weighted toward consumer goods. Because of this, there is a tendency among the less savvy on Wall Street to extrapolate changes in the PPI to changes in the CPI. Note, however, that this can be a very dangerous thing to do, at least from month to month. In particular, if you try to use this month's PPI numbers to predict changes in this month's CPI, and then use that prediction to enter a trade, you may be in for a very rude surprise.

The reason why this can be hazardous to a trader's health is that, at least on a month-to-month basis, the PPI and CPI are not particularly well correlated. This is partly because the PPI is more volatile than the CPI, but it is mostly because of two key differences in the CPI and PPI weighting schemes. In particular, the PPI reflects the cost of very few services, whereas services account for more than half of the CPI. In addition, the actual weights used in the PPI for different goods are very different from those used in the CPI. For these reasons, at least in the short run, there can be considerable divergence between the CPI and the PPI.

FIGURE 15-3   Slices of the PPI pie.

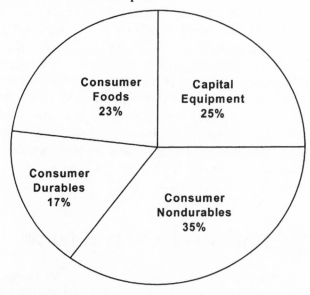

Having said this, it is nonetheless true that over the longer time frame of a few months or a year, the two indexes are much more highly correlated, so in a very real sense the PPI does give you an earlier heads-up on inflation than the CPI. That's why, in many ways, the PPI is a better inflation indicator than the CPI and why a macrowave investor with a longer-term horizon will find watching this indicator so very useful.

Now, let me make several other macrowave investing points about the PPI before we move on to our next inflation indicator. First, as with the CPI, Wall Street tends to focus on the PPI excluding food and energy, and for the same reason. Both the energy and food components of the PPI are highly volatile. They can go up for a few months and then come right back down. Accordingly, the PPI excluding food and energy is a much better measure of the core rate of inflation and demand-pull inflation, and the Street knows that the Fed is more apt to react much more strongly to demand-pull pressures than to cost-push inflation due to energy or food spikes.

To relate this crucial point back to our earlier story about Ernest Hunter, recall that when the PPI numbers came out hot, Ernie shorted the market. However, this turned out to be a really big mistake. That was because the inflationary spike was due merely to a boost in energy and food prices, while the core PPI rate was relatively cool. The market took this as a very positive sign that the Fed would not boost interest rates further and rallied. Of course, Ernie lost a bundle because he didn't understand this.

Now, as a second macrowave investing point, you should also be aware that the PPI is sometimes prone to volatility spikes *even after food and energy are excluded.* For example, auto prices tend to jump up in the fall with the introduction of new models, while tobacco prices can spike at least several times a year. These kinds of price spikes can buffet the PPI in a way that generates false inflationary signals. So when you review the PPI, don't just swallow the whole finished goods number, take a look at each of the categories and try to determine where any movements are coming from. Obviously, Alan Greenspan and the Fed are not going to stress out over a PPI spike caused by a tobacco blip.

OF ECONOMIC FLAT TIRES AND THE GDP DEFLATORS

The stock market headed lower yesterday in more active trading due to a sharp drop in bonds and the dollar, which in turn sparked program selling.... "The gross domestic product deflator was up more than expected and that bombed bonds, which in turn bombed stocks," said market analyst Alfred Goldman of A.G. Edwards Inc. in St. Louis.

INVESTOR'S BUSINESS DAILY

The GDP deflators are the broadest measures of inflation. They cover price changes for over 5000 items in every sector of the economy, from consumer products and capital goods to foreign imports and the government sector.

In all, there are three GDP deflators—a *chain-price* index, a *fixed-weight* deflator, and an *implicit* deflator. They are reported quarterly as part of the broader report on the gross domestic product, which is issued by the Department of Commerce on the third or fourth week of the month after the end of the quarter.

In the greater scheme of things on Wall Street, the GDP deflators are of only mild interest, rating no more than two, or perhaps three, stars. At least part of the reason is that the deflators are only reported quarterly rather than monthly. Also, they are generally regarded as lagging, rather than leading, indicators. In assessing the impact of the GDP deflators on the financial markets, it is important to know that these deflators typically reflect a lower rate of inflation than the CPI. This is because the prices of capital goods, which are included in the GDP deflators but not in the CPI, tend to be less expensive than consumer goods. Having said this, all three key inflation indicators—the CPI, the PPI, and GDP deflators—all tend to move in the same direction over time.

Now, here's a second important macrowave investing point. The GDP deflators can react quite deceptively, as well as very counterintuitively, to a spike in the price of imported oil or other imported goods. The reason: All goods and services not produced in the U.S. such as imported oil are subtracted from the GDP—remember that the "D" in the GDP stands for "domestic." Now here's the problem with this: When import prices rise, a *greater* dollar value of imports is taken from the GDP and the deflator goes *down*. Frankly, this is just plain goofy, since both consumers and businesses are paying higher prices for their imports and it would seem that any inflation index worth its salt should reflect that. But the GDP deflator doesn't—so just be on the lookout for this kind of problem when you evaluate the data.

WATCHING OUT FOR WAGE INFLATION

> An unexpected spike in an important inflation warning signal that tracks labor costs spooked financial markets yesterday.... [B]oth the stock and bond markets fell sharply after the Labor Department reported that the employment cost index rose 1.1 percent from the first to the second quarter of the year, its biggest gain in eight years.
>
> *THE NEW YORK TIMES*

While the CPI and PPI are appropriate instruments to ferret out whether inflation is of the demand-pull or cost-push variety, there are two additional economic indicators that are absolutely essential in revealing the presence of *wage inflation*. These indicators are the *Employment Cost Index* and *average hourly earnings*. Both should be closely watched by the macrowave investor, but be forewarned—both also contain their own traps for the careless conclusion and ill-timed trade.

The Department of Labor reports average hourly earnings one week after the end of every month as part of the broader jobs report. Because these are usually the first inflation data of the month, Wall Street eagerly awaits the average hourly earnings news. There are, however, at least three major problems with these data, and being unaware of them can get a macrowave investor's capital balance into deep trouble.

One problem is that a sharp increase in overtime hours in any given period can send a false signal that wages are rising. This is because of the way average hourly earnings are calculated. It's simply total payroll divided by total hours worked, as reported by each industry. This means that if a worker puts in 40 hours of regular time and another 5 hours at time and a half pay, average hourly earnings will rise even though the worker's base wage hasn't. A second problem that can likewise generate a false inflationary signal is that average hourly earnings do not adjust for changes in the composition of workers. Thus, for example, if manufacturers begin to substitute higher-skilled and higher-paid workers for lower-paid workers, it will appear that wages are rising when, in fact, the only thing that has changed is the composition of the work force.

Because of these two problems with accounting for overtime and the composition of the labor force, the average hourly earnings numbers can be highly volatile, and no self-respecting macrowave investor should ever take them at face value, much less base a major trade on them. Still, the third problem with the average hourly earnings data may be the most serious.

In particular, the average hourly earnings yardstick only measures wage changes while ignoring changes in benefits. However, in the modern labor market, benefits ranging from vacation and sick pay to insurance and retirement plans have become an increasing part of the total compensation package. As a practical matter, this means that even if wages are rising very slowly, rapid increases in the benefits package can still signal significant wage inflation. That's why both Wall Street and the Federal Reserve value the Employment Cost Index as a second important indicator of wage inflation. It counts both wages and benefits. Indeed, even though this index is only reported quarterly, it has entered the top tier of economic indicators ever since the chairman of the Federal Reserve first extolled its virtues in 1995.

As a final point on the Employment Cost Index, even though it is less volatile than average hourly earnings, it nonetheless can be subject to occasional misleading spikes as well. Thus, it is important to always review these numbers within the context of the trend, as well as the broader economy. In this regard, note that a wage spike in an overheated economy is more likely to be a true signal of wage inflation than a similar spike in a cooling economy.

READING THE OTHER INFLATION TEA LEAVES

For the stock market, the final score of last week's barrage of economic news seemed to be Bulls 9, Bears 4.... Nine of the week's reports suggested the economy is slowing and inflation is not a problem. Four left some doubt as to just how slow that is, and whether inflation is really as benign as it seems. Those reports, and others to be released in coming weeks, will weigh heavily in the Federal Reserve's decision to raise or not raise interest rates again when its policy-making committee meets May 20 and 21.

THE ATLANTA JOURNAL AND CONSTITUTION

While the indicators we have discussed measure the rate of inflation *directly,* there are a myriad of other more *indirect* economic indicators that can be useful in reading the inflation tea leaves. In fact, in an overheated economy in which inflationary pressures are percolating, Wall Street will carefully watch other economic indicators from retail sales and industrial production to housing starts, durable goods orders, and capacity utilization. In such a boom context, any sign of a slowdown in these indicators short of a full-blown recessionary signal will be considered anti-inflationary and good news on Wall Street—often to the dismay of Main Street. That's why the prudent macrowave investor follows all the different economic indicators.

THE MARKET'S REACTION TO INFLATIONARY NEWS

Now let's turn to a discussion of how the stock, bond, and currency markets react to inflationary news. And let's start with the stock market. This is simple.

Any inflationary news that increases the probability that the Federal Reserve will increase interest rates or tighten the money supply will drive stock prices down, along with the broader Dow and Nasdaq indexes. This is because higher interest rates augur lower earnings. End of story.

As for the bond market, this is a bit more complicated. This is because the specter of a Fed rate hike can have both an *interest rate effect* and an *equity effect* on bond prices. Moreover, each of these two effects pushes bond prices in the *opposite* direction so the *net* effect of inflationary news on the bond market is not always predictable. In this regard, the interest rate effect is most direct. It stems from the fact that the prospect of a Fed rate hike will push bond prices *down* as yields on existing bonds must rise to match the rate increase. On the other hand, the prospect of a Fed rate hike may drive panicky investors away from the stock market into the relative safety of bonds—the so-called "flight to quality." The resultant equity effect will push bond prices *up* because of increased demand for bonds. In fact, we saw a classic example of this phenomenon during the April 14th Nasdaq crash in the year 2000. When the CPI numbers came out very hot in the morning, bond prices immediately plummeted on fears of a Fed rate hike—that was the interest rate effect working. However, as panicky investors bailed out of the stock market into bonds, bond prices recovered nicely and actually closed up for the day—that was the equity effect. The broader point is that the macrowave investor will be very aware of these two conflicting forces.

As for the currency markets, the prospect of a Fed rate hike will tend to drive the value of the dollar up, at least in the short run. This is because higher interest rates in the United States will attract additional foreign investors into the U.S. bond market. However, before a foreign investor can buy U.S. bonds, she must first convert her yen or euros or pesos into dollars. This increases the demand for dollars and therefore puts upward pressure on the dollar.

Of course, we know all of this about the stock, bond, and currency markets from earlier chapters of this book. But what we really don't know yet is the all-important answer to this question: Which sectors of the stock market are likely to be the most reactive and which are likely to be the least reactive to inflationary news? At least one answer to this question may be found in Table 15-2. This table is based on the results of a study I conducted with a colleague at the University of California. In this study, we examined how the stock market has historically reacted to major announcements of *unexpected* changes in the core rate of inflation. In our sample, we included events in which the inflationary news was unexpectedly bad, as well as cases in which it was unexpectedly good. What we found was a very predictable and systematic reaction among the various sectors to such news.

Take a look at Table 15-2 to see what I mean. From the table, you can see that the results are quite intuitive. For example, in the *most reactive* column, the banking, brokerage, financial services, and home finance sectors all sell products whose price is essentially measured by the level of interest rates. When the expectation of higher interest rates goes up, so, too, does the expected price of the sectors' products—whether these products are a loan for the banking industry, margin interest on stocks for the brokerage sector, or credit card carrying charges for the financial services sector. And as the prices of these products rise, fewer loans are issued, fewer stocks are traded, fewer credit card purchases are made, and the profits in these sectors fall. Of course, as expected profits fall, so, too, do stock prices.

TABLE 15-2.   How Selected Stock Market Sectors React to Inflation

Most Reactive	Most Defensive
• Banking	• Energy
• Brokerage and investment	• Gold
• Financial services	• Industrial materials
• Home finance	• Paper and forest products

Now, what about those sectors in the *most defensive* column? Looking over these sectors, you can see that the results are equally intuitive. For example, both gold and oil are generally regarded as excellent inflation hedges, meaning that in times of rapid inflation, they are likely to hold their value much better than a depreciating currency. The same is true to a lesser extent for commodities like industrial materials.

Now, looking at Table 15-2, it should be obvious as to how you can take this kind of information to the macrowave investing bank. Indeed, armed with this kind of information, you will be much better prepared to trade on the anticipation of inflationary news. For example, suppose the latest CPI numbers are about to come out, and you are very concerned that they may be unexpectedly hot. In such a case, you might want to go short on some weak stocks in the banking or brokerage sector. Alternatively, if you are holding stocks in any of the most reactive sectors, you might want to simply go flat or move into stocks in the most defensive sectors. The point is, such information can help you be like Jack of the old nursery rhyme—both nimble and quick.

THE ARCHANGEL OF PRODUCTIVITY

*A*s soon as Gabriela Michaels heard on CNBC that the *Department of Labor was reporting a significant drop in productivity and sharp rise in unit labor costs, she immediately shorted several thousand shares of stocks in the banking and brokerage sectors. Her reasoning? With productivity falling and unit labor costs on the rise, this must be evidence of wage inflation. And whenever the Federal Reserve sees any evidence of wage inflation, it has a strong tendency to raise interest rates. Since both the banking and brokerage sectors are highly interest rate–sensitive, stocks in this sector must fall on the bad productivity news; so shorting such stocks should earn Gabriela a bundle.*

In fact, Gabriela had used precisely this kind of logic to make a killing not one year ago on a similarly bad productivity report. But that was then when the economy was still booming, and this was now when the economy was in a very different part of the business cycle and sliding into a recession. Because the times had been a-changin', Gabriela's shorted stocks not only didn't drop on the news, the stupid things went up. So what went wrong?

———————

W hile the last chapter was one of the longest in this book, this will be one of the shortest. In fact, I could have tucked this brief discussion of productivity comfortably into the end of our last chapter on inflation. This is because rising productivity is the best antidote to inflation, even as the Federal Reserve views falling productivity as one of the most dangerous signs of a coming inflationary spike. Nonetheless, tucking our discussion of productivity away into the end of another chapter would have given all too short a shrift to the single most important determinant of prosperity—not just for America but also for every nation on the planet. So let's give the archangel of productivity its due right here and right now, and let's begin with these observations about why increasing productivity matters so much to the stock market.

First, increasing productivity allows the gross domestic product to expand at a much faster rate without fear of inflation. As a practical matter, this means the U.S. economy can sustain a growth rate of 4 percent to 5 percent rather than 2 percent to 3 percent. And while a couple of little percentage points may not seem like much year to year, those little increments mean that the size of the economy can double in less than 20 years rather than in more than 30 years. Of course, for the corporations providing the bricks and clicks and mortar to fuel that faster growth, higher productivity means higher earnings and, of course, that leads to higher stock prices.

Second, increased productivity is also the only way that workers can enjoy increases in their real, inflation-adjusted wages. The equation is straightforward: If workers want to see a boost in their paychecks, they must produce more during every given hour. Increased productivity allows them to do this; this, too, has a profound implication for the stock market. When workers have more money in their pockets, they consume more, and, collectively, this consumption leads to more products produced, more products sold, more profits made, and yes, of course, higher stock prices.

TECHNOLOGICAL CHANGE—THE ULTIMATE GROWTH HORMONE

Now to drive home each of these points, let me show you the results of one of the most famous studies ever done in economics. Professor Edward

TABLE 16-1.   Productivity As the Key to Economic Growth

More Workers and Equipment	
• More workers	34%
• More machines and equipment	<u>17%</u>
	51%
Increases in Productivity	
• A better-educated workforce	13%
• Economies of scale	8%
• Improved resource allocation	8%
• Technological change	<u>26%</u>
	55%
Miscellaneous	<u>−6%</u>
Total	**100%**

Denison at the Brookings Institution conducted the study. He looked at the sources of economic growth in the United States over a 50-year period. The results appear in Table 16-1, which measures the percentage contribution to growth of the GDP of various factors such as the number of workers and machines and the level of education.

From this table, we see quite clearly that productivity growth has been a major driving force underlying economic growth in the United States. Indeed, more than half of all the gains in the GDP have been the result of increases in productivity. We can also see exactly which factors have been most instrumental in increasing labor productivity. Clearly, a better-educated workforce, economies of scale, and improved resource allocation have all been important. However, the most important factor, which accounts for a full 26 percent of increased GDP growth, has been *technological change.*

Indeed, from the industrial revolution of the steam engine, light bulb, and automobile to the digital revolution of computers, fiber optics, and semiconductors, the road to prosperity has always been paved with technological change. Of course, the role of technology in promoting a high and sustainable noninflationary rate of growth has not gone unnoticed by the chairman of the Federal Reserve. Here is just one of many of Alan Greenspan's pearls of wisdom regarding productivity:

In the last few years it has become increasingly clear that this business cycle differs in a very profound way from the many other cycles that have characterized post-World War II America. Not only has the expansion achieved record length, but it has done so with economic growth far stronger than expected. Most remarkably, inflation has remained largely subdued in the face of labor markets tighter than any we have experienced in a generation.

A key factor behind this extremely favorable performance has been the resurgence in productivity growth. Since 1995, output per hour in the nonfinancial corporate sector has increased at an average annual rate of 3-1/2 percent, nearly double the average pace over the preceding quarter-century. Indeed, the rate of growth appears to have been rising throughout the period.

Our immediate goal at the Federal Reserve should be to encourage the economic and financial conditions that will best foster the technological innovation and investment that spur structural productivity growth. It is structural productivity growth—not the temporary rise and fall of output per hour associated with various stages of the business cycle—*that determines how rapidly living standards rise over time. [emphasis added]*

Now, as a practical matter, anything that soothes the soul of the chairman of the Federal Reserve is likely to also soothe the soul of Wall Street. In this regard, perhaps the most important thing I can tell you about the impact of productivity statistics on the stock market is this: Productivity is not only driven by the longer-term considerations of capital investment, better education, improved management, and technological change that were identified in Professor Denison's famous study; as Chairman Greenspan alludes to in his quotation above, *the rate of productivity is also strongly affected by short-run movements in the business cycle.*

This is an absolutely crucial observation for the savvy macrowave investor because the Federal Reserve will react much differently to a rise or fall in the rate of productivity depending on where the economy is in the business cycle. That's something that Gabriela Michaels in our earlier story clearly didn't understand, and it cost her dearly. Here's the issue.

When the economy begins to contract and enter a recession, productivity tends to fall. This is because as the economy begins to falter, businesses tend to cut back on production at a faster pace than they lay off workers. At the same time, as factories and businesses operate with more and more idle capacity, businesses must spread their fixed costs over a smaller level of output. Together, these two factors drive up costs even as production is falling so that the *unit costs* of labor must rise.

But note, now, that in such a case, the Federal Reserve is unlikely to interpret this increase in unit labor costs as a symptom of inflationary pressures. Rather, the Fed knows that this apparent rise in wage inflation is merely an artifact of the recessionary phase of the business cycle the economy is in. Accordingly, in this phase, a "bad" productivity report is unlikely to increase the probability of a Fed rate hike. In fact, using contractionary monetary policy when the economy is sliding into a recession would be like pouring water on a drowning man, and no one knows this better than the chairman of the Federal Reserve.

But now consider the opposite case, when the economy is in the expansionary phase of the business cycle. As the economy enters this phase, productivity will tend to lead the expansion even as unit labor costs begin to fall. At this point, as factories increase their capacity, they will begin operating more efficiently even as the same amount of workers employed produce more output.

In this case, so long as productivity gains continue to rise at a pace fast enough to prevent unit labor costs from rising, the Fed's Board of Governors will be very happy campers and leave interest rates alone. However, later in the business cycle, as labor markets get tight and the cost of energy and raw materials also increases, the threat of inflation forces the Fed to look at negative news on the productivity and unit labor cost fronts much more closely. Indeed, at this stage of the business cycle, if unit labor costs outstrip productivity gains, this is likely to be viewed as strong evidence of wage inflation by the Fed and equally likely to be met by a Fed interest rate hike.

So, to summarize the point that Gabriela Michaels failed to grasp in our little story leading off this chapter, a fall in productivity and rise in unit labor costs can sometimes be viewed simply as a benign by-product of an economy in recession unworthy of any interest rate hikes. But at other times, a fall in productivity and rise in unit labor costs may be a clear danger sign to the Fed and be met with swift contractionary policy medicine.

THE PRODUCTIVITY REPORT—TOUCHED BY AN ANGEL

Productivity surged in the American workplace during the spring and labor costs dipped, a powerful signal that the record-long U.S. economic expansion still packs plenty of momentum to lift profits and wages. It also provided further evidence that the economy maintains the resilience to grow without kindling inflation.... The data were far better than Wall Street had expected. Treasury bond yields, which are especially sensitive to inflation and Federal Reserve policy, declined on the belief that the news is another indication that the Federal Reserve will leave interest rates untouched at its Aug. 22 policy meeting. The Dow Jones industrial average rallied, climbing 109.88 points to close at 10,976.89.

LOS ANGELES TIMES

The Department of Labor releases its quarterly report on productivity and unit labor costs around the 7th of the second month of the quarter for the prior quarter. In this report, the calculation for productivity is simple. It is measured as the ratio of worker output to the number of hours worked. However, the calculation of unit labor costs is a bit more complex.

First, worker compensation per hour must be determined. Such compensation not only includes wages and salaries but also commissions, payments in kind, and employer contributions to taxes and worker benefit packages. Then, unit labor costs equal compensation per hour divided by output per hour. Now, looking carefully at this relationship, we can see that unit labor costs will increase as compensation rises without any offset in output per hour. However, as long as productivity rises, it pushes up the denominator in the unit labor cost equation and thereby reduces unit labor costs or, at least, helps to offset any increase in unit labor costs.

Now I'm going to surprise you. Here goes. Given that productivity is so important in driving long-term growth—and indeed, it is almost an obsession with the chairman of the Federal Reserve—you might think that the productivity report is deserving of a top five-star billing. *Au contraire, mon* macrowave investor. The reasons number three, and after our lengthy discussions of other economic indicators in previous chapters, they all should be very familiar to you. The first problem is that the data are highly volatile. The second is that the data only come around quarterly. Third, and perhaps most important, since the previously released GDP report provides a pretty good heads-up on the state of productivity growth, the productivity report is rarely fresh.

Having said all this, it is nonetheless important to point out that the unit labor cost section of the productivity report can significantly move the markets. In times of inflationary concerns when the economy is in an expansionary stage of the business cycle, rising unit labor costs can look like Devil's horns and prompt the Fed to immediately hike interest rates as a means of fighting wage inflation. It is also true, as the quotation from the *Los Angeles Times* leading off this section clearly indicates, that very strong productivity reports at key points in the business cycle can indeed move the markets.

SLAYING THE
BUDGET DEFICIT
DRAGON

Last month, the Treasury Department surprised everybody by announcing that the federal government has been in surplus for the past year. Just a puny $2.5 billion in the black, but it's the first budget surplus in almost 30 years. And it's likely to get bigger this year—as high as $30 to $40 billion.

Los Angeles Times

What is perhaps most interesting about this news excerpt from 1998 is that just a few short years before, virtually every economist on the planet seemed to agree on two things: The U.S. budget deficit posed the gravest of threats to the entire global economy, and there was no really painless way to slay the budget deficit dragon.

Of course, we now know that an incredible surge of productivity and growth in our technology-driven new economy did, indeed, come to the nation's fiscal rescue. At least for the foreseeable future, it appears that the U.S. will continue to enjoy large budget surpluses. It is equally true, however, that in some not-too-distant future, the deficit problem may well reassert itself as both tax cuts and the forces of recession chip away at the surplus. Accordingly, in this chapter, we want to get a much better handle on how the stock, bond, and currency markets react to news about the Federal budget. To do so, we need to answer these questions:

- *What is the scope of the budget deficit problem, and what is an appropriate benchmark for measuring the associated public debt?*

- *What is the difference between a structural versus a cyclical budget deficit and why is a structural deficit so much more dangerous to the stock, bond, and currency markets?*

- *What options does the government have to finance deficits and disburse surpluses, and how does each option affect the markets?*

WHAT'S YOUR MEASURING STICK?

To begin, then, let's take a look at Fig. 17-1. It tracks annual budget deficits and surpluses by presidential administrations from the time of Richard Nixon right up until the budget went into surplus in 1999 under President Bill Clinton. Note how these budget deficits soared, particularly in the 1980s under the administrations of Ronald Reagan and George Bush. The primary reason: When the Reagan supply-side tax cuts were passed by Congress in the early 1980s, there were few or no offsetting reductions in government outlays. That was a guaranteed recipe for explosive deficit growth.

Now take a look at Fig. 17-2. It depicts the size of the U.S. government debt after decades of chronic and accumulated budget deficits. From the figure, you can see how that this debt grew almost exponentially to a peak of almost $5 trillion. But how big, really, is this debt? Which is another way of asking ourselves: How dangerous to the financial markets might such a debt be?

To answer that question, we need a benchmark of comparison, and here's the way economists like to think about it. They like to relate any nation's debt to the size of its gross domestic product. The reason is simple: In the abstract, a $5 trillion national debt is a very large number. However, such a debt would pose a far more crushing burden to a small nation such as Thailand than it would to the United States.

FIGURE 17-1   A history of U.S. budget deficits.

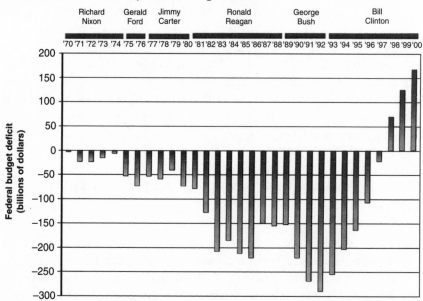

FIGURE 17-2   How chronic budget deficits lead to a huge public debt.

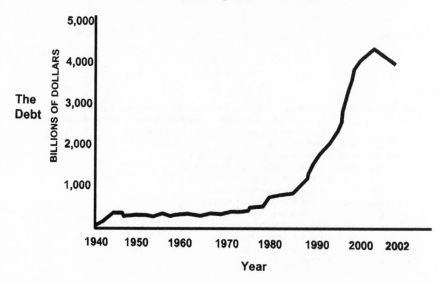

Accordingly, comparing the debt to the GDP gives us a measure of a nation's ability to produce, and therefore, of its ability to pay off its debt. When we make such a comparison, the news about the national debt is somewhat less grim, as illustrated in Fig. 17-3. From this figure, we see that even though the United States may have the largest public debt in *absolute* terms, on a *relative scale,* it actually ranks towards the bottom on a debt-to-GDP basis. Indeed, it is above only Britain, Finland, and Australia, while it happily ranks far below nations like Belgium and Italy that owe more than 100 percent of their GDP.

THE STRUCTURAL VERSUS CYCLICAL DEFICIT—A CRUCIAL DISTINCTION

Okay. Now that we have answered our first question about the scope of the deficit problem, let's turn to our second one: What is the difference between a structural versus a cyclical budget deficit and which is more dangerous?

What may be most interesting about this seemingly esoteric question is this: If you were to ask a thousand Wall Street professionals what the difference is between a structural budget deficit and a cyclical one, you would wind up staring into 2000 blank eyes. Given this level of ignorance, the distinction I want to alert you to here might seem like a distinction without a difference. Nonetheless, just the opposite is true. The reason: Structural

FIGURE 17-3 Public debt around the globe.

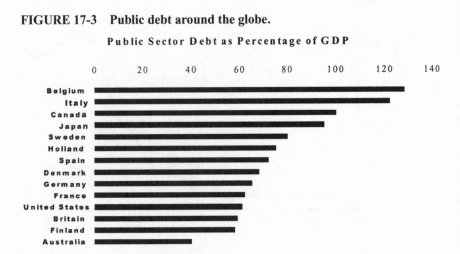

Source: Organization for Economic Cooperation and Development.

deficits are much more dangerous to the health of Wall Street than cyclical deficits. Let me show you why.

The *structural deficit* is that part of the actual budget deficit that would exist *even if the economy were at full employment.* It is due to the existing structure of tax and spending programs. Accordingly, the structural part of the budget is thought of as *active.* It is determined by discretionary fiscal policies that the President and the Congress enact like tax cuts or increased defense spending or the approval of new Medicare benefits.

In contrast, the *cyclical* or *passive* deficit is that part of the actual budget deficit *attributable to a recessionary economy.* It results at least partly from the government's so-called *automatic stabilizers.* These are the increased income transfers that kick in during a recession on such things as unemployment compensation, food stamps, and other welfare benefits. However, the cyclical deficit results primarily from the shortfall of tax revenues that arises when the economy's resources are underutilized, such as in the downward portions of the business cycle. That, of course, is why they call it the "cyclical" deficit.

Now the reason why the distinction between the cyclical and structural deficit is so important is that it helps both the Federal Reserve and Congress distinguish between *long-term* changes in the budget caused by discretionary policies and short-run changes caused by the business cycle. This distinction helps provide the President, the Congress, and the chairman of the Federal Reserve with a policy guide for tackling the deficit problem.

For example, for the Congress or the Federal Reserve to use expansionary fiscal or monetary policy in the presence of a structural budget deficit would be to throw gasoline on an inflationary fire. And when the fires of inflation burn, Wall Street always goes up in smoke. In contrast, since we can grow our way out of a cyclical deficit simply by reaching full employment, expansionary fiscal or monetary policies may well be appropriate in a sluggish economy. Moreover, the failure to engage in such expansionary policies may also prolong any recession—which is never good news for Wall Street.

To drive this point home, let's go back in time to two different presidential administrations and see how each coped with its own budget problems. And let's start with President Dwight Eisenhower way back in 1957.

IKE'S DOGMA RUNS OVER NIXON'S KARMA

At that time, in the middle of a recession, the Eisenhower administration was running a deficit—totally cyclical in nature—of $10 billion. Vice

President Richard Nixon was deeply concerned that a stagnating economy and a faltering stock market would make him vulnerable in the upcoming 1960 presidential election. Accordingly, Nixon vigorously advocated an expansionary tax cut to stimulate the economy and bolster the financial markets. However, President Eisenhower wanted to balance the budget before he left office and rejected such a tax cut for fear it would balloon the deficit. Absent any stimulus, Wall Street and the economy limped into the presidential election season, John F. Kennedy seized on the slogan "let's get the country moving again," and Kennedy squeaked by Nixon in one of the tightest presidential races in history.

Now here's the irony: If Eisenhower had listened to Nixon and cut taxes, the result would not only have been strong economic growth and a booming stock market; Eisenhower would have left office basking in the glow of a budget surplus of about $5 billion—more than enough to have paid for Nixon's tax cut! This is because the additional economic growth would have generated billions of dollars of additional tax revenues.

GEORGE BUSH GETS RUN DOWN BY HIS ADVISORS

Now, let's fast forward from the 1950s to the 1990s and watch as another Republican presidential candidate loses to a Democrat because of a failure to address a cyclical deficit in a timely way. The year is 1990, Republican George Bush is president, a recession has begun, and the cyclical portion of the budget deficit has begun to soar into the hundreds of billions of dollars.

To any red-blooded Keynesian economist, this onset of recession and an increasing cyclical deficit would have been a clear signal to engage in expansionary fiscal policy. However, in the Bush White House, Bush's conservative economic advisors flatly rejected any Keynesian quick fix to reverse the deepening recession and reduce the cyclical deficit. Because George Bush was so alarmed by the soaring budget deficit, and perhaps because he was not fully cognizant of its large cyclical component, Bush took this advice, the economy limped into the 1992 presidential election and, like Richard Nixon in 1960, Bush lost to a Democrat promising to get the economy moving again.

Now the broader point of these examples for the macrowave investor is simply this: It's not just the budget deficit itself that matters. It's also the kind of budget deficit—cyclical or structural—and how it is handled by the President, the Congress, and the Fed.

PAYING THE DEFICIT PIPER

Let's turn now to our third set of questions, which is where the biggest pay-off of this chapter lies: What options does the government have to finance deficits and disburse surpluses, and how does each affect the stock, bond, and currency markets?

In theory, the government can finance a budget deficit by raising taxes, selling bonds, or printing money. However, in practice, the "raise taxes" option is rarely used because politicians around the world are loath to do so. That generally means that the government must either sell bonds or print money to finance its deficits. Which method is actually chosen has huge implications for the stock and bond markets, because each option not only affects the ability of businesses in the private sector to borrow their own funds in the capital markets, it also has grave implications for inflation. Let's see how this works.

With the "borrow money" option, the U.S. Treasury sells IOUs in the form of bonds or Treasury bills directly to the private capital markets and uses the proceeds of the sales to finance the deficit. Note that in this case, *the Federal Reserve is out of the loop.* Note, also, that the U.S. Treasury is competing directly in the capital markets with private corporations that may also be seeking to sell bonds and stocks in order to raise capital to invest in new plant and equipment. In order to compete for these scarce investment dollars, the Treasury typically must raise the interest rate it is offering in order to attract enough funds. This is because in the "borrow money" option, running a deficit is largely a zero-sum game: The money used to finance the deficit is money that would otherwise have been borrowed and spent by corporations and businesses on private investment. In this case, deficit spending by the government is said to "crowd out" private investment. More specifically, crowding out is the offsetting effect on private expenditures caused by the government's sale of bonds to finance expansionary fiscal policy.

Now here's the bigger point: Both the stock and bond markets hate crowding out, and perhaps for obvious reasons. For stocks, crowding out will shrink a company's earnings by raising its capital costs; for bonds, higher interest rates in the capital markets mean lower bond prices.

LETTING THE PRINTING PRESSES ROLL

At least in theory, it's possible to avoid crowding out altogether with the "print money" option. With this option, the Federal Reserve is said to *accommodate* the Treasury's expansionary fiscal policy.

In particular, the Fed simply buys the Treasury's securities itself rather than letting these securities be sold in the open capital markets. To pay for these deficit-financing Treasury securities, the Federal Reserve simply "prints new money" in the form of expanding reserves in the banking system.

The problem with this option, of course, is that the increase in the money supply can cause inflation—an undesirable result, in and of itself. Moreover, if such inflation drives interest rates up and private investment down—as it is likely to do—the end result of the "print money" option may be a crowding-out effect, as well. Now do you see why Wall Street has such an aversion to budget deficits?

AN EMBARRASSMENT OF RICHES—WHAT TO DO WITH A BUDGET SURPLUS

Now, what about the opposite situation—how to disburse a budget surplus? While this may seem to be one of the happiest of problems, it, too, raises thorny issues for Wall Street. In fact, there are three basic ways to handle a surplus: Cut taxes, increase spending, or use the surplus to retire the existing government debt.

Of course, you may think that Wall Street would always prefer option one: using the surplus to cut taxes. After all, any such tax cuts will be expansionary, and when the economy is expanding, that must always be bullish. Wrong! The problem here is that if the economy is already at or near full employment, any further stimulus will not only be expansionary, it will also be highly inflationary. And we already know how Wall Street reacts to any increase in inflationary expectations. Crash!

So what about option two: using the surplus to increase government spending? It is interesting that here we face the same problem as with tax cuts, only more so. What I mean is that using the budget surplus to increase government expenditures is even more expansionary than tax cuts; therefore, if such an action is taken when the economy is already humming along, the clear danger again is the dreaded "I" word, inflation.

Hmmm. So I guess that leaves us with option three: using the budget surplus to buy down the existing public debt. While this would seem to be the most fiscally conservative option, it, too, is not without problems. The best way to see these problems is to recall the events of the year 2000 during which Fed Chairman Alan Greenspan was trying to cool down a very overheated economy. And how did he do this? By significantly raising interest rates. But here's the irony. During this time, another branch of the Federal government, namely, the U.S. Treasury, was steadily buying back bonds in the market with funds from the ever-growing budget surplus. Because the government was a net buyer of bonds rather than a net seller, this had the perverse effect of putting downward pressure on interest rates, and therefore worked at cross-purposes to the Fed's policy.

The upshot of this discussion is that, while Wall Street certainly prefers budget surpluses to budget deficits, each has its own problems that can affect the stock, bond, and currency markets in a major way. That's why the savvy macrowave investor not only pays attention to the size of the deficit or surplus, but also carefully monitors how deficits are financed or how surplus funds are disbursed.

Enough said. Let's end this chapter with a quick summary of how you can follow the budget numbers.

THE TREASURY BUDGET REPORT—'TIS THE SEASON

The U.S. budget deficit narrowed in February as the robust economy generated strong revenues—keeping the government on course for its first annual surplus in three decades.

February's deficit totaled $41.750 billion, down from [last year's February] deficit of $44.010 billion, Treasury figures showed. A deficit was expected because February isn't a month—like April—in which the government gets large tax receipts....

In late New York trading today, the bond rose 1½ point, pushing down its yield 2 basis points to 5.88 percent. Stocks climbed to records and the Dow Jones Industrial Average rose 103 points....

BLOOMBERG BUSINESS NEWS

The U.S. Treasury releases the Treasury budget report about the third week of every month for the previous month. The report summarizes both the revenues and expenditures of the various government agencies. These are illustrated in the twin pie charts in Fig. 17-4.

On the expenditure side of the equation in the left-hand chart, the three biggest categories include defense, social security, and, perhaps most interestingly, the payment of interest on the debt. In addition, Medicare consumes almost 10 percent of the budget, while the catchall "other" category of expenditures includes a smorgasbord of energy, environmental, health, education, and law enforcement programs.

FIGURE 17-4   Slices of the Treasury budget pie.

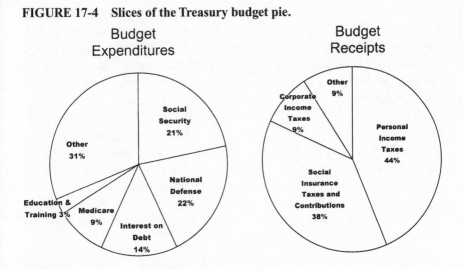

In the right-hand chart, you can see that Uncle Sam's biggest revenue source is the personal income tax, which accounts for almost 45 percent of revenues. At 38 percent, the social security and insurance system isn't far behind with its complex system of taxes and contributions. As for the corporate income tax, it contributes another 9 percent or so to government coffers, while the remainder of receipts comes from sources like excise and estate taxes and customs duties.

Now here is a rather large irony regarding the Treasury report: While large budget deficits or surpluses can have an enormous effect on the stock, bond, and currency markets, this monthly report typically garners very little interest from Wall Street and barely warrants one star as a market mover. A major problem is that the government's pattern of spending is highly seasonal. For example, revenues tend to increase during the months of January, June, September, and December because quarterly tax payments are due in these months. Similarly, there is a large revenue spike in April when most people file their taxes. Because the Treasury Department neither seasonally adjusts nor annualizes these data, they are subject to very large month-to-month fluctuations.

Note, however, that from a macrowave investing perspective, there is at least one useful technique to get around the inherent volatility of the budget data. The thing to do is to compare the *current* month's receipts and outlays to the same monthly data from *the year before*—as, in fact, the *Bloomberg Business News* reporter in the news story leading off this section wisely does. Thus, if the budget deficit is smaller this month than it was a year ago at the same time, that may be a signal that it is declining.

THE TRADE
DEFICIT TRAP

If there is any one economic report that always bedevils Richard Hume, it is the monthly report on international trade. Over the years, Richard has seen the dollar rise sharply on news of an unexpected increase in the trade deficit, but he has also seen the dollar fall equally hard on quite similar news. At the same time, Richard never knows how the stock and bond markets will react. What he does know is that stock and bond prices often rise when the trade deficit falls; but that is something he can never really count on, because sometimes just the opposite occurs. That's why Richard Hume is so very leery of the trade numbers and will often go flat and into cash the day before the numbers are to be released. But is his caution really warranted?

Absolutely. That's because the impact of the trade numbers on the stock, bond, and currency markets is the most difficult thing of all to predict. The reason is that there are many different forces that push and pull and push again on the markets when the trade numbers are released. Some of these forces are quite benign and pose little or no threat to Wall Street;

others can send even the most brave-hearted of bulls scurrying out of the market ring with their tails between their legs—bringing the markets down with them.

The purpose of this chapter is to help you better understand the complex nature of the trade deficit and its effects on the markets. Our ultimate goal is to help you to sort out all of the disparate forces that bear down on the global economy and the international monetary system, and to use that knowledge to your advantage in the trading arena. Because this will be a bit complicated, I want to give you a brief road map for this chapter. Our first task will be to examine the scope of the trade deficit problem within the context of some basic balance of payments accounting. Learning the difference between the current account and the capital account, and also why these two accounts must balance, is essential for understanding the deficit issue and the trade report.

The second task will be to explain what exchange rates are and, more important, to explain why the values of currencies like the dollar, yen, and euro move relative to one another. Here, we will see how factors such as economic growth, the rate of inflation, and the level of interest rates in the different countries all conspire to determine the value of their currencies.

For the third task, we will look at the actual trade report released monthly by the Department of Commerce. The important thing to recognize here will be this: The size of the trade deficit per se is *not* the most significant piece of information for the financial markets to digest. Rather, Wall Street analysts look carefully at the numbers to determine whether the movements in the trade deficit are due more to changes in exports or in imports.

Why is this information about exports and imports so important? We will answer that question in the process of completing our fourth and final task. This will be to systematically work our way through a set of different scenarios in which the trade deficit unexpectedly rises—but each time for a different reason. For example, in one scenario, the trade deficit will increase because of a recession in Europe and a collateral drop in European exports. In a second scenario, the trade deficit will spike because of rising oil prices. In yet a third scenario, the deficit will jump because of robust growth in the United States, even while Europe and Japan grow quickly, as well, albeit at a slightly slower pace.

In each of these different scenarios, the stock and bond markets will react quite differently to what is seemingly the same kind of deficit news. Of course, the important point we will want to take away from this exercise is that how the markets react to the trade data is very much scenario-dependent. For the savvy macrowave investor, this is an absolutely crucial point, and it is a point that our fictional trader leading off this chapter, Richard Hume, has yet to fully understand.

THE WORLD'S BIGGEST DEADBEAT

Let's begin, then, by examining Fig. 18-1. It traces imports and exports as a share of the gross domestic product from 1929 to the present.

From the figure, you can see how American imports and exports have steadily increased over time as the U.S. has become more and more dependent on trade. Note also the dip in trade during the trade wars of the 1930s, the large export spike during the European reconstruction after World War II, and the large import spike with the OPEC oil increases of the 1970s. Finally, note the rapidly growing gap between imports and exports in the late 1980s. This is the trade gap that has turned not Brazil or Mexico or some other Third World country, but the good old U.S. of A., into the world's largest debtor nation. In fact, at last

FIGURE 18-1   An exploding trade deficit.

count, the United States owed the rest of the world almost $2 trillion. To understand why this debt and the deficits fueling it are of such concern to Wall Street, we next have to master some balance of payments accounting.

A PRECARIOUS BALANCE OF PAYMENTS INDEED

Table 18-1 presents a simplified U.S. balance of payments schedule for a typical year. As you scan this table, please note three things.

First, there is a *current account*, which consists of both goods and services and net investment income. Second, there is a *capital account*, which tracks the flows of capital both into and out of the U.S. Third, and most important, *the current account and the capital account balance.* That is, if a country runs a trade deficit in its current account, it must balance that deficit

TABLE 18-1.   The U.S. Balance of Payments for a Typical Year

	Credits	Debits	Net
Current Account			
Merchandise trade balance			−191
• U.S. goods exports	612		
• U.S. goods imports		−803	
Fees for services			+80
• U.S. exports of services	237		
• U.S. imports of services		−157	
Net investment income			−19
• Income earned by U.S. investors holding foreign assets	206		
• Income earned by foreigners holding U.S. assets		−225	
Current Account Balance			**−130**
Capital Account			
• Foreign purchases of assets in the United States	+517		
• U.S. purchases of assets abroad		−387	
Capital Account Balance			**+130**

with inflows into its capital account. This is the basic *trade identity equation,* and it is a very important concept for the savvy macrowave investor to grasp, because it explains much about how trade flows affect both the values of currencies and the levels of interest rates across countries.

THE CURRENT ACCOUNT—A STUDY IN SCARLET

Now let's take a more detailed look at our table. In it, we can see that the *merchandise trade balance* is by far the biggest item in the current account. It reflects trade in commodities such as food, fuel, and manufactured goods, and shows a deficit of $191 billion in the table. Note that when you read in the newspaper that the U.S. is running its trade balance in the red, it is this merchandise trade balance to which journalists often are referring—but this is only part of the total picture.

The second item in the current account is *fees for services.* Such services include shipping, financial services, and foreign travel. While this fees category is much smaller than the merchandise trade balance, it has been growing in recent years as the U.S. has shifted from a manufacturing economy to a more service-oriented economy. This growth has helped to offset at least some of the large merchandise trade deficits, as is evident from the table. In particular, the service fees received by the U.S. are $237 billion and fees paid out are $157 billion, yielding a net surplus of $80 billion.

Still a third item in the current account is *investment income.* The table shows a credit of $206 billion. This represents the amount of income earned by Americans holding foreign assets, while the debit of $225 billion represents the amount of income earned by foreigners holding U.S. assets. Historically, this category has run a small surplus for the U.S. However, as foreigners have continued to accumulate more and more U.S. assets, this category has now started to run in the red, further exacerbating the trade deficit.

Now, summing these items in the table, we wind up with a deficit in the current account of $130 billion. According to the basic trade identity equation, this deficit must be offset by a net surplus in the capital account. In other words, enough capital must flow into the U.S. to offset the expenditures reflected in the current account. But in order for that to happen, *the level of interest rates in the U.S. must be high enough to attract enough foreign investment.* This is a crucial point because, as we now know, when interest rates move, so too do stock and bond prices.

THE CAPITAL ACCOUNT—BLACK TO THE FUTURE

As for the capital account, it tracks the purchases of both *real* assets, like hotels and factories, and *financial* assets, like stocks and bonds.

For example, foreign purchases of U.S. assets represent capital *inflows* and might include the purchase of government bonds by a German pension fund, the buying of American stock by a Dutch mutual fund, or the acquisition of a factory in Pennsylvania by Japanese investors. In our table, we show a credit of $517 billion.

Similarly, when U.S. investors purchase assets abroad, like hotel chains or foreign stocks, this results in capital *outflows* and a debit such as the $387 billion represented in the table. And summing U.S. and foreign purchases of assets, we wind up in the black with a surplus of $130 billion in the capital account. Of course, this is just enough to offset the deficit in the current account.

THE EXCHANGE RATE RIDDLE—A YEN FOR THE DOLLAR

The euro has dropped 26% against the dollar since its creation in January 1999. That has hurt U.S. companies that do business in Europe and must convert euro earnings into higher-priced dollars. Profits at U.S. blue chips, such as McDonald's, Colgate-Palmolive and Gillette, also have suffered because of the weak euro.

USA TODAY

From our earlier discussion, we now know that when a country buys more goods and services than it sells, it runs a deficit in its current account. We also know that any country doing this must raise its interest rates to a level high enough to attract enough foreign capital to offset the current account deficit. The next question this dynamic raises is, How might rising interest rates affect the value of a country's currency? The answer to this question lies in more broadly understanding how the exchange rates of currencies like the dollar and euro are determined in the international arena.

An *exchange rate* is simply the rate at which one nation's currency can be traded for another nation's currency. For example, when the euro was first introduced into the international monetary system in 1999, one euro exchanged for about a dollar and twenty cents. However, by the year 2000, the slumping euro was exchanging for only about 80 cents. More broadly, exchange rates can move very quickly and in very large steps. For example, during the Asian crisis of 1997–98, the Thai baht, Philippines peso, and South Korean won all lost more than 40 percent of their value relative to the dollar within a few short months. But why do exchange rates move? The answer lies in three basic reasons.

The first reason has to do with the *differing rates of economic growth* in the different countries. If, for example, the U.S. gross domestic product is growing faster than the Japanese GDP, the U.S. dollar will *depreciate* relative to the Japanese yen. This is because robust growth in the U.S. will attract relatively more Japanese imports. This, in turn, will lead to a surplus of dollars relative to the yen and put downward pressure on the dollar.

The second reason why exchange rates move may be traced to *changes in relative interest rates*. Thus, for example, when the Federal Reserve raises U.S. interest rates relative to, say, British interest rates, the dollar will appreciate relative to the British pound. The reason: Higher U.S. interest rates will attract relatively more British investment. But in order to invest in America, the British must first buy dollars with their pounds. This drives the value of the dollar up relative to the pound.

The third reason why exchange rates move has to do with *different rates of inflation*. If, for example, the rate of inflation in Mexico is higher than in the U.S., the Mexican peso will *depreciate* relative to the U.S. dollar. This is because exchange rates in the *currency* markets reflect *real* inflation-adjusted price differences in the *goods* markets. Thus, if inflation raises the price of, say, an auto made in Mexico relative to the price of an identical auto made in the U.S., there must be a corresponding adjustment in the exchange rate so that the *real,* inflation-adjusted prices of the two autos remain the same. Economists, by the way, call this the *law of one price.*

Okay. We are now finished with the heavy conceptual lifting in this chapter and are almost ready to engage in our scenario-building and some real profit-making opportunities. But before we do that, let's first go over the mechanics of the trade report.

THE INTERNATIONAL TRADE REPORT—WHERE BOTH SIDES OF THE LEDGER MATTER

Wall Street's Dow industrials rallied Tuesday to their best levels since the October crash...after the Commerce Department reported that the seasonally-adjusted trade deficit fell to $9.89 billion in April, its lowest level in more than three years and far below the $12-plus billion that market watchers had been anticipating. The report also sparked a rally in the bond market and helped push the dollar higher against the major currencies.

THE LOS ANGELES TIMES

The Department of Commerce releases the trade report around the 20th of every month, and this four-star report contains a wealth of data. Specifically, it includes detailed information on imports, exports, and the trade deficit, as well as trade flows by category and country.

The data are reported on a seasonally adjusted basis, as well as in both current and inflation-adjusted dollars. However, in general, it is better to look at the inflation-adjusted data. This is because monthly fluctuations in both the value of the dollar and the prices of goods and services can obscure changing trends in the trade flows. Note that upon the release of this report, the news media typically focus primarily on whether the trade deficit has been rising or falling. However, as we shall see in the scenarios below, it can be even more important to look carefully at the individual export and import data.

For example, by looking at the export data, it is possible to assess whether U.S. companies are gaining or losing competitive advantage in the international arena. These export data also help shed light on whether the economies of America's trading partners are strengthening or weakening. In both cases, there are important implications for corporate earnings and stock prices. Similarly, the import data can be a key indicator of the underlying strength of the domestic economy.

Besides looking closely at the export and import data in the aggregate, it can be very useful to look at movements among the broad categories of industry. These range from oil and agriculture to industrial supplies, capital goods, consumer products, and autos. The basic idea here is to determine whether movements in exports and imports are broad-based or more sector-specific.

As a final comment on the trade report, when looking at the merchandise trade balance, it is very important to examine this balance excluding oil imports. In fact, oil imports account for about a third of the merchandise trade deficit. This means that even small changes in oil prices can obscure important movements in the non-oil segment of the current account.

AROUND THE WORLD IN FOUR SCENARIOS

Let's look now at how currency, stock, and bond prices are likely to react to the trade report, starting with currency prices. At the simplest level, we can say that an increase in the trade deficit will tend to weaken the dollar, while a fall in the deficit will tend to strengthen the dollar. This is because as the deficit increases, more dollars accumulate in foreign hands. When foreigners attempt to exchange these dollars for euros or yen or pesos, that puts downward pressure on the dollar.

Note, however, that the reactions of the stock and bond markets are much more ambiguous. To see why, consider these different scenarios.

Scenario 1: The U.S. Trade Deficit Rises Because of Robust U.S. Economic Growth

In this scenario, both Europe and Japan are growing at a moderate-to-healthy rate. However, the U.S. economy is growing at an even faster rate and is sucking in imports. In this case, the stock market is unlikely to react to the news of a rising deficit and may even rally. This is because robust economies around the world augur well for corporate earnings and thus news of a rising deficit can be decidedly bullish.

As for the bond market, if it foresees a weakening dollar from the rising deficit, or if it interprets the news as a sign that the U.S. economy may be overheating, it will fear inflation and bond prices will fall. Otherwise, there will be little reaction.

Scenario 2: The U.S. Deficit Rises Because of Recession in Europe or Japan

Here, when the U.S. trade deficit rises, the problem will not be rising imports but rather a falloff in U.S. exports to the faltering economies in Europe or Asia. This is a much more bearish scenario for the stock market, particularly for those sectors of the market which are export-dependent. So look for the stock market to fall on this kind of news, with the export-dependent sectors like aerospace, agriculture, autos, industrial equipment, and telecommunications leading the decline.

As for the bond market, it typically prefers a trade deficit due to weakening exports as opposed to increasing imports. The reason is that the weakening of U.S. export industries will slow the U.S. economy down as well as lessen the credit demands of these industries, and therefore put downward pressure on interest rates.

Scenario 3: The U.S. Trade Deficit Rises Because of an OPEC Oil Price Shock

In this scenario, the actual quantities of imports or exports comprising the deficit may not have changed at all. Rather, because of a tight oil market, OPEC has been able to successfully raise its prices and thereby gouge U.S. businesses and consumers. The stock market as a whole cannot possibly be happy about this. However, at the sector level, energy stocks may rise on the anticipation of increased profits while those stocks in defensive sectors like food and pharmaceuticals may benefit from some sector rotation.

As for the bond market, participants will try to assess whether the oil price shocks are temporary or more permanent. If they are temporary, the news may actually cause the bond market to rally. This is because it will view the OPEC shocks as dissuading the Fed from raising interest rates. In addition, the shocks will be seen as recessionary, and such recessionary pressures must drive interest rates down.

On the other hand, if bond market participants see the shocks as more permanent, they may fear that the Fed will raise interest rates to prevent higher oil prices from pushing up the core rate of inflation over time. This fear will cause bond prices to fall.

Scenario 4: The U.S. Trade Deficit Rises Because the Federal Reserve Has Raised Interest Rates

When the Fed hikes interest rates, the value of the dollar increases relative to other currencies. This makes exports more expensive to sell and imports cheaper to buy. That's a recipe for a rising trade deficit. It also spells big trouble, both for U.S. export industries like aerospace and pharmaceuticals and for multinational corporations like IBM, Gillette, and McDonald's that derive a large share of their sales and profits from abroad. Indeed, for these multinationals, a strong dollar cuts right into their profits—at least those profits earned in the now weaker currencies like the euro. This is because the weak euros must be exchanged for strong dollars before being claimed as earnings. Accordingly, an increase in the trade deficit precipitated by rising interest rates and a strengthening dollar will be bearish for both the stock and bond markets.

Note, however, that the story hardly ends here. In fact, the ultimate reaction of the financial markets to this scenario will depend on how Wall Street expects foreign governments to react to the spillover effects of the Fed's rate tightening. Here's the problem. When the Fed raises interest rates to strengthen the dollar, investment capital seeking a higher return will, for example, leave Europe for American shores. On the negative side of the ledger, the Fed's actions will therefore weaken the euro. This will, in turn, exacerbate inflation within Europe. On the positive side, however, the weakening euro will also help those industries in Europe that are export-oriented—from chemical products and clothes to mobile phones and wine—and this will be expansionary for the European economy.

Now here's the ultimate question this scenario raises for Wall Street: Will the Europeans respond to a Fed rate hike by raising their own interest rates or, alternatively, will they leave European interest rates alone? The answer to that question will typically depend on the state of the European economy at the time. If the European economy is weak, it will be very difficult for the Europeans to counter the Fed's interest rate hike with a hike in interest rates of their own. On the other hand, if the European economy is growing fairly robustly and inflation looms as a problem, the Europeans will almost certainly match the Fed rate hike.

On the whole, Wall Street generally prefers that the Europeans *not* counter the Fed moves with interest rate hikes of their own. The reason is that any increase in European interest rates will only amplify the contractionary effects of the Fed's rate hikes. Indeed, such a countermove will typically heighten concerns over a worldwide recession. So, perhaps you can see once again why it has often been said that when the Fed Chairman sneezes, Europe often catches a recessionary cold.

A Bloomberg Sampler

The four scenarios that I have presented to you are hardly exhaustive. Nonetheless, it should be clear at this point that this kind of scenario building can be of enormous help in honing your macrowave investing skills. Accordingly, I strongly urge you to incorporate this kind of global macrowave thinking into your assessment of the overall market trend and the underlying trends in the various sectors. Towards this end, I'm going to conclude this chapter with some excerpts from the Bloomberg News Service. These excerpts are taken from Bloomberg's coverage of the trade report over the last decade, and they should shed some further light on both the complexities and crosscurrents that swirl around the market numbers.

- U.S. bonds posted their worst loss in two weeks after the government said imports and exports surged to records in March, fueling concern the Federal Reserve will raise interest rates soon to ward off inflation. Stocks fell.

- The trade report likely will have little effect on Treasury bond prices because the statistics suggest the economy will continue to grow at a subdued pace.... Exports, a key engine of domestic growth, declined in December. Imports, a gauge of consumer and business spending, rose to a monthly record as oil prices rose to an almost six-year high. That combination points to more subdued growth in the U.S. economy.

- The U.S. trade deficit widened 6% in January...as the recession overseas caused exports to retreat from a record high to a five-month low.... The dollar tumbled against most currencies today, hitting a record low against the yen, as traders expressed concern about the strength of the U.S. economic recovery.

- The dollar initially slumped on the trade deficit news and then came roaring back later in the morning as investors concluded export sales were limited by unusual events such as winter storms and a now-settled strike against Boeing Co.

- The U.S. trade deficit in goods and services fell by almost a third.... Exports set a record.... Imports, meanwhile, fell to $79.7 billion as fewer new cars were shipped to the U.S. from Canada.... Stocks, bonds and the dollar all surged on the news.

- The U.S. trade deficit widened to a record $14.5 billion in April as exports and imports fell...a sign that sagging demand from overseas is slowing the U.S. economy. U.S. bonds rose, snapping a two-day decline....

- U.S. Treasuries fell as a report of record-high imports and exports underpinned expectations the Federal Reserve will raise interest rates more than once in the coming months to slow consumer demand and curb inflation faster.

THE FOUR
HORSEMEN OF
THE APOCALYPSE

*A*s macrowave traders go, Ron Vara is in a league of his own—a
very major league. In fact, this Dark Prince of Disaster has
made a very large fortune making the very best out of very bad
situations.

It all started back in 1986. At the time, Ron was a struggling
doctoral student in economics at Harvard working on his thesis in
utility regulation. As part of his research, Ron had come to the
inalterable conclusion that nuclear power no longer had a future in
the United States and that any utility company that was heavily
reliant on nukes was in for a very serious financial meltdown.
Based on that observation, Ron had used some of his tuition money
to short two stocks—Long Island Lighting, which was struggling
under the weight of its nuclear program, and Westinghouse, which
was a major manufacturer of nuclear power plant equipment.

Two days after Ron entered his trades, the Chernobyl nuclear reactor caught fire and spewed radiation over a 1000-square-mile stretch of some of the most fertile grain lands in the Soviet Union. Over the next few days, both Westinghouse and Long Island Lighting swooned along with the stock of virtually every nuclear-dependent U.S. utility, and Ron made a bundle. To Ron, however, the most interesting aspect of the whole episode was not that utility stocks had fallen on the Chernobyl news. That was a pretty obvious result. No. It was to a more subtle macrotrading aspect of the Chernobyl disaster that Ron was drawn.

In particular, Ron noticed that the stocks of food processing companies like General Mills, Quaker Oats, and Pillsbury had all taken a big hit on the news, as well. The reason, as Ron thought through it, was simply this: Fears over possible grain shortages from a catastrophe in the Russian breadbasket began to drive up prices in the world-wide grain futures market. Shortly thereafter— but with an interval long enough for a savvy trader to exploit—the stock prices of grain processors like General Mills and Quaker began to fall in reaction to the prospect of their profit margins being squeezed by higher grain prices.

To Ron, that wasn't just a valuable insight, it was a macrowave epiphany. And ever since that time, Ron has dedicated himself to finding stocks that are most likely to move sharply up or down whenever and wherever any one of the Four Horsemen of the Apocalypse is on the gallop.

Y ou may recall that in the first chapter of this book, I noted that the Chinese symbol for crisis consists of two characters: one for danger and the other for opportunity. The dangers of which I will speak in this chapter are many and varied. They include natural disasters like earthquakes, droughts, and floods; they also encompass more man-made cataclysms ranging from bloody wars and African coups to more bloodless forms of violence such as Internet vandalism and that perennial force through the decades, oil price shocks. And of course, when speaking of perennial dangers, let's not forget disease and pestilence—be it an AIDs epidemic, a virulent new strain of wheat fungus, or a nonnative species like the Formosan termite invading new territory.

As for determining the opportunities inherent in each of these dangers, it takes a very special kind of macrowave thinking—one that must be as prescient as it is thoroughly grounded in research. Perhaps the best way to understand this particular kind of macrowave thinking will be to analyze some of Ron Vara's most lucrative macroplays. As we do so, note the common threads of macrowave logic running through each of the Dark Prince's trades. First, each macroplay begins with some kind of unexpected disaster. Next, the macroplay travels along an often winding trail of facts and assumptions. Finally, the macroplay winds up at its destination—a stock, a group of stocks, or a sector poised for a sharp movement up or down.

THE SHAKE HEARD ROUND THE SEMICONDUCTOR WORLD

When a mammoth earthquake registering 7.6 on the Richter scale shook the tiny island of Taiwan, it not only killed more than 2000 people, it also led to power blackouts that shut down production at many of Taiwan's factories.

Upon receiving news of the quake, Ron Vara's mind immediately churned through the following scenarios. Knowing that Taiwan accounted for production of about 15 percent of the world's supply of dynamic random access memory (DRAM) chips, he immediately understood that the quake would cause a worldwide DRAM shortage. From this assumption, Ron further assumed that the shortage would benefit other leading producers of DRAM chips like Samsung and Hyundai because they would now be able to substantially raise their prices.

At the same time, Ron figured that a halt to production at many of Taiwan's computer manufacturing facilities would hit computer makers like Apple and Dell particularly hard. This is because Ron knew that Dell always ran on very low product inventories as a means of cutting costs and therefore would be particularly vulnerable. As for Apple, it was in the midst of introducing its new G4 Power Mac computer, which was contract-manufactured in Taiwan.

Based on this set of assumptions, Ron immediately opened 5000-share long positions in Samsung and Hyundai and closed these positions a day later with a 10 percent gain in each. In addition, Ron also shorted 5000 shares each of Apple and Dell and was pleased to see their share prices each fall by around 20 percent within a month.

THE WINTER OF SADDAM'S DISCONTENT

When Iraq invaded Kuwait, this put one of the largest oil producers in the world at the mercy of a megalomaniac dictator. This was a dictator intent not only on the destruction of Israel, but also on the abject humiliation of that Great Satan of the planet, otherwise known as the United States.

As a then much younger Captain Ron Vara watched the war unfold and wondered whether his reserve unit would be called up, he ran through several different scenarios. To Ron, the most obvious macroplay would be something in energy stocks as the price of a barrel of oil would surely skyrocket. More subtly, Ron also knew that the war would also disrupt civilian air travel in the Mideast, and this would likely hurt certain carriers like Air France and Trans World. Still, neither the energy or airline gambits had much appeal to him. Indeed, it wasn't until CNN first reported that Iraq was launching deadly, germ-tipped Scud missiles into Israel that Ron truly got his inspiration. It would turn out to be one of his simplest yet most elegant and lucrative macroplays—5000 shares of Raytheon. His reasoning: Raytheon was the main manufacturer of the Patriot missile, the first line of defense against the Iraqi Scuds.

As CNN reported that Patriot after Patriot had destroyed Scud after Scud, Ron knew without a doubt that he could make small fortune on this play. Of course, he did. After the first Patriot was fired on January 18, there was a 7 percent rise in Raytheon stock within three days; within two months, Ron's total gain was 18 percent. That's when Ron cashed out, and he didn't trade in Raytheon stock again until the war ended a few months later in June. On a hunch, he used all the profits he had made on the first trade to short Raytheon. Interestingly enough, he picked up another 10 points on the short side within just a couple of weeks.

SO WHO INSURES THE INSURANCE COMPANIES?

When Hurricane Andrew smashed into southern Florida, it did so with winds of up to 145 miles per hour and a ferocity that few people ever experience in their lives. Fool that he sometimes was, Ron Vara had refused to join the long line of cars evacuating Miami. Instead, he simply hunkered down on his houseboat, which he had named "the Patriot" in honor of the trade that had paid for the boat. It was almost a fatal mistake.

As flying coconuts smashed against the sides of his houseboat like cannon balls hitting a frigate, his home sweet home began taking on significant amounts of water. Frantically running his bilge pumps to avoid a sinking and even fearing for his life, Ron could take consolation in only two things. First, he had an excellent insurance policy that would protect his beloved boat no matter what happened. Second, several weeks before, in celebration of the annual hurricane season, Ron had shorted more than 10,000 shares of several different insurance companies, including Aetna, Cigna, Geico, and, in what would turn out to be his biggest score, Continental. Indeed, while all of these insurance companies would see their stock prices fall as the extent of Hurricane Andrew's damage and the size of the claims became clearer and clearer, Continental's stock would drop the farthest and fastest—more than 30 percent in less than a month.

THE CHECKPOINT CHECKMATE

When Ron Vara heard that Palestinian demonstrators had captured four Israeli soldiers and slaughtered two of them, he was as shocked and appalled as anyone in the United States. Ron's outrage didn't stop him, however, from logging on to his computer so he could short 5000 shares of Checkpoint Software. He knew this was a very safe bet for at least two reasons.

First, the broad market would likely crash for a day or two, caught as it would be in the grip of fears about a new Arab-Israeli war and skyrocketing oil prices. So Checkpoint would likely fall along with most other stocks just by the pure law of averages.

Second, and more to the macroplay point, Ron also knew that many of Checkpoint's operations were based in Israel. That meant that if the conflict escalated, many of Checkpoint's engineers and executives would be called up for duty in the Israeli army. Since this might slow down or even cripple operations, Ron figured that a Checkpoint short might be a pretty good bet. It was. The stock fell by more than 10 percent within a day.

A MUCHAS GRACIAS MACROPLAY

When Mexico devalued its peso in December of 1994, it was a nasty little Christmas present to the rest of the world. As for Ron Vara, he knew that this wouldn't sit well with the whole banking sector. The problem as he saw it was that the Mexican devaluation would likely lead to other devaluations around Latin America—from Columbia and Peru down to Chile and Argentina. These devaluations would likely occur because these other countries would want to be competitive with Mexico in global markets. But these devaluations and an ensuing instability in the monetary system would, in turn, substantially increase the credit risk of any banks holding major loans in Latin America.

Based on these assumptions, Ron promptly shorted 10,000 shares of both Citibank and the Bank of Boston—both of which were heavily invested in Latin America. As scores go, it certainly wasn't Ron's biggest; but it did earn him over $30,000 in just a couple of days.

VANDALS ON THE INFORMATION SUPERHIGHWAY

Ron Vara actually received the "love bug" computer virus himself. In fact, he was one of its first victims outside the Philippines—the country where the love bug was born. The funny part about the whole thing is that even as this vicious little virus was bursting out of his e-mail system and boring into the guts of his computer, Ron was already on the phone to his broker opening long positions in three of the leading companies in antivirus software—Symantec and Network Associates in the United States and Trend Micro out of Japan. To Ron, anything that could so thoroughly destroy a hard drive was worthy not only of respect but also a large investment.

As it would turn out, the love bug virus would be the most virulent virus ever to hit the Information superhighway. It would wind up inflicting over $8 billion of damage to computer systems and companies around the globe. It would also inflate the shares of Trend Micro by more than 50 percent, even as the sales for Symantec and Network Associates products also soared.

THE OPEC DEVIL MEETS THE RISING SUN

Using his training at Harvard as an energy economist, Ron Vara has developed a very straightforward theory of how the stock market is likely to react to oil price shocks. As he sees it, any oil price shock will come at the markets in at least four different, and often conflicting, ways.

First, higher oil prices put downward pressure on the dollar and raise the specter of inflation. This will bolster both gold stocks and other precious metals because the market sees these as inflation hedges.

Second, and perhaps equally obvious, when oil prices rise, the stock prices of oil-dependent sectors like the airlines, autos, and entertainment are likely to fall on the prospect of higher costs and lower profits. At the same time, the stock prices of companies in the energy sector—from drilling outfits and oil service companies to alternative energy providers—are likely to rise on the prospect of higher prices and more lucrative profits.

Third, rising oil prices often signal the approaching end of the expansionary phase of a business cycle and a collateral entry into the early bear phase of the stock market cycle. As Ron sees it, this becomes an open invitation to begin to rotate investment funds into more defensive sectors like health care and pharmaceuticals.

Fourth, and finally, Ron also knows that the emergence of oil price shocks may significantly alter the behavior of the Federal Reserve. As Ron sees it, one or a few shocks will likely deter the Fed from raising interest rates, and that's good for inflation-sensitive sectors like brokerage and finance. However, if higher oil prices persist and lead to a rise in the core rate of inflation, Ron also knows that the Fed will move swiftly to raise interest rates as a means of containing inflation, and that's bad for financial sector stocks.

Based on this theory, Ron engaged in a suite of macroplays during the energy crisis that emerged in the summer and fall of the year 2000. While he made at least some money going long on pharmaceuticals and shorting brokerage and finance stocks, his favorite trade of all was a 25,000-share long position in a small company called Astropower. Small though this company was, Astropower was also the largest U.S.-owned maker of solar electric power products. And at the height of the oil crisis, its share price absolutely caught fire. In fact, in just a little more than two months, Astropower rose from the $20 per share at which Ron had bought it to the $60 per share at which he sold it—all for a net gain to Ron of 40 points and a very cool $1 million.

C H A P T E R

BIG BROTHER
AND YOUR
PORTFOLIO

*B*en Graham started delivering the Washington Post as a
sophomore in high school, and he was one of the few
paperboys who actually read the Post after the end of his long,
early morning route. At the breakfast table, Ben would give his
older brother the sports section and his younger sister the
cartoons. Then Ben would get down to the business of seeing what
was happening in the two worlds he loved most—business and
politics.

It didn't take young Ben long to see how these two worlds were
ineluctably intertwined. Indeed, he first noticed the intersection
when the major drug stocks began to yo-yo wildly during President
Bill Clinton's ill-fated attempt to nationalize health care. After that
experience, Ben began to notice more broadly how a new bill in
Congress could push a stock or an industry up or down, and
particularly how bad news from a regulatory agency like the Food

and Drug Administration or the Federal Trade Commission could absolutely squash a stock price.

From these observations, Ben soon figured out that political events do indeed move the markets, and the beauty of his insight was that it all fit into his broader master plan. This plan was to make $10 million in the stock market before he was 35 years old and then use his deep pockets to get elected to Congress. By the time of his 30th birthday, Ben was already halfway to his financial goal. The best part was that he had found a way to combine his two passions for business and politics into one style of trading. Ben focused exclusively on political news macroplays.

In my professional life as a professor at the University of California, I have spent a lot of time with business executives seeking the Holy Grail of an MBA degree. The vast majority of these men and women think that if they master the intricacies of topics like accounting, finance, and marketing, they will become better managers. And, of course, they are right.

But it is also true that the very best managers and executives are the ones who also clearly understand the broader political and regulatory environment within which their companies operate. In fact, one of the first things I tell each of my students is this: *Get into politics or get out of business.*

The reason is simple. The government not only giveth and taketh away with its subsidies, taxes, regulations, and consent decrees; its actions and, at times, *inaction* can affect the bottom line of a company to a far greater degree than any 10 competitors. This is an insight that I believe not only can help make any MBA graduate a better executive, but can also help you yourself become a much better trader or investor. Let me show you both how and why by reviewing some of the good, bad, and ugly things that can happen to a stock or a sector when the government Leviathan stirs.

THE TRUSTBUSTERS AND MERGER SPOILERS

Shares of Microsoft Corp. fell 15 percent yesterday and dragged down the Nasdaq Composite Index after federal officials proposed breaking the software giant into three pieces.

THE WASHINGTON TIMES

From a macrowave perspective, there are at least two kinds of antitrust activities that move the markets. The first, embodied in the quotation above, is when the government tries to break up a firm like Microsoft that it believes is engaging in monopolistic practices. While we have already talked about how you can make money on that kind of government intervention—for example, by buying a competitor that might benefit like Sun or Oracle—it is also true that such trust busting macroplays are relatively rare.

Not so, however, with the second type of antitrust action. Every year there are over 5000 mergers and acquisitions, and each of these transactions is subject to the scrutiny of the Federal government. If the government doesn't like what it sees, it may step in to block the merger or acquisition, and that can have profound implications for stock prices.

The fact is: Speculating on merger news can be both dangerous and lucrative. To see why, we have to understand that proposed mergers and acquisitions often experience at least *two* significant price movements. These movements are illustrated in these two news clips, which are several months apart.

Office Depot rocketed 4³⁷⁄₆₄ to 20²⁹⁄₆₄ after Staples agreed to buy it. Staples lost ¾ to 18¾.

THE LOS ANGELES TIMES

Office Depot tumbled 5½ to 17⅛ after the Federal Trade Commission said it would seek to block the company's planned merger with Staples Inc. Staples lost 1⁵⁄₁₆ to 23¼.

THE BUFFALO NEWS

As illustrated in the first news clip, the first price movement occurs when the news of a merger or acquisition first hits the Street. Often the stock price of the acquiring firm or big player in the deal falls while the price of the acquired firm moves up towards the announced acquisition or deal price—as with the proposed acquisition of Office Depot by Staples. Sometimes, if the Street views it as a brilliant coupling, the stock prices of both parties rise. And it is not uncommon for the Street to punish both parties if the joining looks like a real dog.

In each of these cases, trying to exploit these kinds of price movements can be very dangerous because the first price movement occurs almost instantaneously. This is because insiders usually have much better information than the rest of us and can act much more quickly. Accordingly, one likely scenario is that you try to get in on the action but do so just a little late and then you wind up buying at a price that was pushed up too high in the ensuing merger news panic. That's why I believe that speculating on the first price movement is a very dangerous checkers play and one usually to be avoided.

Not so with the second price movement, which is much more of a chess move and potentially much more lucrative. This second price movement may begin as early as the point at which analysts on the Street begin to question whether the proposed merger or acquisition will be approved, and will creep in one direction or the other as a cloud of uncertainty begins to form over the proposed marriage. Alternatively, this second price movement may not hit with full force until a regulatory agency like the Federal Trade Commission actually acts—as in our second news clip above. The game here, then, is for the savvy macrowave investor to put himself in the shoes of the federal antitrust regulators and ask these questions: Is the proposed deal a bad one for the economy and if so, should it be challenged? Here's the way economists like to think about these questions.

On the one hand, consolidations in an industry are very good for the economy because with bigness comes a variety of cost savings and efficiencies. For example, when Wells Fargo acquired rival First Interstate Bancorp, it was able to slash costs by closing almost 300 branches. Similarly, when the nation's largest supermarket chain, Kroger, bought rival Fred Meyer, both companies enjoyed huge savings in advertising costs. This is because the consolidated company could run the same ads hawking coupons and specials over a larger customer base. And, of course, when a company like Cisco acquires a Pirelli or a Geotel, this helps Cisco boost its expertise and reach in areas like optical signaling and distributed call center routing.

On the other hand, consolidation in an industry can also pose a threat to competition and result in higher prices. This can happen when only a few large firms remain to compete in the market. In such situations, it becomes much more likely that these would-be rivals would tacitly collude to fix prices rather than compete fiercely. That's a clear signal for the government to step in and break up the wedding, and that's precisely when the second price movement becomes exploitable.

To see how all of this might work, consider the proposed merger between the two office products giants featured in our news clips—Staples and Office Depot. In fact, as the first clip indicated, Wall Street liked this deal immediately and sent the stock price of Office Depot soaring. That was the first price movement.

But wait. The savvy macrowave investor would have seen, after just a little bit of research, that the merger would have created huge concentration in that industry and been very anticompetitive. This observation would, in turn, have led the macrowave investor to consider shorting Office Depot and then lying in wait for the second price movement. Interestingly, the Federal Trade Commission did indeed challenge the deal and, as you would expect, Office Depot slumped on the news.

Ultimately, the real beauty of this kind of merger news macroplay is that it typically entails little downside risk. In this case, upon the merger news, Office Depot jumped up and, more important, it was unlikely to go much higher while the merger was being scrutinized by the Feds. That meant that the only big direction the stock price could go would be down—which is exactly what it did when the FTC weighed in with its ruling.

THE PATENT PROTECTORS

The public purpose of a patent is to encourage technological innovation, which is an economy's greatest spur to both growth and prosperity. This public purpose is achieved by granting the inventor of a patent—be it an individual or a company—the exclusive rights to a technology or a process for a specified period. Of course, the longer the patent, the more time a company has to exploit its advantage and, conversely, if a patent life is shortened or, far worse, if the patent is overturned, the company loses its advantage and the profits from it.

From these observations, you can immediately see why court decisions regarding patents can have such a powerful impact on a stock price. Here are three examples that illustrate a range of macroplaying possibilities.

> Bristol-Myers Squibb, which made a legal maneuver today that seems to temporarily preserve its patent protection on the blockbuster cancer drug Taxol, rose 1⅞, to 52½. Generic-drug maker Ivax, which was poised to start producing a cheaper, generic Taxol, plunged 13, to 29⅜.
>
> *THE WASHINGTON POST*

> Late today, a U.S. appeals court ruled to strip [Eli Lilly] of patent protection on its blockbuster anti-depressant Prozac sooner than expected. That paves the way for a generic version of the drug to make its way to the market. Eli Lilly expects the ruling to have a financial impact on the company

for the next two years, forecasting single digit earnings a share. The stock was down $32 at 76½.

CNN

Sepracor plunged 11⅝, to 94½, in the wake of a court ruling jeopardizing Eli Lilly's patent protection for the antidepressant drug Prozac. Sepracor and Lilly have an agreement to develop and sell a variation of the drug.

THE NEW YORK TIMES

In the first example, we have a pretty simple checkers macroplay—one winner, Bristol-Myers Squibb, and one big loser, Ivax. It would have been very hard to make money on that macroplay, too, because the price movements were so swift.

In the second example, we've got a slightly more subtle macroplay. Here, we have Eli Lilly crashing on the news of the loss of a key patent. But unstated in the example is that several other big drug stocks like Merck and J&J fell shortly thereafter in sympathy. Thus, while it would have been almost impossible to successfully short Eli Lilly because the stock fell so fast and because of the up-tick rule, it may well have been possible for the savvy macrowave investor to get in a nice short on Merck or Johnson & Johnson, or to short the exchange-traded fund PPH.

Finally, in the third example, we move into the realm of chess. Here, we have a relatively small drug company named Sepracor losing over 10 points after the Eli Lilly decision. But get this. Sepracor's plunge didn't happen until a full *two days* after the court ruling. That's a lifetime in the scheme of Wall Street and a huge opportunity for a savvy macrowaver to exploit.

Now here's a broader question when macroplaying the patent protection news: Is it possible to anticipate a favorable or unfavorable patent decision in the courts *before* it hits the press? If the answer is yes, it should then be possible to better exploit an opportunity or, in some cases, simply protect one's portfolio from unfavorable patent decisions. In fact, some patent decisions can be anticipated, but there are some very important qualifications to that statement.

First, patent lawsuit information is often very hard to find, buried as it usually is in the fine print of annual filings with the Securities and Exchange Commission. Second, even when you find a reference to a lawsuit, a company almost never makes any kind of forward statements about the eventual outcome of the dispute. This makes it very difficult for you to know whether the patent wolf is really at the door.

My bottom line, then, is this: If you are trading in a stock that relies on one or a few patented products, you especially need to do your due diligence research—including researching any news stories or analysts' reports on the company. If the company is indeed facing any stiff patent challenges, factor that risk into your trading decisions. As with Holiday Inns, the best surprise for a patent-dependent stock is no surprise.

POLITICIAN MACROPLAYS

> Several investment firms have gone so far as to create indexes of stocks that they believe will benefit from either a Bush or a Gore win.... ISI's Bush index is weighted toward drug makers, defense contractors, tobacco, Microsoft, and mutual funds.... The Gore index...favors...environmental consultants, Microsoft's competitors, government-sponsored entities such as Fannie Mae, and pharmacy benefits managers.
>
> *BUSINESS WEEK*

The powers of the Congress and the president to tax and subsidize, to regulate or deregulate, and to raise or decrease government expenditures are so enormous that the stock market can literally quake when Congress is in session or when the President is signing executive orders. There may be no better illustration of this point than to summarize some of the very diverse and rampant speculations that occurred on Wall Street in the days leading up to the presidential and congressional elections in the year 2000. Indeed, these speculations offer a beautiful case study in how the markets react *prospectively* to what both the Congress and the president are likely to do.

In this case, as it became more and more likely that Republican George Bush would defeat the Democratic incumbent Al Gore, certain sectors began to prosper:

- Microsoft jumped upward on speculation that a Bush administration would drop its antitrust suit against the software giant, even as the shares of Microsoft competitors like Linux and Red Hat fell.

- The stock prices of defense companies like General Dynamics and Northrop Grumman began to rise on speculation that a Bush-Cheney presidency would be more hawkish and a bigger defense spender.

- Tobacco companies like Phillip Morris and R.J. Reynolds also saw a rebound in stock prices on speculation that a Bush administration would be less aggressive about suing or otherwise restricting Big Tobacco.

- Oil stocks moved upward on the assumption that a president and vice president who made their money in the "oil patch" would be much more friendly to their industry.

- Drug companies like J&J, Merck, and Pfizer all enjoyed healthy advances on speculation that a Bush administration would be far less likely to impose price controls on drugs purchased under Medicare plans.

Equally interesting, each of these sectors also began to bleed quite heavily during those very turbulent days after the election when it looked like Gore might actually emerge as the victor, after challenging the election results in court. The broader point, of course, is that for the savvy macrowave investor, it can be very profitable to carefully follow the political news on the federal legislative and regulatory fronts.

THE PERFECT ELECTRICITY STORM

Three of San Diego County's biggest energy providers reported sky-high profits yesterday, reflecting just how much money was made from the California energy market. Reliant Energy in Houston reaped $319 million in earnings….At the Williams Companies in Oklahoma, profits for the energy marketing and trading…jumped from $10.3 million in the third quarter of 1999 to $143.5 million during the past quarter. Calpine Corp. in San Jose had such a successful third quarter that it announced a 2-for-1 stock split yesterday.

SAN DIEGO UNION TRIBUNE

It's not just regulations and legislation by the federal government that can boost or hammer a stock price. Even actions by state legislatures—from the imposition of insurance rate controls and tort reform to bond issues for major construction projects—can have important repercussions for a company or a sector, and thereby provide the savvy macrowaver with some lucrative trading opportunities. To prove this point, we need look no farther than the "perfect electricity storm" that hit California ratepayers during the great electricity deregulation debacle in the Golden State. And what is perhaps most interesting about this particular macroplay is that, like a fine wine, it took not days or weeks to develop but rather several *years*. Here's what happened.

In 1996, some very powerful lobbyists got in the proverbial smoke-filled back room with members of the California state legislature to cut a deal on electricity deregulation. The deeply flawed result not only left the wholesale electricity generation market vulnerable to price manipulation, it also left the retail market for small consumers subject to monopoly abuses and ultimate collapse. Add to this volatile regulatory mix an electricity power plant shortage in the southern part of the state and a sharp spike in natural gas prices, and you had all the ingredients for a perfect electricity storm.

When that storm hit San Diego—this was the first city to have its rates fully deregulated—it hit with such brute force that San Diego ratepayers saw their rates first double, and then triple. As small businesses collapsed under the weight of these soaring electricity rates and senior citizens sweltered in the summer heat to save their social security dollars, a whole bevy of electricity generating companies saw both their profits and stock prices soar. But what was even more interesting about the situation was that even as companies like Calpine and Reliant and Williams were successfully exploiting the crisis, the state's big three utilities that had helped lobby for the deregulation legislation also found themselves in the finest of messes. This is because they had divested most of their power plants as part of the deal and were now vulnerable to the market's own fallibilities.

Savvy macrowavers who carefully watched all of this unfold could have made an absolute killing going long on Calpine and Reliant, even as they shorted utilities like Southern California Edison and Pacific Gas & Electric.

In closing, I hope I have made the point in this chapter that if you ignore the impacts of Big Brother on the stock market, you do so not only at your own peril, but also at the risk of losing some very lucrative trading opportunities. In this regard, regularly reading daily publications such as *The Los Angeles Times, The New York Times, The Wall Street Journal, Investor's Business Daily,* and *The Washington Post* along with magazines like *Barron's, Business Week, Forbes, Fortune, Money,* and *Worth,* will keep you well ahead of the government's regulatory curve—and keep you out of harm's way from its many curveballs.

THE MACROWAVE INVESTOR'S RESOURCE GUIDE

There are lots of great books, newspapers, magazines, stock picking services, and web sites for the savvy macrowave investor. This is just a very small sample.

ALL THE NEWSPAPERS THAT FIT

Barron's: Simply the best weekly perspective on the markets. Read it or weep.

Financial Times: Any macrowave investor with a globally oriented portfolio will want to add this international paper to the list.

Investor's Business Daily: From its Big Picture column and blow-by-blow sector wrap-ups to its features on emerging stocks and solid fundamental analyses, the IBD powerhouse is required reading for anyone who truly wants to graduate to the level of master macrowave investor.

The Wall Street Journal: Even if it weren't so useful, it would still be worth reading because the writing is so very, very good.

The Los Angeles Times, New York Times, or **Washington Post:** Depending on where you live and how your tastes run, one of these newspapers will be right for you to keep abreast of the latest political events.

BEST BETS FOR YOUR BOOKSHELF

Market Wizards and **New Market Wizards:**   Jack Schwager interviews some of the best traders in the business, and the result is a trading philosophy tour de force. Miss these two companion volumes, and you will completely miss the macrowave investing boat.

Reminiscences of a Stock Operator: Edwin Lefevre writes a thinly veiled biography of one of the most successful stock speculators of the 1920s, the legendary Jesse Livermore. Above all else, this book is an exclamation point to the importance of following the broader macroeconomic and market trends when investing. It's also damn funny at times—although you should know that the hero of this book wound up broke and dead by his own hand in a seedy hotel room.

The Education of a Speculator: Victor Niederhoffer had one of the most distinguished trading careers on Wall Street—as well as one of the spectacular of trading wipeouts. He reveals all with inimitable style in this thrilling memoir.

Investment Biker: The legendary international investor Jim Rogers uses the highly entertaining vehicle of a worldwide motorcycle tour to teach us some of the most valuable lessons of successful macrowave investing. This one is an absolute must for any one who trades the global markets. And it's just plain fun to boot.

24 Essential Lessons for Investment Success: This book by William O'Neill—as well as **Investor's Business Daily** that O'Neill publishes—will be two of your most valuable tools in the trading trenches.

How to Get Started in Electronic Day Trading: This best-selling book by David Nassar was one of the first ones to bring the art of day trading to a broad audience. It's still a very good book for both the beginning and intermediate day trader.

THE MACROWAVE INVESTOR'S RESOURCE GUIDE

A Beginner's Guide to Day Trading Online: Toni Turner should be applauded for writing a very clear, concise, and entertaining book for beginning traders. It's a great place for the neophyte trader to start.

Tools and Tactics of the Master Day Trader: Oliver Velez and Greg Capra are the megabrains behind one of the most successful online trading advisory services in the world—The Pristine Day Trader. In this book for intermediate and advanced traders, they reveal many of the secrets of their success.

Strategies for the Online Day Trader: If you are looking for an elegant treatise on the rough and tumble world of online trading, look no farther than this masterfully written tome by Fernando Gonzalez and William Rhee. Besides the utmost respect these authors demonstrate for the importance of a macrowave perspective on the markets, the best things about this book are its crystal clear prose and almost majestic tone.

ChangeWave Investing: Tobin Smith is to technology investing as Deepak Chopra is to spiritual enlightenment—a leading guru with machine gun flashes of brilliance. If you want to learn how to find the right stock in the right space at the right time, and maybe double your money doing it, this book will start you on your way.

Using Economic Indicators to Improve Investment Analysis: Drink lots of water while reading Evelina Tainer's magnum opus on macroeconomic indicators because this is one very dry book. However, it is also absolutely invaluable as a reference volume, so keep it on your shelf.

MACROPLAYS OFF THE MAGAZINE RACK

Active Trader: Hands down, one of the best and most valuable magazines for, you guessed it, active traders.

Bloomberg Personal Finance: High-end advice for sophisticated investors and traders.

Business Week: A big-picture perspective on the world of business as filtered through the lens of the political economy.

The Economist: This monthly clinic on both the microeconomy and the macroeconomy is, in itself, an exercise in macrowave thinking. Gets us out of the American perspective rut, too.

Forbes: This heartbeat of the new Republican America still manages to keep it all fresh.

Fortune: As in, "worth a…."

Inc: Read it to avoid the red ink.

Individual Investor: A solid independent look at the markets.

Money: As valuable as it is venerable.

Red Herring: With almost as many pages as a Manhattan phone book, this magazine is jam-packed with useful tidbits and techbits.

Technical Analysis of Stocks and Commodities: For the hard-core techie, but well worth your money. Just don't forget to check your fundamentals, too.

Time/Newsweek: Pick at least one of these staples to stay abreast of popular thinking and culture.

Worth: A rarity in our age, this one actually lives up to its title.

THE BUSINESS BOOB TUBE

Bloomberg TV: Does for TV what the *Financial Times* does for newspapers: Provides a refreshing, in-depth international perspective on the markets. Too bad it's on only a few hours of the day in most TV markets.

Bulls and Bears: True to its demographic roots, this Fox News channel entry targets younger traders and investors. Does a very good job of it, too.

CNBC: Great commentators. Great market coverage. Buy an extra TV set just to keep it tuned to this. Just bring a macrowave perspective to the table.

CNN Moneyline: Excellent evening market wrap-up.

Wall Street Week: An oldie but still a goodie. Not for the MTV crowd.

GURUS, KAHUNAS, AND OTHER STOCK-PICKING SERVICES

There are thousands of stock-picking services and newsletters out there. Follow any of them blindly, and you will sooner or later find yourself in the poorhouse. That said, here are just a few services that can be an excellent source of ideas—provided you maintain your macrowave perspective and discipline. (Note that all charge a subscription fee.)

ChangeWave: A great place to identify the top stocks in the new economy. But be especially careful here when the market trend is down and the tech sector is tanking. (http://www.changewave.com)

eGoose: One of my absolute favorites for two reasons. The recommendations all begin from a macroeconomic perspective and the service also frequently counsels subscribers to move to cash when conditions warrant, rather than to just trade their brains out as many stock-picking services do. (http://www.egoose.com)

Market Edge: Pure, unadulterated technical analysis with great buy and short lists. Just be sure to bring all your macrowave knowledge to bear when acting on any of this information. (http://www.marketedge.com)

Maverick Investing: This is the house that Doug Fabian built. Fabian is a member of the Smart Money 30 Club, which lists the most influential individuals in the mutual fund industry. He espouses an interesting sector and basket trading approach. (http://www.fabian.com)

Pristine: More a conglomerate than a mere Web site at this point, Pristine offers a daily stream of picks and pans for day, swing, and position traders. (http://www.Pristine.com)

HURTLING AROUND THE WORLD WIDE WEB

There are a bunch of great Web sites out their for the savvy macrowave investor, and this list is hardly exhaustive. But it will give you a good start.

Best Calls: Avoid any earnings traps by listening in to the conference calls held between analysts and company executives. (http://www.bestcalls.com)

Bigcharts: Gotta go somewhere for your charts. This is a great place to start. (http://www.bigcharts.com)

CBS Market Watch: Great site to stay abreast of breaking news. (http://www.marketwatch.com)

CNET Investor: Search message boards around the Web in one easy window. (http://www.investor.cnet.com)

The Dismal Scientist: A secular data Mecca for the macrowave investor. Timely, top-notch analysis and commentary on virtually

every economic indicator discussed in this book. Check it daily.
(http://www.dismalscience.com)

Earnings Whisper/Whisper Number: Two great sites to track whisper numbers during earnings season. (http://www.earningswhisper.com, http://www.whispernumber.com)

The Motley Fool: Comic relief with a very serious purpose. (http://www.fool.com)

Online Trading Academy: This site is a great resource center in and of itself. You can also find out how to enroll in one of their legendary trading boot camps. (http://www.tradingacademy.com)

Quote Tracker: This handy little site allows you to track stocks with real-time quotes and graphs. It's a nice complement to an Ameritrade, Datek, or other online account that doesn't give you access to Level 2 quotes. (http://www.quotetracker.com)

Redchip: Great source to do your research on small-cap stocks. (http://www.redchip.com)

Silicon Investor: The market insight columnists are high quality. (http://www.siliconinvestor.com)

Smart Money: Gotta love that map of the market. (http://www.smartmoney.com)

TheStreet.Com: Keep this one open in a window all day long for news, commentary, charts, and columns by notables such as James J. Cramer, Gary B. Smith, and Adam Lashinsky. (http://www.thestreet.com)

Wall Street City: Excellent tools to evaluate and screen stocks based on both fundamental and technical criteria. (http://www.wallstreetcity.com)

Yahoo Finance: A veritable wealth of information. (http://finance.yahoo.com)

Zacks: Great summaries of all of the analyst recommendations for thousands of stocks and a lot of other great stuff. (http://my.zacks.com)

Great Trading!

EPILOGUE

A macrowave perspective can help you become a better trader or investor no matter what your style of trading or investing is. That has been the basic premise of this book, and I hope I have delivered on its promise.

I also hope you have enjoyed reading this book as much as I have enjoyed writing it. There really is no more interesting game than following the stock market from a macrowave perspective, and I myself have found both thinking and writing about this endeavor to be enormously satisfying.

In this regard, my last piece of advice to you is simply to focus on trading well, rather than just trying to grab a fistful of dollars. This advice works on two levels.

First, if you are only in this game to make a fast buck, chances are that this will cloud your judgment. Fear will grab you at all the wrong times, and greed will eventually be your undoing.

Second, if you approach trading and investing more as an art, craft, and science to be mastered than simply as a vehicle to fill up your bank account, your appreciation of the mysteries and nuances of the market will deepen. This, in and of itself, will guide you to a better result.

In closing, I would like to say that now you have listened to me, I want to listen to you. Not just about what you thought of the book; but over the years, I also want to hear from you about the many different ways that this book may have helped you.

So stay in touch. I can be reached at my web site, *http://www. peternavarro.com.* I would love to hear from you.

Peter Navarro
San Diego, California

Index

About the Author

Peter Navarro holds a doctorate of economics from Harvard University and is an associate professor of economics and public policy at the Graduate School of Management, University of California-Irvine. Dr. Navarro is the author of several nationally acclaimed books, including *The Policy Game* and *The Dimming of America*, and has also created a multimedia CD-ROM and website called The Power of Economics (http://powerofeconomics.com). His articles have appeared in publications ranging from the *Harvard Business Review*, *BusinessWeek*, and *Journal of Business* to the *Wall Street Journal*, the *New York Times*, *Los Angeles Times*, and the *Washington Post*.